Neo4j

A Graph Project Story

Written under the direction of Sylvain Roussy

by
Nicolas Mervaillie
Sylvain Roussy
Nicolas Rouyer
Frank Kutzler

D-BookeR
éditions

Neo4j - A Graph Project Story
by Nicolas Mervaillie, Sylvain Roussy, Nicolas Rouyer, Frank Kutzler
written under the direction of Sylvain Roussy

ISBN (paper) : 978-2-8227-0747-3

Published by Éditions D-BookeR, Parc des Rives créatives de l'Escaut, Nouvelle Forge, 80 avenue Roland Moreno, 59410 Anzin, France
www.d-booker.com
contact@d-booker.fr

Original title : Neo4j : des données et des graphes - 2. Déploiement
Original ISBN : 978-2-8227-0382-6

Examples (downloadable or not), unless otherwise indicated, are the property of the authors.

Logo Neo4j : reproduced with the kind permission of Neo4j, Inc. (https://neo4j.com)
Artworks : by efix based on Guillaume Desbiolles's drawing
Translation from French : by Nicolas Mervaillie, Nicolas Rouyer and Frank Kutzler with the contribution of DeepL
Layout : made with Calenco / XSLT developed by NeoDoc (www.neodoc.biz)
Dépôt légal (France) : Mai 2019

Date of publication : 05/2019
Edition : 1
Version : 1.00

Table of Contents

Acknowledgements

Because there would be no book without the support, assistance and encouragement of people other than the authors, each of us would like to thank those helped us throughout this project.

From Nicolas Mervaillie:

I'd like to thank Alice for her everyday support and help, Sylvain Roussy who took me on this book writing adventure, and my colleagues from GraphAware for their valuable feedback (special thanks to Miro Marchi!). Last but not least, thanks to the awesome Neo4j community, which makes my everyday work so exciting!

From Nicolas Rouyer:

First of all I have a special thanks for my wife and kids who have been very supportive during this project. Sincere thanks to Benoît Simard, Neo4j consultant, for his technical advice and product expertise, and to Michael Hunger, Head of Developer Relations at Neo4j, for his quick responses. Last but not least, my deepest gratitude to Cédric Fauvet, Neo4j France sales manager, for his constant encouragement.

From Sylvain Roussy:

I'd like to thank Nicolas, Nicolas and Frank for their involvement. Please accept my deepest gratitude. Also, I'd like to thank all the people who participated in this book from near and far, Jim Webber, for the forewords and help, Guillaume Desbiolles and Efix for the illustrations, Christophe Willemsen, who was available at all hours everyday to lend a hand, Jérôme Bâton for the title of this book and the start-up of this translation project, and finally to Luna, my daughter, who had to deal with my lack of availability.

From Frank Kutzler:

I'm very grateful to Eric Spiegelberg for hooking me up with this unique opportunity to help with some writing while learning a new technology. Also, I greatly appreciate my co-authors' patience—they spoke English in all our conversations. I wish I'd been even the tiniest bit competent in speaking French so I could have made it easier for them!

Thanks to the whole Neo4j community, you rock, guys!

Foreword

by Dr. Jim Webber

Chief Scientist at Neo4j, Inc.

We have awoken to the fact that relationships are where true value lies in data. We have seen the large Web companies - Facebook, Google, LinkedIn, eBay to name but a few - deploy graph technology to devastating advantage. By using graphs they have become the dominant players in their domains. Neo4j - the first and leading graph database - allows enterprises and startups alike to deploy graph technology like those Web giants.

Neo4j is the product of over 10 years of continuous research and development, pioneers of the property graph model, and the de facto standard in graph databases. It allows users to store complex networks information (called graphs) that model the real world in high fidelity. Those graphs can be queried by a sophisticated graph query language called "Cypher" which provides the basis for gaining insight into the connected data.

But learning about graphs and Neo4j is one part of successfully deploying a next-generation platform. To succeed we also need to understand the mechanics of the database: how to import data, how to communicate with the server securely and performantly, and how to configure the system for dependable runtime operation. This is a sophisticated task.

This book marks an important milestone: leading experts in the Neo4j community to take your graph projects all the way to production. The authors have condensed their considerable expertise operating Neo4j with expert guidance on deployment choices clearly captured and trade offs competently assessed. The authors attention to detail and pragmatic approach will guide any Neo4j deployment through to a successful conclusion.

The future of Neo4j is one of innovation and possibility: Mervaillie, Roussy, Rouyer and Kutzler have written an accomplished work that will help you to unlock that future.

London, April 2019

About Neo4j and CYPHER

Although you need basic knowledge about Neo4j and CYPHER to make this book truly understandable, maybe you got here without having had the chance to do so. So, in this spirit, we wrote this introduction to Neo4j, with the hope of making the following chapters more easily readable.

If you already have some basic knowledge about Neo4j and CYPHER, you can go directly to the chapter *Welcome to GraphITs.Tech!*.

If not, take a little time to read on. This introduction is not intended to be exhaustive training, but we hope it can help you form a good perspective of what Neo4j does, and how to go about making Neo4j database queries.

1. What is Neo4j?

Neo4j is basically like other database systems. We store data in it, and then retrieve this data as quickly as possible. Neo4j's speciality is to store data natively into a *graph*, a set of nodes (aka vertices or points) connected by edges (or arcs or lines). This is more than merely a visual representation of the data, but rather a technical way to store the data structure, one which makes of use of *graph theory*. Unlike the more traditional RDBMS (Relational Database Management Systems, in other words, SQL systems), there is no notion of *foreign keys*. Because with Neo4j, every entity *knows* its *neighborhood*.

The concept of *neighborhood* may be a bit fuzzy for you at this point... but it should become more clear. OK, let's talk about major concepts in Neo4j.

Graph, Nodes, Relationships

A *Graph* is composed of a set of *nodes* which are linked by *relationships*. The relationships play the important role of organizing the nodes in the graph.

Data is stored as *properties* (key/value pairs) in the nodes or in the relationships.

Figure 1 : Graph, Nodes, Relationships, Properties

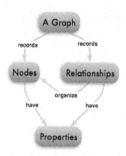

It is useful to visualize these nodes as entities, entities which are likely to be connected to other entities. The first level of connected nodes is the direct relationship. The nodes connected to a particular node, say node A, is called the *neighborhood* of node A!

Now let's talk about relationships. As mentioned above, the relationships are the links between nodes. In Neo4j, the relationships are directed (*from* one node *to* another), so the graph is called a *digraph*, short for directed graph. The relationships are *typed* with a name suggesting the nature of the relationship between the two nodes. For example, in a social graph, two nodes might describe two different people. A relationship between them might be called *friend of* which means: a *person is a friend of some other person.*

Labels

Labels are like tags we put on nodes. They don't contain any information other than their name, but a well-chosen name (chosen by the Neo4j user) contains valuable information, such as the type of the node. For example we might label a node as "User" or as "Book". Additionally, a node might have more than one label. Or none at all, though it's a best practice to have at least one label on every node to indicate its basic meaning in the graph.

When should we use Neo4j?

As Neo4j is a database, its fundamental goal is to store and retrieve data. But because Neo4j is a native graph store, it is particularly useful where the data entities are strongly interconnected to one another.

Social networks, analysis of networks, recommendations, master data management or detection of fraud rings are all common use cases related to Neo4j. But, that's not an exhaustive list!

So, consider using Neo4j:

- when relationships are as or more important as your entities, and are an important feature of the business case;
- when knowledge of the relational structure is important;
- when data traversals are important to your business use cases.

2. What is CYPHER?

Just as SQL is the language used by relational databases, you can think of CYPHER as the SQL of Neo4j. This is the query language of Neo4j. The syntax of CYPHER differs from SQL, but it has many similar principles: we ask for some data (selection) which matches constraints (restrictions) in a formal structure to return (projection). Also we can count or collect the data (aggregation), or query for the connected data. This is where CYPHER shows its most powerful features.

We're now going to attempt a quick summary of the comparisons and contrasts between the RDBMS/SQL and Neo4j/CYPHER in the table below:

Table 1 : RDBMS/Neo4j comparison

RDBMS	Neo4j
Based on the relational algebra.	Based on the graph theory.
Data is stored in tables, and rows contain information for an object, e.g., a book.	Data is stored in nodes and relationships, which can have 0 to n labels (usually at least one). A set of nodes with the same label(s) might be (very loosely!) thought of as similar to a RDBMS table.
Tables need to modeled before storage.	Nodes and relationships can be modeled and stored at runtime.
Each row in a table has the same properties (columns), although a property might be null for some rows.	Nodes and relationships, even those with the same label(s), can hold a completely different set of properties as key-value pairs. There's no real formal type of entity (like a table). Labels might be useful to group entities, but the structure is basically unformal.

RDBMS	Neo4j
Foreign keys are used to normalize the data. Objects in different tables relate to one another through a primary key.	There are no foreign keys at all. Connections between nodes are handled explicitly through relationships.
A join table containing two foreign keys is used to create a many-to-many relationship. This table may also have additional properties, such as start and end dates for the relationship.	The relationships can have properties like any other node.
Finds, inserts, updates, and deletions are handled through SQL.	Finds, inserts, updates, and deletions are handled through CYPHER.
SQL keywords such as SELECT, JOIN, WHERE, UPDATE, INSERT, DELETE, etc. form the basis of the language.	CYPHER has analogous keywords, e.g. (MATCH for SELECT, CREATE for INSERT). The exception is JOIN. There is no JOIN concept in CYPHER.
SQL uses boolean AND, OR, NOT, and XOR operators.	CYPHER also uses AND, OR, NOT, and XOR operators.
SQL provides functions such as COUNT(), AVG().	CYPHER provides a similar set of functions.
Uses indexes to enhance performance. Indexes help to locate rows in a table for SELECT and UPDATE.	Also uses indexes to enhance performance. Indexes speed the process of finding the starting node for a CYPHER query. The related nodes can be very quickly located from that starting node.
Ideal for data which is not highly related, tables which contain few, if any, foreign keys. This leads to simple SQL queries with few, if any, JOIN statements.	Ideal for data which is highly related, especially many-to-many relationships. The lack of the expensive JOIN process leads to better performance.

And now, let's see some practical examples comparing SQL and CYPHER.

Selection—Simple way: unique type of data

The selection is the way we pull data from tables and, in SQL, virtual tables formed from JOIN statements. Here, we're focusing on the simplest case of selection, without joined data.

Imagine we have a Users table, and we want all user data from that table. In SQL, we would write:

```
SELECT * FROM Users
```

In CYPHER, we would to match all the nodes which have the label `User` (remember, there is no concept of tables in Neo4j!).

```
MATCH (:User) RETURN *
```

`MATCH` is the keyword for the selection. Nodes are represented by the content in the parentheses, e.g. `(:User)`, and `:User` matches on the node label. In this example the label is `User`.

`MATCH...RETURN` has the same meaning as `SELECT`.

Projection—Returned data

The projection is what data we choose to see, that is, which properties in the global dataset.

Continuing to use the `Users` table as an example, to get the last names of users, we'd write in SQL:

```
SELECT Users.lastName FROM Users
```

In CYPHER, this is the syntax to do the equivalent select, indicated in the `RETURN` keyword:

```
MATCH (u:User) RETURN u.lastName
```

Here `u` is an identifier used to reference each node (record). Then `RETURN u.lastName` means *Return the last name property value of each node matching the selection*.

Restriction—Constrained data

We filter data by using restrictions on the properties.

For instance in the `Users` table, we might write SQL in the following way to filter the data based on the `lastName` property:

```
SELECT * FROM Users WHERE Users.lastName='Neo4j'
```

In CYPHER, we use almost exactly the same syntax:

```
MATCH (u:User) WHERE u.lastName='Neo4j' RETURN u
```

Here the CYPHER WHERE keyword works just like like SQL WHERE clause.

But there's another way in CYPHER to do the same thing, but without the WHERE. We can write restrictions directly on the MATCH part of the query like this:

```
MATCH (u:User {lastName:'Neo4j'}) RETURN u
```

We can think of the {...} as an object, with a property lastName and its associated value matching the literal Neo4j. In this case, we are using this object like a filter expression, and this filter is placed just behind the label of the node.

Yet another way is to filter nodes is by using labels, as we did previously in the section *Projection—Returned data*. A label is useful to identify a kind of node, but with Neo4j, a node can have more than one label. So, we can filter nodes with multiple labels, like this:

```
MATCH (u:User:Database) RETURN u
```

In this example, the last query exposes two labels: User and Database. This means *We want to get the nodes with labels User AND Database, a user of the database.*

We can also combine multiple labels with a property filter:

```
MATCH (u:User:Database {lastName:'Neo4j'}) RETURN u
```

This gives us all the nodes with the labels Database and User, and with a lastName value that equals Neo4j.

Selection with multiple types of related data

Returning to the Users database model, we now want to identify the databases the users have access to. Assuming we have a Database table and a many-to-many relationship table called DatabaseUsers, we can write in SQL like:

```
SELECT Users.lastName, database.name
FROM Users
INNER JOIN DatabaseUsers ON Users.id=DatabaseUsers.userId
INNER JOIN Database ON Database.userId=DatabaseUsers.id
```

In CYPHER the User nodes would be connected to the Database nodes with a HAS_AC-CESS relationship. And the query would look like:

```
MATCH (u:User)-[:HAS_ACCESS]->(db:Database)
RETURN u.lastName, db.name
```

This treatment of related data is the strong point of CYPHER. The CYPHER query is shorter than the corresponding SQL query. It is also more explicit and readable, too.

Why?

Because the CYPHER syntax doesn't have to deal with foreign keys, because they don't exist! There are also no intermediate tables (like the DatabaseUser table in the SQL above). In RDBMS these tables exist solely to simulate relationships. With CYPHER, the technical people can speak a language which is very similar to the language of the business people.

Let's take a closer look at this query, focusing on this part:

```
-[:HAS_ACCESS]->
```

Parenthesis are used to indicate nodes in the other parts of the query, but this piece uses square brackets and describes a relationship. The type of the relationship HAS_ACC-CESS is preceded by a colon :, as we saw earlier with labels. A name like HAS_AC-CESS has semantics indicating the type of relationship, and is very descriptive, isn't it?

Ignoring for the moment the [] characters, the -->, indicates the relationship direction. The symbol <-- means a FROM (incoming) relationship, and the symbol --> means a TO (outgoing). We are using ASCII as a kind of emoji art!

To complete this introduction to relationships, you also need to know how use identifiers to get properties of the relationship itself. For example, imagine the HAS_ACCESS relationship has a property called subscriptionDate, which indicates when the user gained access to the database. We could then write the following query to return user, databases and the subscription dates:

```
MATCH (u:User)-[r:HAS_ACCESS]->(db:Database)
RETURN u.lastName, db.name, r.subscriptionDate
```

Here, r, just like u and db, is simply an identifier for the query, which gives us a handle to reach properties, e.g. r.subscriptionDate.

Aggregation

Aggregation functions are useful in obtaining statistics on the data. The basic computing operators are `Min`, `Max`, `Count` and `Avg`.

In SQL, `GROUP BY` is used to group the data prior to applying an aggregation function. The following example results in the number of databases each user can access:

```
SELECT Users.lastName, count(Database.name)
  FROM Users
  INNER JOIN DatabaseUsers ON userId.id=DatabaseUsers.userId
  INNER JOIN Database ON Database.userId=DatabaseUsers.id
GROUP BY Users.lastName;
```

With CYPHER, we do the same thing using the `COUNT` function:

```
MATCH (u:User)-[r:HAS_ACCESS]->(db:Database)
RETURN u.lastName, count(db)
```

If we need to show the database names, we could *try* a query like this:

```
MATCH (u:User)-[r:HAS_ACCESS]->(db:Database)
RETURN u.lastName, COUNT(db), db.name    // broken--won't work!
```

But the aggregation doesn't work here—the count always returns 1 for each database name, and there will be one row per Database node.

CYPHER provides an accumulator, the `COLLECT` function, to handle this case:

```
MATCH (u:User)-[r:HAS_ACCESS]->(db:Database)
RETURN u.lastName, COUNT(db), COLLECT(db.name) AS dbs
```

The `COLLECT` function adds each database name to an array (called a list or a collection). Now the results table contains one row per user lastName.

Relationships and paths

The goal of this section is to show how CYPHER deals with relationships. There's no equivalent in the SQL standard.

Earlier we showed how to find related entity types:

```
MATCH (u:User)-[:HAS_ACCESS]->(db:Database)
```

```
RETURN u.lastName, db.name
```

But the scope of this relationship can be extended to more than one traversed relationship:

```
MATCH (u:User)-[:*0..5]->(n)
RETURN u.lastName,n
```

In the above relationship description the additional `-[:*0..5]->` indicates that we traverse zero to five relationships from the `User` node in order to find its connected nodes. This is an important CYPHER capability, because we can query farther into the neighborhood of the node without significantly increasing the complexity of the query. Even better, we'll get good query performance, too. Nice, right?

And to achieve this information, you need to understand how CYPHER works with paths. But what is a path? A path is simply the initial node, the final node, and all traversed intermediate nodes and relationships along the way:

```
MATCH path=(u:User)-[:*0..5]->(n)
RETURN path
```

Again, `path` is just an identifier, and this identifier takes the values of possibles paths (nodes and relationships) which leads from the `User` node to the `n` node.

Then, thinking about the nature of the path naturally leads us to... the shortest path!

```
MATCH path=shortestPath((u:User)-[:*0..5]->(n))
RETURN path
```

The `shortestPath` function is an embedded algorithm that CYPHER provides for finding, as the name implies, the shortest path among all possible paths. The Neo4j extensions like `APOC` or `Algorithms` complete the CYPHER arsenal.

Conclusion on CYPHER

CYPHER is not a SQL like, to be sure, but it is a powerful query language well adapted to graph databases. This quick introduction cannot claim to demonstrate all of CYPHER —we only hope to give you a taste of its capabilities.

Remember, CYPHER syntax is a bit different from SQL syntax, but the things we can do with SQL can also be done with CYPHER. Many keywords are common between the two languages, but we have the luxury of forgetting about foreign keys or joins. Think graph nodes, not tables.

If you need to dive deeper into CYPHER, you can study CYPHER on Graph Academy from Neo4j website [http://d-booker.jo.my/neo4j-graphacademy].

A CYPHER reference card is also provided at the end of this book in the annex *CYPHER Reference Card.*

Welcome to the graph world! Enjoy it!

Book examples

You can find the sources of the examples in the book GitHub repository [http://d-booker.jo.my/neo4j-book-sources].

Shortened URLs

For the purpose of readability, and to be able to stay current, we made the decision to replace all internet addresses with so-called "shortened URLs". Once you've reached the target page, we suggest you register it with a bookmark if you want to return frequently. You will then have the direct link. If it disappears you can go back through the shortened URL. If the shortened URL also fails, tell us!

Welcome to GraphITs.Tech!

Welcome to the strange and wondrous land of GraphITs.Tech!

In this place software engineering is generated by self-described engineering geniuses (although none of them ever agree with any other and are not at all timid about vocalizing their differences). Interns learn a lot of things, some of them are even correct. Developers rail at sloppy code, ignorant of the memory that they themselves originally wrote said hacks. Project managers are cyclicly anxious, despondent, reassured, and euphoric. Sometimes even salespeople verge on technical hysteria. All this is overseen by a bipolar management team. Some members of this team have commented that REST endpoints sound relaxing, others have been know to say "vixen" when they mean "maven", and one or two need to be reassured that a stack overflow isn't going to get their shoes wet. Talking to management, the engineers mentioned above will sometimes ask if "B2B clients" means "business to business clients" or "2859 clients" (after converting hexadecimal to decimal in their heads). In short, a development environment which is somewhat less dysfunctional than the norm.

In other ways, too, GraphITs is unlike other companies. It works mainly on projects for which the objects represented by the data are strongly connected. It offers a variety of services like fraud detection and recommendations, or the technical architecture of social networks. Though grumbling can sometimes be heard, and is sometimes impossible not to hear, everyone takes quiet pride in belonging to this innovative company.

And it is in this raucous climate, on a beautiful morning, in a beautiful month, in a beautiful year, that a new client crosses the doors of GraphITs. This client has a need, and that's good. Because here, they just love to meet needs.

The client in our story is a technical book publisher known as ACME Publishing. ACME Publishing wanted to meet the GraphITs team in order to explain problems it has been experiencing with their data. And this is where our story begins. Once upon a time...

Characters

Varsha, *salesperson*

Jackie, *project manager*

Tiago, Iryna, *technical experts*

Ashley, *DevOps and network expert*

Brian, *trainee*

Client, ACME Publishing, a company specializing in technical book publishing

Warning › *We have purposely exaggerated the personality of each character for educational, and, we hope, entertainment purposes. Any resemblance to actual persons, living or dead, or actual events is purely coincidental.*

1. Kickoff meeting

Varsha, salesperson at GraphITs.Tech, greets the client in the large meeting room. The entire team is present.

Varsha: Good morning and welcome to GraphITs Services. We're delighted to meet with you and eager to hear about your needs and concerns. Help yourself to the doughnuts and coffee.

ACME Publishing: Hi. Thanks for the warm welcome. As you may know, ACME Publishing is becoming the uncontested leader in technical book publishing in the domain of computer science. These books are published in several formats such as paper, EPUB, PDF and HTML. We are also beginning to translate our books for export to other countries. We'd like to make improvements to our information system and update it to meet new challenges.

Varsha: Good, and what was it that drew your interest to us?

ACME Publishing: We've heard you're working in NoSQL data stores?

Varsha: That's right. But is there something in particular that leads you to believe that NoSQL will help you solve your problems?

ACME Publishing: Actually I'm not too sure, but I'm even less sure what the future holds. In short, I've heard that NoSQL could be a foundation for a more agile, more flexible system. As it stands, every time we need to change the structure of our SQL databases, it hurts like the dickens!

Varsha: That's partly true. But it depends to some extent on what we are talking about. NoSQL does not remove the need to have a well thought-out upstream design. A NoSQL system can simplify certain tasks, such as structural changes. But again, the mileage you get may vary depending on the details of your data.

REMINDER: The four types of NoSQL

- *Key-Value store,* data stored as key-value pairs;
- *Column store,* data stored as tables (also known as *Big Table*) shaped as columns and super columns;
- *Document store,* data stored as compound objects (generally as JSON or XML);
- *Graph store,* data stored as graphs.

ACME Publishing: So you do deal with graph storage, don't you?

Varsha: Correct. But please continue.

ACME Publishing: Well... other companies seemed quite uncomfortable when we've talked about data structures that haven't been completely designed yet. They propose that we store some data in a relational database, and the rest of unstructured data in a NoSQL system.

Varsha: That is quite common, to take advantage of both types of databases in information systems.

ACME Publishing: Well, I'd prefer a transactional system. And the rigid aspect of relationships in SQL databases slow us down when building new services.

Varsha: You seem to be surprisingly aware of technical problems!

ACME Publishing: As I said before, we've had major problems making changes to our applications. My team is pretty skilled, and they've briefed me about problems they've encountered.

Varsha: Terrific! I suggest that you detail what you'd like to do and then we'll set up a round table presentation of our team.

ACME Publishing: Here, in a broad outline, is our requirement: in order to better manage our growing orders, I would like to implement a process that would allow our customers to track the status of their transactions, from order to shipping. Also I'd like to see my catalog of books related to the order process. There are fuller details in some documents we have brought with us, but that's the 10,000 foot view.

Varsha: Of course. I think we've captured the essence of it for now. Let me introduce the members of our team. This is Jackie, who will act as project manager. Jackie, any opinions you'd like to share at this point?

Jackie: Good morning. It seems to me that this isn't a single requirement but several smaller ones. If I understand correctly you need a catalog of books and a way to manage the order process.

ACME Publishing: Exactly.

Varsha: This is Tiago, Iryna and Ashley, our technical experts.

Tiago, Iryna and Ashley: Hi!

Varsha: And this is Brian, our wannabe developer... hey, where is Brian?

Ashley: In the kitchen, of course!

Varsha: Hmmm, Brian is one of a kind. OK, guys, how about you start working on the first drafts. Let us know when you have an implementation proposal.

ACME Publishing: Isn't my requirement a bit too "classical" for your team?

Varsha: We hope to prove to you that graph databases can not only solve a classical requirement, but then can also ease system maintenance!

Jackie: Yes, it's well known that Neo4j, being a NoSQL database, allows to start with data structures yet unrelated and imperfect, then evolve to more polished things. Neo4j support database schemas with strong constraints. Moreover, it is also a transactional ACID database, therefore highly coherent, which also offers a particularly advanced relationship management between entities. But whoever runs can also walk... usually...

ACME Publishing: If I understand well, the advantages of NoSQL without the downsides.

Jackie: Well, imagine that in the past your goal was only to store data. Now, your goal is to do more. Hence your presence here.

ACME Publishing: You sure are selling me a good night's sleep and sweet dreams. But can your technical teams deliver? How can I know my project will be successful?

Varsha: Expertise is our team's strong point, which is why you came to us. Once you've been shown the power of our technology solution, we think there's a good chance that you will decide to employ our graph database technologies. Our job will be to show you, step by step, how this success is possible. Once you've seen that by approaching the problem differently (and with fewer technical constraints), you'll be pleasantly surprised by the results.

ACME Publishing: Well, I'll let you get to work. Varsha, let's you and I talk contracts.

2. Debriefing

Varsha, Jackie, Tiago, Iryna, Ashley and Brian gather to discuss the project roadmap.

Varsha: So, what are your thoughts about this project?

Tiago: For the catalog part, not very complicated. We could almost do that with a relational database.

Iryna: Why not go with CSV files, while we're at it?! Even if that's true, we're not going to do it like that. Who wants to manage two systems when one can do the job?

Jackie: I'm with Iryna. Just because it could work with a SQL database doesn't mean we have to go that way, even if the advantages of storing the catalog in a graph is less obvious than for the other scenarios. Why don't we talk about the technology stack?

Tiago: As for the catalog, the domain model isn't going to be very dynamic, so we could use OGM (Object Graph Mapper) or even SDN (Spring Data Neo4j).

Jackie: Cool. What about the rest?

Iryna: For the other parts, I suggest we use CYPHER directly, without necessarily using *object mapping*; potentially we'll use APOC procedures[1], to optimize processing between Neo4j and our business services. We could use Bolt as the database driver, which is more efficient than the HTTP API.

---

[1] Awesome Procedures On Cypher

Jackie: But what if they want to connect it to their BI tools?

Iryna: CYPHER requests over JDBC should be fine, but we'll double check that.

Jackie: They will surely have legacy data to ingest...

Tiago: We have several options in Neo4j to do some data import/export, even on large volumes.

Ashley: I hate to bring this up guys, but the client wants to go international with several languages!

Tiago: So what's the problem?

Ashley: Have you heard of Europe? This minor continent with a 6 hours time difference from here.

Jackie: I still don't get your point.

Ashley: My point is that it's always the high-traffic time somewhere on the globe. We really can't afford to be down any time of the day. Which means High Availability (HA) which means clusters of Neo4j servers and hot backups.

Jackie: Not a bad point!

Brian: Wow, there's a sh...buttload of stuff to do. Where do we even begin?

Tiago and Iryna: With some methodology and design!

Iryna: This is going to be a blast. Once in a while we might even be on the same page.

Varsha: OK, I see you are off and running. I'll come back later for the next step.

The agenda: next steps

- Some methodology and design: Or how to go from requirements to graph structure design;
- Interactions with Neo4j: About setting up systems to talk and interact with Neo4j;
- Data import: For each graph, import legacy data;
- Operations: How to achieve high availability with clusters of Neo4j servers;
- Security: Securing the cluster and its data.

1
A Little Bit of Method and Analysis

The first step in your project is to implement your ideas in order to make sure they work. This *proof of concept* involves the model (data structure), the services your application provides, and infrastructure which this system will be based on. In general, the proof of concept is an exercise of building an end to end working solution, starting from the data and proceeding through the UI rendering. This is done for a representative portion of the whole project. In this way we can evaluate the viability of the engineering choices, and see if they can scale at the whole project level.

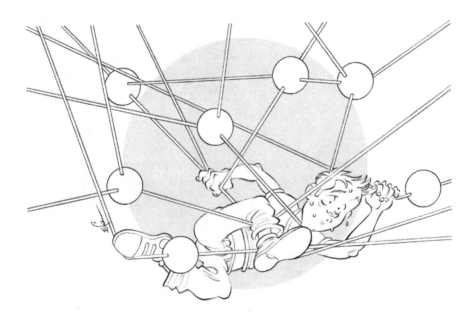

In this chapter, we will focus on modeling graphs. It's a bit like designing the model of a classic relational database, but with a more flexible model: we often talk about a Neo4j graph as *schema free*. This makes the graph easy to change. But the more correct the first design is, the fewer the number of iterations required to get a graph which fulfills the requirements and simplifies optimization.

1.1. Briefing

Jackie, Tiago, Iryna, Ashley and Brian start their analysis work together.

Brian: Where to begin?

Jackie: I suggest we read the specification and split it into sections. If the scope of our proof of concept is too large, we'll likely drown in a mass of details. Instead, let's try to extract potential business services and to split our complex problems into smaller, simpler operations.

Brian: Wait, we were talking about graphs, but now we're talking about services. I'm lost already.

Jackie: No worries. You see, every service we're going to provide will match a business domain. And each service will be responsible for its own data. Moreover, data from a particular domain can also be related to different data from different domains.

Brian: Uh...okay...so...

Ashley: Let there be light...

Jackie: All right, let's get back to basics. Starting with the client requirements, I came up with two major services: a catalog and an order process. Here is a small diagram that I created from it (Figure 1.1).

Figure 1.1 : Domains and Services

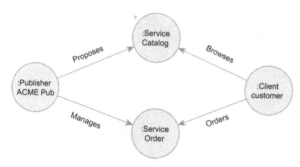

Jackie: On the website, the customer browses the catalog proposed by the publisher. We need a dedicated service which allows the customer to browse catalog contents. Then, the customer completes the order by selecting items from the catalog, and going through check out. The order service will implement the appropriate steps to fulfill the order.

Brian: Ah! So we're gonna need two graphs, right?

Jackie: That's right.

Ashley: ... and there *was* light!

Jackie: Now let's analyze these services and try to develop their *metagraph*.

CONCEPT: Metagraph

A metagraph is a graph which describes another graph, similar to a graph pattern.

Jackie: Let's whiteboard something. The catalog will be the basic domain of the system, because it will be used by the order process. So let's start with it.

1.2. Analysis of the graph catalog

Tiago: I prefer to start by finding entities and the relationships between them, and deal with the details the information they convey later.

Jackie: Agreed.

Nodes and relationships

Tiago: I had a look at the dataset the client gave us, and started drawing the graph shown in Figure 1.2. The graph does not seem very complex at first glance: *people are authors of books.* Let's sketch it on the white board.

Figure 1.2 : Book and Author

Brian: Yup, very simple stuff. But what are the two dots in front of the nodes?

Tiago: As in Jackie's graph, I assign a type to my nodes by using a label. You remember what a label is?

Brian: Ah, yeah...it's a...you know...a label kind of thing that labels the thing that is labelled, speaking label-wise.

FURTHER DETAIL: The labels

A label is a kind of tag. Labels allow us to group together some nodes based on distinct, arbitrary information about the data carried by nodes. Labels are stored within nodes but, unlike properties, are not accessible. They are similar to categories, or types of nodes, but do not convey information other than their name (for example, we can't add properties to labels).

In a CYPHER query, labels are prefixed by a colon.

```
MATCH (publication:Book:ComputerScience)
RETURN publication
```

Here, `Book` and `ComputerScience` are labels.

Tiago: But what the customer actually buys is a specific format (EPUB, HTML, PDF, paper)...

Brian: So it's really very simple! Just use a label for every publishing format and add them to the `Book` node!

Tiago: ...Let me finish and you'll realize how much more there is to it! Every publishing format of a book has its own particular ISBN number, price, etc.

Brian: Oh yeah, and you can't put properties on a label...

Tiago: Exactly. So I'll create a `Product` node:

Figure 1.3 : *Book, Product and Author*

Tiago: This means: one or several persons are authors of one or more books published as one or more products. As you can tell by the awkwardness of that description, we do not worry much about cardinalities because we consider everything as potentially many-to-many, that is, *n,m*. The concept of foreign keys doesn't exist in Neo4j, which makes life easier. We'll see below how to ensure uniqueness of a relationship if need be.

Brian: So we're done already? Great! Happy Hour, anyone?

Tiago: Almost. We are still lacking some pieces. Our Catalog service should, as the name implies, provide a catalog of products.

Brian: Well... we just return the list of products and, voila, Bob's your uncle. Right?

Tiago: No, Brian, Bob's not our uncle yet – there's still more to do. We prefer a Catalog entity for many reasons – the product price may change from time to time, some products may be removed from the catalog, etc.. So we'll create a node type `Catalog`.

Figure 1.4 : *Book, Author, Product and Catalog*

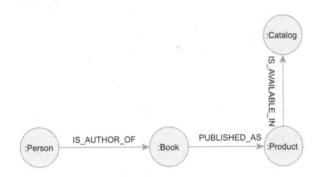

If the `Catalog` life cycle is yearly, each year we'll make a new `Catalog` node. Each of the `IS_AVAILABLE_IN` relationships will carry the price of the product. With this structure, we'll be able to fulfill, for example, the query: *Here is the list of products available in the 20xx catalog related to the book "A Graph Project Story"*.

Iryna: However you are forgetting something: the current catalog.

Tiago (sighs): Not at all. The current catalog is simply the one for the current year!

Iryna: I disagree, that's not good enough. First, if we proceed this way we'll have to handle dates. Second, our client will probably need to start designing a new catalog while the previous one is still active.

Tiago (grouchily): So what! We just add two properties: a start date and an end date, and it all activates automatically.

Iryna: But that's what I'm arguing, we'll need to mess with date ranges! And on top of that, we'll have to develop a scheduled job to activate the new catalog and deactivate the old one. Not to mention that the client will absolutely need to have the new catalog ready before the expiry date of the active one. Seems quite fragile to me...

Tiago (piqued): Doesn't seem fragile to me.

Iryna: Okay, I think we can do better. I suggest we create a `Publisher` node linked to all catalogs. The first benefit is that this will be multitenant.

CONCEPT: Multitenant

The term *software multitenancy* refers to a software architecture in which a single instance of software runs on a server and serves multiple tenants. A tenant is a group of users who share a common access with specific privileges to the software instance. With a multitenant architecture, a software application is designed to provide every tenant a dedicated share of the instance – including its data, configuration, user management, tenant individual functionality and non-functional properties. Multitenancy contrasts with multi-instance architectures, where separate software instances operate on behalf of different tenants.

(Source Wikipedia [http://d-booker.jo.my/neo4j-en-multitenant])

Iryna: If, for some reason, another publisher wants to use the same solution we will be ready. Then we will use a *pointer*, i.e. a relationship that will go from the `Publisher` node to one (and only one) `Catalog` node. This relationship will point to the active catalog, the one currently being sold, solving that problem.

Tiago (reluctantly growling): Yeah...

Iryna: So here's more detail:

Figure 1.5 : *Book, Product, Author, Catalog and Publisher*

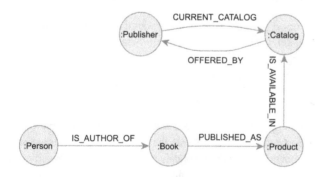

The catalogs are offered by a publisher, and the publisher indicates which catalog is active. A simple query is all that is needed to move the CURRENT_CATALOG relationship from one Catalog node to another Catalog node. Simple, right? You'll notice that I didn't use an action verb for this relationship. That's because this relationship is a pointer–its purpose is to maintain a state. I'll talk about pointer relationships later and show you how they work.

Brian: So now we're done, finally? I'll head out and grab us a table at the brew pub.

Tiago: Almost. Hang in there, Brian.

Tiago hurriedly tries to erase the publisher/catalog portion from the whiteboard. But he is too late, as Jackie has already recorded it on her tablet.

Jackie: We need to address the categorization of books. A user must be able to find all books with a common topic, same as for the publisher website. As of now, the website design allows a book to belong to only one category. Our client would like us to fix this —it should be possible for a book to belong to several categories.

Tiago: I've been giving this some thought. I see two ways of doing this: either we use labels on Book nodes to represent categories, or we associate a weight to the link with the category. For example, the book *A Graph Project Story* is primarily a book about databases, but secondarily a book about programming. Our graph should represent this. The relationship HAS_CATEGORY could be weighted using a matching property indicating relevance.

Figure 1.6 : Book, Product, Author and Category

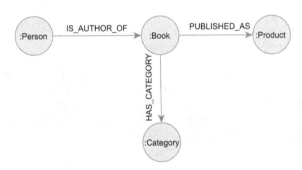

Jackie: Hey, I like that proposal! I'll discuss it with the client.

Brian (suddenly enthusiastic): Yeah, and wouldn't that make it easy to recommend books to readers based on their favorite topics?

Tiago (impressed): Check out the big brain on Brian! Recommendation engines are made for graph databases, and vice versa! But that's another project, so let's just put a pin in that.

Jackie: Awesome idea! Let's keep it in mind, but I will need to first check with the client... Let's move on and discuss what's in our nodes and relationships.

Property analysis

Jackie: Well, let's start on the uniquely identifying properties.

Brian: Wait. I know that properties are the data contained in nodes and relationships. But how would they be uniquely identifying?

Jackie: Let's take a step back and think about this. Unique properties are important properties of our nodes, because they allow us to locate certain nodes. These properties are often indexed to optimize our CYPHER queries.

Brian: Why not just simply index them all? Plus, we can search the labels!

Iryna: Mmmm, not quite. An index is used to quickly retrieve a set of data for a particular value. If you have the same amount of data in your index as you have in your graph, you won't get much benefit from using indexes. Using labels is a good idea, but less performant than using an index. A CYPHER query starts from one or more nodes (the leftmost ones in a MATCH clause) to find the starting points [1]. The time required to find them depends on the type of scanning that Neo4j performs. For example, when we execute the following query:

```
MATCH (n:Book {title:"Neo4j - A Graph Project Story"})
RETURN n
```

If the title property is not indexed, Neo4j will first search for all the nodes with the Book label. Then it will browse *all* entries in this intermediate result (which is, in this case, *all* books!) to find those entitled "Neo4j - A Graph Project Story". Alternatively, if we index the title property of the Book nodes, then Neo4j will use the index for the nodes referring to the value "Neo4j - A Graph Project Story".

---

[1] Actually the query planner chooses the best entry point based on the database statistics.

FURTHER DETAIL: Scanning the entry point of a query

Every CYPHER query starts with an entry point defined in the MATCH clause. Neo4j's query optimizer is designed to improve this lookup by determining the best strategy (using indexes or labels), even before doing pattern matching.

- If the entry point has no nodes using a label or an index, we perform a *full scan* of the graph (AllNodesScan operation).
- If the entry point can be found using a label, we perform a *label scan* (operation NodeByLabelScan).
- If the entry point can be found using an index, we perform an *index scan* (operation NodeIndexSeek or NodeUniqueIndexSeek).

For a given amount of data, generally speaking, index scanning is more performant than label scanning, which in turn is more performant than full scanning. We'll talk more about query performance tuning later in this chapter.

Tiago: Fine, I'll consider each type of node and first figure out the unique constraints we'll want to set up. Jackie and I talked about his, and we established that an email address would serve as a unique identifier for people.

Iryna: Sounds good.

Tiago: Brian, remember how you specify a uniqueness constraint with CYPHER?

Brian: Uh...of course. We politely say "Siri, ask CYPHER to put a uniqueness constraint on".

Tiago: Let's try something like this first.

FURTHER DETAIL: Creating a unique constraint

In the same way as for indexes, a unique constraint can be associated with a label/property pair.

```
CREATE CONSTRAINT ON (identifier:MyLabel)
ASSERT identifier.property IS UNIQUE
```

The creation of this constraint automatically triggers the creation of an index for this label/property pair. The constraint can be removed using a syntax close to the one used for its creation.

```
DROP CONSTRAINT ON (identifier:MyLabel)
ASSERT identifier.property IS UNIQUE
```

Note › We can lookup the list of constraints and indexes by using the **:schema** command from the Neo4j browser.

Tiago: It's slightly more complicated for books because the title is not necessarily unique. For example, the book *A Graph Project Story* might have two volumes with the same title but a different subtitle. The first volume might be subtitled *1. Getting to production,* the second *2. Advanced use cases.* The problem is that Neo4j does not support the uniqueness constraint for two or more properties.

Iryna: That's not quite true anymore...

Tiago: True. Since version 3.2 of Neo4j, we are able to apply composite constraints by using the *NODE KEY* constraint. However, some Neo4j projects haven't upgraded to this version yet, so I think it's important to know an alternate way to accomplish this.

NEW: Creating a composite constraint

The *NODE KEY* constraint makes it possible to enforce the existence and uniqueness of a node using several properties for a given label. This type of constraint is only available in the enterprise edition of Neo4j from version 3.2.

Declaration of a *NODE KEY* constraint:

```
CREATE CONSTRAINT ON (identifier:MyLabel)
ASSERT (identifier.property1, identifier.property2) IS NODE KEY
```

Removal a *NODE KEY* constraint:

```
DROP CONSTRAINT ON (identifier:MyLabel)
ASSERT (identifier.property1, identifier.property2) IS NODE KEY
```

Jackie: Actually, our client doesn't do things that way. Instead, the title is the combination of the title of a set of modules and each module title. A module can be a book, a chapter or something else, like an appendix for example.

Tiago: Ah, I didn't understand that... So building on that, for books we add indexed properties but without unique constraints: the title of the whole set, which might be called the *master title*, the subtitle that corresponds to the module title. And why not also use a property corresponding to the edition, such as "first edition", "second edition", etc. Thus we have a property `title` with unique value, which is the concatenation of these three fields.

Jackie: That works!

Iryna: Mmmmm, I think it's a bit fragile... How about we make the model more robust by using the constraints which verify the existence of a property, available in the enterprise version of Neo4j? This way we can ensure the existence of the `title` field, because the `title` field is *calculated*. Real data, in the strictest sense, should be precisely given, not calculated. It's easy to forget this difference, especially when importing data from some other source. Moreover we can do the same for the fields used in the field's calculations.

Jackie: That works even better!

FURTHER DETAIL: ASSERT EXISTS

The `EXISTS` constraint was included with version 2.3 of Neo4j (but only on the enterprise edition). It ensures when a node is created that a necessary property is present at creation time.

```
CREATE CONSTRAINT ON (identifier:MyLabel)
ASSERT EXISTS (identifier.property)
```

It is also possible to place this type of constraint on a property belonging to a relationship:

```
CREATE CONSTRAINT ON ()-[myRelation:MY_RELATION]-()
ASSERT EXISTS (myRelation.property)
```

Tiago: Let's continue with the uniquely identifying property of `Product` type nodes. Earlier we said that, obviously, the ISBN will serve as identifier.

Ashley: Uh... For my personal enlightenment, what is an ISBN?

Jackie: An International Standard Book Number that uniquely identifies every edition of every book published.

Tiago: We could identify the `Catalog` by a reference value based on a date and an issue number, couldn't we?

Jackie: Perfect.

Tiago: The `Publisher` can be uniquely identified by the corporate name concatenated with the a corporate category.

Jackie: So far this all seems good, right?

Tiago: Let's do it!

Jackie: Here is the complete metagraph:

Figure 1.7 : *Catalog—complete metagraph*

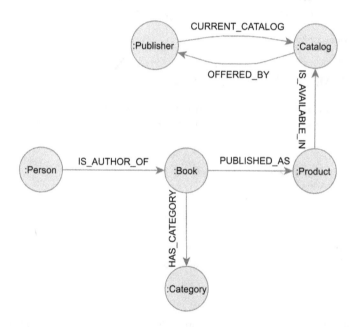

...and some of the uniquely identifying properties:

Table 1.1 : *Catalog—uniquely identifying properties*

Object	Identified by	Constraint
:Person	email	unique
:Book	title	unique, exists

Object	Identified by	Constraint
:Book	mainTitle	indexed, exists
:Book	subTitle	indexed, exists
:Category	title	unique
:Product	isbn	unique
:Product	module	indexed
:Catalog	reference	unique
:Publisher	id	unique
:Publisher	name	indexed

I believe this is a good start!

Let's do some checks

Tiago: Let's start. I'll create indexes and constraints using only features available on the community edition:

```
CREATE CONSTRAINT ON (p:Person) ASSERT p.email IS UNIQUE;
CREATE CONSTRAINT ON (b:Book) ASSERT b.title IS UNIQUE;
CREATE INDEX ON :Book(mainTitle);
CREATE INDEX ON :Book(subTitle);
CREATE CONSTRAINT ON (c:Category) ASSERT c.title IS UNIQUE;
CREATE CONSTRAINT ON (pr:Product) ASSERT pr.isbn IS UNIQUE;
CREATE INDEX ON :Product(module);
CREATE CONSTRAINT ON (ca:Catalog) ASSERT ca.reference IS UNIQUE;
CREATE CONSTRAINT ON (pub:Publisher) ASSERT pub.id IS UNIQUE;
CREATE INDEX ON :Publisher(name);
```

Brian: Neo4j complains when I copy and paste this into the Neo4j browser as it is... Do you have to do them one by one?

Tiago: From the Neo4j browser? Up to version 3.4.2, yes. Newer versions now allows execution of multiple statements.

Ashley: You can also put your query in a .cql file by enclosing it with keywords :begin and :commit (realizing these two keywords are case sensitive), as follows:

```
:begin
CREATE CONSTRAINT ON (b:Book) ASSERT b.title IS UNIQUE;
CREATE INDEX ON :Book(mainTitle);
CREATE INDEX ON :Book(subTitle);
CREATE CONSTRAINT ON (c:Category) ASSERT c.title IS UNIQUE;
```

```
CREATE CONSTRAINT ON (pr:Product) ASSERT pr.isbn IS UNIQUE;
CREATE INDEX ON :Product(module);
CREATE CONSTRAINT ON (ca:Catalog) ASSERT ca.reference IS UNIQUE;
CREATE CONSTRAINT ON (pub:Publisher) ASSERT pub.id IS UNIQUE;
CREATE INDEX ON :Publisher(name);
:commit
```

Then you can load it into Neo4j with the online `cypher-shell` tool using the command:

```
[NEO4J_HOME]$> cat myfile.cql | bin/cypher-shell
                -u neo4j
                -p password
                --format plain
```

TECHNICAL: cypher-shell

The `cypher-shell` command allows us to manipulate a Neo4j graph from the command line.

```
cypher-shell [-h]
[-a IP ADDRESS AND PORT]
[-u USERNAME]
[-p PASSWORD]
[--encryption {true,false}]
[--format {verbose,plain}]
[--debug]
[--non-interactive]
[-v]
[--fail-fast | --fail-at-end]
[cypher]
```

The available options are detailed below:

Table 1.2 : cypher-shell—options

Option	Description
cypher	Execute a CYPHER query.
-h, --help	Displays help
--fail-fast	Stop reading the file when the first error is encountered and return an execution report (default).
--fail-at-end	When reading a file, return the report at the end of the execution.
--format {auto,verbose,plain}	Desired Output Format auto (default) displays results in tabular form, verbose displays results in

Option	Description
	tabular form with additional execution statistics, `plain` display results in minimal form.
`--debug`	Display additional information, disabled by default (`false`).
`--non-interactive`	Force non-interactive mode (useful only when auto-detection is failing), disabled by default.
`-v, --version`	Display the cypher-shell tool version.
`-a, --address`	Specify the Neo4j server to connect with(default: `http://localhost:7687`).
`-u, --username`	Specify the user to be used to connect to the Neo4j server.
`-p, --password`	Specify the password to be used to connect to the Neo4j server.
`--encryption {true,false}`	Specify whether the connection to the Neo4j server must be encrypted or not. This parameter must be consistent with the configuration of the Neo4j server. Encrypted by default. (`true`).

Some keywords which are interpreted by the cypher-shell tool:

Table 1.3 : cypher-shell—keywords

Keyword	Description
`:begin`	Opens a transaction.
`:commit`	Validates the current transaction.
`:exit`	Exits the shell.
`:help`	Displays keywords.
`:history`	Displays the list of last commands executed.
`:param`	Sets the value of a CYPHER query parameter.
`:params`	Displays the CYPHER query parameters.
`:rollback`	Rollback the current transaction.

The `.cql` extension is convention for a *Cypher Query Language* file, but it's really just an ordinary text file.

Tiago: Once these operations are completed, we can check that the constraints and indexes are correct with the command :schema in the Neo4j browser.

```
Indexes
ON :Catalog(reference) ONLINE (for uniqueness constraint)
ON :Category(title) ONLINE (for uniqueness constraint)
ON :Publisher(name) ONLINE
ON :Publisher(id) ONLINE (for uniqueness constraint)
ON :Book(mainTitle) ONLINE
ON :Book(subTitle) ONLINE
ON :Book(title) ONLINE (for uniqueness constraint)
ON :Person(email) ONLINE (for uniqueness constraint)
ON :Product(module) ONLINE
ON :Product(isbn) ONLINE (for uniqueness constraint)
Constraints
ON (product:Product) ASSERT product.isbn IS UNIQUE
ON (person:Person) ASSERT person.email IS UNIQUE
ON (book:Book) ASSERT book.title IS UNIQUE
ON (category:Category) ASSERT category.title IS UNIQUE
ON (catalog:Catalog) ASSERT catalog.reference IS UNIQUE
ON (publisher:Publisher) ASSERT publisher.id IS UNIQUE
```

Now I'm going to enter some data:

```
CREATE
(sylvain :Person{name:"Sylvain", email:"sylvain@graphits.tech"}),
(nicolas :Person{name:"Nicolas", email:"nicolas@graphits.tech"}),
(frank :Person{name:"Frank", email:"frank@graphits.tech"}),
(book :Book {mainTitle:"Neo4j",
 subTitle:"A Graph Project Story",
 title:"Neo4j - A Graph Project Story"}),
(catDB :Category {title:"Databases"}),
(catProg :Category {title:"Programming"}),
(prodPaper :Product {isbn:"9782822703826", module:"Printed Edition"}),
(prodDigital :Product {isbn:"9782822702591", module:"Digital Edition"}),
(catalog2017 :Catalog{reference:"2017-1", year:2017}),
(catalog2018 :Catalog{reference:"2018-1", year:2018}),
(publisher:Publisher {id:"AcmeId", name:"Acme Publishing"}),
(sylvain)-[:IS_AUTHOR_OF]->(book),
(nicolas)-[:IS_AUTHOR_OF]->(book),
(frank)-[:IS_AUTHOR_OF]->(book),
(book)-[:PUBLISHED_AS]->(prodPaper),
(book)-[:PUBLISHED_AS]->(prodDigital),
(prodPaper)-[:IS_AVAILABLE_IN]->(catalog2018),
(prodDigital)-[:IS_AVAILABLE_IN]->(catalog2018),
(catalog2017)-[:OFFERED_BY]->(publisher),
(catalog2018)-[:OFFERED_BY]->(publisher),
(publisher)-[:CURRENT_CATALOG]->(catalog2018),
(book)-[:HAS_CATEGORY {matching:1}]->(catDB),
(book)-[:HAS_CATEGORY {matching:0.3}]->(catProg)
```

This creation query will give us the following graph:

Figure 1.8 : Catalog—some data

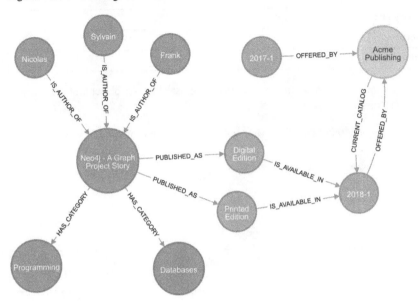

Brian: Woot, woot!

Iryna: Yeah, it works. Then again, it's not exactly rocket science...

Jackie: Ok, now let's query the graph to verify we can answer the basic questions. I'll ask a question and, Tiago, you answer it, ok?

Tiago: Yeah, sure.

Jackie: I'll pretend I'm a user who is visiting the website. The main page displays the following information: a menu with the list of categories...

Tiago: Child's play:

```
MATCH (category:Category) RETURN category.title
```

Table 1.4 : Catalog—categories

category.title
Databases
Programming

Jackie: So now I click on a category, wanting the list of books about that category in descending order of relevance...

Tiago: There's only one book right now, but I can give you a query that works:

```
MATCH (category:Category{title:"Databases"})<-[r:HAS_CATEGORY]-
(book:Book)
RETURN book.title
ORDER BY r.matching DESC
```

Table 1.5 : Catalog—books by category

book.title
Neo4j - A Graph Project Story

Iryna: How about we add some fake Book node just for a test viewing?

```
MATCH (category:Category{title:"Databases"})
WITH category
CREATE (book2:Book {title:"A sample book"}),
  (book2)-[r:HAS_CATEGORY{matching:0.85}]->(category)
WITH category
MATCH (category)<-[r:HAS_CATEGORY]-(book:Book)
RETURN book.title  ORDER BY r.matching DESC
```

Table 1.6 : Catalog—books by category

book.title
Neo4j - A Graph Project Story
A sample book

Tiago (exultantly): Yes! It works!

Iryna: Looks like it. I'm going to try reversing the sort order now...

```
MATCH (category:Category{title:"Databases"})<-[r:HAS_CATEGORY]-
(book:Book)
```

```
RETURN book.title
ORDER BY r.matching ASC
```

Table 1.7 : Catalog–books by category

book.title
A sample book
Neo4j - A Graph Project Story

Tiago does a brief but vivid victory dance...

Iryna: Okay, okay, it works fine. Let's delete the test book.

```
MATCH (book2:Book {title:"A sample book"})
DETACH DELETE book2
```

Jackie: Now let's get more complicated. Give me the list of categories of books published by ACME Publishing in its active catalog.

Tiago: Yeah, give me two seconds... And voilà!

```
MATCH (publisher:Publisher{name:"Acme Publishing"})-[:CURRENT_CATALOG]-
>(catalog:Catalog)<-[:IS_AVAILABLE_IN]-(product:Product)<-
[:PUBLISHED_AS]-(book:Book)-[:HAS_CATEGORY]->(category:Category)
RETURN DISTINCT category.title
```

Table 1.8 : Catalog–active catalog categories

category.title
Databases
Programming

Iryna: I think your current design has a couple of flaws, but we'll tackle that later. Jackie, ask another...

Jackie: Now tell me what books and authors for a given category are available in the active catalog for ACME Publishing.

Tiago: OK, I'm on it...

```
MATCH (publisher:Publisher{name:"Acme Publishing"})-
[:CURRENT_CATALOG]->(catalog:Catalog)<-[:IS_AVAILABLE_IN]-
```

```
(product:Product)<-[:PUBLISHED_AS]-(book:Book)-[:HAS_CATEGORY]-
>(category:Category{title:"Databases"}),
(author:Person)-[IS_AUTHOR_OF]->(book)
RETURN DISTINCT category.title, book.title, author.name
```

Which returns:

Table 1.9 : Catalog—active catalog categories

category.title	book.title	author.name
Databases	Neo4j - A Graph Project Story	Nicolas
Databases	Neo4j - A Graph Project Story	Sylvain
Databases	Neo4j - A Graph Project Story	Frank

Iryna: Okay. Now, it's time to clear something up...

Tiago: What's that?

Iryna: First of all, your query will be difficult to maintain because it's not very readable. The problem is really not that difficult.

Tiago: Well, yeah, but it's a first draft...

Iryna: I get that. We'll take this as a teaching moment to show others about checking and correcting a query.

Jackie: Iryna, you said *first of all*, so I take it you have other issues?

Iryna: In essence, I am not convinced the system will use the indexes correctly. This is not important with a small volume of data, but might become relevant with a larger volume.

Tiago: We can check this out with PROFILE.

Iryna: Ding, ding, ding! You said the magic word!

FURTHER DETAIL: PROFILE and EXPLAIN

The keywords EXPLAIN and PROFILE have the same function: when added before a CYPHER query, they cause Neo4j to provide the execution plan for a query. After all, A CYPHER query is just a bit of text. When Neo4j receives a CYPHER query, it parses it and locates the expressions that are useful for choosing *operators*, that is, the set of instructions that are equivalent to this text. The *execution plan* describes all the operators used for a query, as well as the order in which they are executed.

EXPLAIN presents a probable execution plan but does not execute the query. In this way, one may check write queries without actually altering the graph or check the reach of a query without waiting for the results.

PROFILE executes the query and presents the execution plan that was actually used.

Tiago: The query is read-only (and so won't change the graph) and also has a very low data volume, so we can just use PROFILE:

```
PROFILE
MATCH (publisher:Publisher{name:"Acme Publishing"})-
[:CURRENT_CATALOG]->(catalog:Catalog)<-[:IS_AVAILABLE_IN]-
(product:Product)<-[:PUBLISHED_AS]-(book:Book)-[:HAS_CATEGORY]-
>(category:Category{title:"Databases"}),
(author:Person)-[IS_AUTHOR_OF]->(book)
RETURN DISTINCT category.title, book.title, author.name
```

Figure 1.9 : Query CYPHER - PROFILE

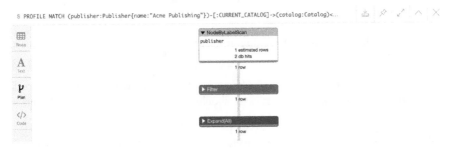

Iryna: You see? The operator used to find the publisher is a NodeByLabelScan, not a NodeByIndexScan.

Tiago: So Neo4j apparently isn't using the index as the starting point of the query?

Iryna: Right. And I think I know why... Let's check out the schema:

```
Indexes
[...]
ON :Publisher(name) ONLINE
ON :Publisher(id) ONLINE (for uniqueness constraint)
[...]
```

We declared two indexes for the `Publisher` label and I suspect multiple indexes will confuse the `COST` planner. It doesn't know which one to pick...

Tiago: The what planner...?

Iryna: The *planner* is the mechanism which builds the implementation plan. I'll come back to this. First let me explain my reasoning and focus for now on this ignored index. I'm going to explicitly tell Neo4j which index to use. To make that easier to edit, I'll have to rewrite the query.

Tiago: I think we're all groping in the dark here. Could you be a little more explicit?

Iryna: Sure. As I said earlier, the query is correct but difficult to read and manipulate. I'll start by making it easier to edit.

```
MATCH (publisher:Publisher{name:"Acme Publishing"})
MATCH (publisher)-[:CURRENT_CATALOG]->(catalog:Catalog)
MATCH (catalog)<-[:IS_AVAILABLE_IN]-(product:Product)
MATCH (product)<-[:PUBLISHED_AS]-(book:Book)
MATCH (author:Person)-[IS_AUTHOR_OF]->(book)
WITH DISTINCT author,book
MATCH (category:Category{title:"Databases"})<-[:HAS_CATEGORY]-(book)
RETURN category.title,author.name,book.title
```

Tiago: Uh, yeah...but several `MATCH` clauses in a row will generate cartesian products, won't they?

Iryna: And cartesian products are evil, I know. But they won't necessarily be generated. If we restart this query with a `PROFILE`, we should see that the execution plan is similar to what we had before.

Ashley: But why do you choose to use mostly `MATCH` clauses instead of `WITH` clauses here?

Iryna: Because I'm not changing data, I'm just doing *pattern matching*. I'm trying to be as simple as I can. But if you look closely, I actually do use a `WITH` clause to search for the category. Indeed, I can distinguish two paths to get the books: a path from the publisher (catalog, etc.) and a path from the provided category. It is natural to separate them in the query. Another interesting point, I'm reducing the number of books upstream through my DISTINCT clause, in order to match the category.

Tiago: And now we can expect to see the index being used?

Iryna: Right. If you remember, we can specify which index we want CYPHER to use.

FURTHER DETAIL: USING SCAN and USING INDEX

These two keywords are used to force the scanning type that Neo4j must perform.

USING SCAN allows you to force label scanning for a particular label when multiple labels are assigned to a node.

USING INDEX allows you to define the index to be used to find a node.

Checking this change:

```
PROFILE
MATCH (publisher:Publisher{name:"Acme Publishing"})
    USING INDEX publisher:Publisher(name)
MATCH (publisher)-[:CURRENT_CATALOG]->(catalog:Catalog)
MATCH (catalog)<-[:IS_AVAILABLE_IN]-(product:Product)
MATCH (product)<-[:PUBLISHED_AS]-(book:Book)
MATCH (author:Person)-[IS_AUTHOR_OF]->(book)
WITH DISTINCT author,book
MATCH (category:Category{title:"Databases"})<-[:HAS_CATEGORY]-(book)
RETURN category.title,author.name,book.title
```

Bam! There it is, using the index!

Figure 1.10 : Query CYPHER - USING INDEX

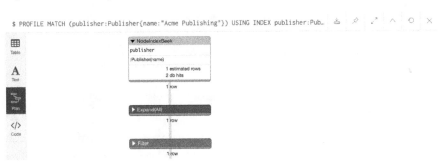

Tiago: There's the operation `NodeIndexSeek` for the query's starting point. We have our index back! But the response time didn't get faster......

Iryna: With so little data we can't expect much performance improvement. Moreover, the COST planner tries to select the best operators to construct its implementation plan.

Tiago: I still don't understand what the COST planner is...

Iryna: I'm getting there.

Jackie: Light on the detail, ok? We have other things to do as well...

Iryna: Ok, in a nutshell, the query planner is the Neo4j component that computes the execution plan of the CYPHER query. There are two of them: the RULE planner and the COST planner. These two planners use different operators to build their plans.

Jackie: Okay, so far, so good.

Iryna: The RULE planner is Neo4j's legacy planner, now deprecated. Briefly, it chooses its operators using only what's in the query, i.e. without worrying about other factors, such as the volume of data in the database, for example.

Jackie: I suppose that the COST planner behaves differently...

Iryna: Exactly. The COST planner will query information from Neo4j internal statistics. Thus it can select the most judicious operators for its execution plan. The COST planner has replaced the RULE planner.

Ashley: How do you choose which planner you want use?

Iryna: You can tell CYPHER which planner to use for a query as follows:

```
CYPHER planner=RULE
PROFILE
MATCH (publisher:Publisher{name:"Acme Publishing"})
MATCH (publisher)-[:ACTIVE_CATALOG]->(catalog:Catalog)
MATCH (catalog)<-[:IS_AVAILABLE]-(product:Product)
MATCH (product)<-[:IS_PUBLISHED]-(book:Book)
MATCH (publisher)-[:ACTIVE_CATALOG]->(catalog:Catalog)
MATCH (catalog)<-[:IS_AVAILABLE]-(product:Product)
MATCH (product)<-[:IS_PUBLISHED]-(book:Book)
MATCH (author:Person)-[IS_AUTHOR]->(book)
WITH DISTINCT author,book
MATCH (category:Category{title:"Databases"})<-[:HAS_CATEGORY]-(book)
RETURN category.title,author.name,book.title
```

Iryna: As you can see, with the RULE planner, the operators used are different. It is also simpler. This planner finds the index to use for the node Publisher all by itself:

Figure 1.11 : *CYPHER planner=RULE*

CYPHER: The CYPHER directive

```
CYPHER[version][planner=COST|RULE]
[runtime=interpreted|slotted|compiled]
```

This directive is used to specify how the CYPHER interpreter works, with arguments defined as follows:

- `[version]`: this option ensures backward compatibility. If the given CYPHER version number is not supported by the Neo4j system used, then a response indicating usable versions will be returned. For example, with Neo4j 3.0: *Supported CypherVersion values are: 2.3, 3.0.*

- `planner=[COST|RULE]`: this option allows the user to specify the use of a specific planner. The RULE planner is deprecated, and the COST planner relies on an internal statistics service at Neo4j to compute the best possible execution plan.

- `runtime=[interpreted|slotted|compiled]`: this little used option allows to choose how cypher queries will be handled by the database: dynamically interpreted, interpreted with more optimizations (default), or converted to compiled code (deprecated).

Iryna: That's basically all you need to know about planners.

Jackie: Thanks. Anything else about the catalog graph analysis?

Iryna: No, it's fine now as far as I'm concerned.

Jackie: So, if I'm summarizing properly, the main steps of this method are:

- Analysis of the client requirements and modelling the graph: at this stage we model the graph on a whiteboard, for example.
- Identification of uniquely identifying properties, to determine the required indexes and constraints.
- Check by exercising on data, enter sample data and run CYPHER queries similar to what we expect to use in production to see if everything works as expected. Write queries, check their behavior using EXPLAIN or PROFILE instructions, and optimize, if necessary.

I think we have the essence of what we need, so let's now move on to the *order process*.

1.3. Analysis of the order process graph

Brian: What do you mean by *order process*?

Iryna: Basically, a process is a series of tasks. An *order*, from a customer perspective, is a set of products he wants to buy. After payment, the publisher gets a list of items and the *order process* is the set of tasks carried out to finalize an order. Here's an example:

Figure 1.12 : Order process

Jackie: Iryna, you said you had some ideas about the order process graph...

Iryna: That's right. And now that we've worked out a process to describe our graphs, I'm going to go a little deeper and focus on modeling.

Tiago: Oh, I see! We built something and now you're going to rework it in your own way!

Iryna: Come on, no, that's not my intent. It's just the graph modeling is an important step and this part is a little more complex than the *Catalog* graph. Trust me, I'm not going to undo anything we've already done. So, anyway, my analysis can be broken into these steps:

- Domain objects, where I'll describe the entities not involved in order process, per se.
- Linked lists, where I'll discuss what linked lists are and describe how they can be manipulated.

- Process without procedure, where I'll demonstrate how a linked list is used in a process.

- Process with procedure, where I'll detail the procedures, a kind of template for the process scale.

Domain objects

Iryna: So I define domain objects as entities that are not directly involved in the execution of the process itself. I intend to come back to this notion of process later [40]. Basically, we define our nodes and relationships as before, which seems to me to give something like:

Figure 1.13 : Order process–domain objects

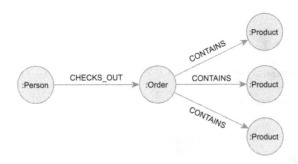

To sum up, a person completes (CHECKS_OUT) an order composed of products. The only new node type is the Order object. It will be assigned a uniquely identifying property of type order identifier. This order identifier must be unique and will be provided by the customer website through an external call.

Brian: How do you get the total cost of the order? Can you show us an example?

Iryna: Later, but let's focus on this for a few minutes. On the previous graph we can enforce the order identifier uniqueness:

```
CREATE CONSTRAINT ON (o:Order) ASSERT o.orderId IS UNIQUE
```

Next we can add some test data. But first, we need to set product prices on the relations binding products to catalogs, i.e. the relations of type IS_AVAILABLE_IN.

```
MATCH (p1:Product{isbn:"9782822702591"})-[r1:IS_AVAILABLE_IN]-
>(c:Catalog)
```

```
SET r1.price=25
WITH p1, r1, c
MATCH (p2:Product{isbn:"9782822703826"})-[r2:IS_AVAILABLE_IN]-
>(:Catalog)
SET r2.price=35
RETURN c.reference as Catalog, p1.module, r1.price, p2.module, r2.price
```

Having done this, we can now add an order to the graph. Let's pretend it is composed of the two previous products and, Brian, you're the client:

```
MERGE (client:Person {email:"brian@graphits.tech"})
 ON CREATE SET client.name="Brian"
MERGE (order:Order {orderId:"20170330-1"})
MERGE (order)<-[:CHECKS_OUT]-(client)
WITH order, client
MATCH (p1:Product{isbn:"9782822702591"})
MERGE (order)-[:INCLUDES]->(p1)
WITH order, client, p1
MATCH (p2:Product{isbn:"9782822703826"})
MERGE (order)-[:INCLUDES]->(p2)
RETURN client, order, [p1,p2]
```

Here's the result. There's nothing new yet.

Figure 1.14 : Order process—domain data

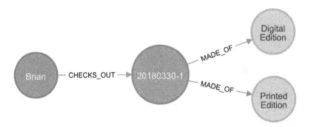

Ashley: Ok, but, you're certainly not going to write your query like you've done here, are you?

Iryna: What do you mean "your query like you've done here"?

Tiago: What Ashley means is that it'd be crazy to do a separate MATCH... MERGE... WITH... for each ISBN code.

Ashley: Correct.

Iryna: Oh yeah, I see. I was doing it quick and dirty. Ultimately we'll use a FOREACH loop...

Ashley: Can you demonstrate this?

Iryna: Of course, and anyway it will be useful for later on:

```
MERGE (client:Person{email:"brian@graphits.tech"})
 ON CREATE SET client.name="Brian"
MERGE (order:Order {orderId:"20170330-1"})
MERGE (order)<-[:CHECKS_OUT]-(client)
WITH order, client, ["9782822702591","9782822703826"] as products
FOREACH (product IN products |
  MERGE (order)-[:INCLUDES]->(:Product{isbn:product}))
```

Iryna: As you can see, the ISBN numbers are in an array. Later we'll bind this array to a parameter $isbn whose value will be provided by an HTTP request from our client's website.

Ashley: That's handy!

Iryna: I know, right?! Now, let's calculate the total for the order that Brian was asking about. To do this, we have to extract the products composing our order. Nothing all that complicated at this stage:

```
MATCH (n:Order)-[:INCLUDES]->(p:Product)
RETURN p
```

Then we lookup the catalog containing these products (the active catalog actually, but I'm simplifying my query for this example). We'll use the relations linking them:

```
MATCH (n:Order)-[INCLUDES]->(p:Product)-[r:IS_AVAILABLE_IN]->(c:Catalog)
RETURN sum (r.price)
```

The total is exactly 60. Finally, we'll display the details and the total:

```
MATCH (n:Order)-[INCLUDES]->(p:Product)-[r:IS_AVAILABLE_IN]->(c:Catalog)
RETURN p.module as module, r.price as price
UNION
MATCH (n:Order)-[INCLUDES]->(p:Product)-[r:IS_AVAILABLE_IN]->(c:Catalog)
RETURN 'Total' as module, sum (r.price) as price
```

Table 1.10 : Order—modules and prices

module	price
Printed Edition	35
Digital Edition	25
Total	60

Iryna: Work for you, Brian?

Brian: I guess so.

Iryna: Good, then let's take the next step.

Linked lists

Brian: Hey, I think I know! These are lists which are linked to one another!

Iryna: Not quite, but close. *Linked lists* is something of a misnomer because we're actually going to focus on the elements that make up one list. A linked list, the name commonly used in computer science, instead means a list with linked elements. By long-standing habit I use the term *collection* to refer to a list. A list is composed of items, for example a shopping list containing items to buy. A linked list is composed of elements linked to each other in such a way that from a given *current* element you can find the *next* element.

Brian: Ok, I'm almost with you it, but...

Iryna: Look, let's consider the shopping list example again. Imagine that you've optimized your route in a store and that you know you must start with the packaged food department and finish with the fresh produce department, in between going through other departments in the order you think is the best.

Brian: Okay.

Iryna: I'll start by creating a list of shelves to visit and I represent it with a node.

```
CREATE (list:List {name:"Shelves to visit"})
RETURN list
```

Brian: Why create a node? Are you storing the definition of the list?

Iryna: That's right, I am. On one hand, I'll be able to store data in the node if I need to, and on the other hand it will help to maintain state. Let's go on by adding the shelves to visit to our list:

```
MATCH (list:List)
WITH list, ["Fresh Food","Canned Food","Drinks"] as shelves
FOREACH (s IN shelves |
  CREATE (shelf:Shelf{name:s})-[:IS_ELEMENT_OF]->(list))
RETURN list,shelves
```

This gives us the following graph. The shelves are linked to the list with IS_ELEMENT_OF relationships:

Figure 1.15 : Linked list–the list and its elements

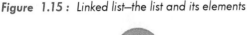
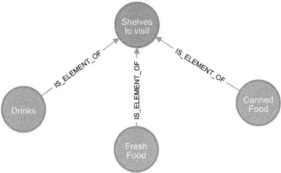

Now I will link the list items together with the others:

```
MATCH (s:Shelf)-[:IS_ELEMENT_OF]->(:List)
WITH s ORDER BY s.name
WITH COLLECT(s) AS shelves
FOREACH (n IN RANGE(0, SIZE(shelves)-2) |
  FOREACH (previous IN [shelves[n]] |
    FOREACH (following IN [shelves[n+1]] |
      MERGE (previous)-[:NEXT]->(following))))
```

FURTHER DETAIL: Reading/Writing with FOREACH

CYPHER provides a mechanism to iterate on a collection and modify the graph accordingly. The general syntax takes the following form:

```
FOREACH (variable IN collection | command)
```

where `variable` is an identifier whose scope is limited to the clause FOREACH; `collection`, the collection to be processed; and `command` the mutation operation to be performed, either: CREATE, MERGE, SET, DELETE or REMOVE.

Let's dissect that query. The MATCH clause returns the items that make up the list. The first WITH clause sorts them alphabetically (an arbitrary choice). The second WITH clause gathers the shelves we found into a collection. Then the query goes through this collection omitting the last element (first FOREACH) and processes the current element of my list (second FOREACH) and the element that follows it (third FOREACH). Finally I link them with my MERGE clause.

Figure 1.16 : Linked list–linked elements

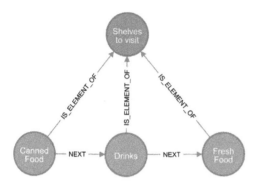

Tiago: Okay, but what does that do for us?

Iryna: Let me first finish this part and then I'll show you the use case. I still have to setup a pointer that will track the current status of my shopping. I'll create this pointer with a relation, exactly as we did in the *Catalog* graph to point to the active catalog of the publisher:

```
MATCH (list:List)
MATCH (s:Shelf) WHERE NOT (s)<-[:NEXT]-(:Shelf)
MERGE (list)-[:CURRENT_ELEMENT]->(s)
```

Iryna: In this way I've positioned the pointer on the first element of the list, i.e. on the element that does not have an incoming relation of type NEXT:

Figure 1.17 : Linked list–pointer

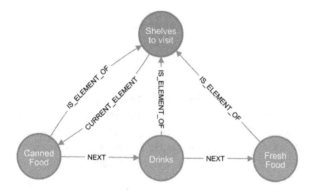

Iryna: Now we are able to iterate on the elements on the list. To do this we have to perform two actions: returning the current element and advancing the pointer to the next element...

Tiago: Something like what we do with the `iterator.next()` in Java...?

Iryna: Exactly. Note that it is quite possible to perform one operation (return the current element for example) without performing the other (moving the pointer). Here is the query that combines the two operations:

```
MATCH (list:List)-[p:CURRENT_ELEMENT]->(current:Shelf)
MATCH (current)-[:NEXT]->(following:Shelf)
DELETE p
MERGE (list)-[:CURRENT_ELEMENT]->(following)
RETURN current
```

Iryna: As you can see, the CURRENT_ELEMENT pointer moved from the first to the second element of the list.

Figure 1.18 : *Linked list—pointer movement*

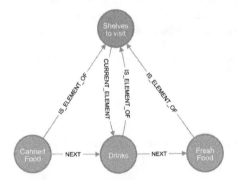

Iryna: I really like this design model. It has proven useful in lots of cases, and it is one of the benefits graphs provide: it's easy to describe and easy to handle technically.

Jackie: Also, if you think about it, it could be used for ISBN numbers.

Ashley: How's that?

Jackie: ACME Publishing, like all publishers, has a sequence of ISBN/EAN numbers provided by the U.S. ISBN Agency.

Ashley: I'm still not getting your point...

Jackie: Once an ISBN number has been assigned to a product, ACME Publishing can no longer use it legitimately–only numbers still available in the pool can be used. Now imagine this sequence of numbers as a linked list, each available number being a node. You could then, applying this mechanism, pull the current number and assign it to a specific product, then move the pointer to the next number...

Ashley: Absolutely! Great use case! That eliminates the risk of using the same number twice.

Jackie: Score one for me!

Process (without procedure)

Iryna: Remember I said that by process I mean a list of tasks to be performed sequentially?

Jackie: How is that different from a procedure?

Iryna: My idea of procedure, and this is my personal use of the word, is that a procedure is a way to define the process. The procedure is, so to speak, the schema (or metadata) used as a template for all processes. The overall behavior is as follows: as each task is performed, the process will query the procedure *I just finished task x, what's next?*

Tiago: So in other words, according to your definition of procedure, you might say a *process* is an *instance of a procedure?*

Iryna: Yes, that's the way I see it. But let's forget the procedure for now, and focus on an order process.

Jackie: So you mentioned linked lists earlier, and just now you mentioned that a process is a list of tasks. I bet you're connecting those two ideas, right?

Iryna: Yup, you got it. Let's take another look at the order process:

Figure 1.19 : Order process

Tiago: That's not much like what you had before!

Iryna: True, I simplified it quite a bit, because I want to focus on the process we want to implement, rather than on the definition of the process itself. Our client didn't go into the details about this. So, in short, let's pretend to be ACME Publishing and determine the tasks we need to carry out to fulfill an order.

Jackie: Okay, so the idea is this: we've received the order and someone has to validate it (for example, was the payment accepted?, are copies available?). Then the order goes to fulfillment, the people responsible for preparing the package, then sent to the shipping department. That's briefly what I'm imagining.

Iryna: Okay, so now we put the two graphs together:

Figure 1.20 : *Control graph*

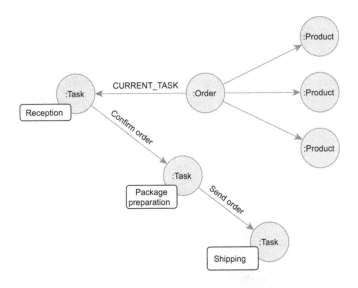

There are lots of ways to do this. One might, for example, split the order process and the order itself. Still, I'm portraying the simplest solution that illustrates my point. Here the order *is* the list (much like the node List in our shopping list examples).

Tiago (rubbing his forehead): Hey, I think I see where you're going with this...

Iryna: So, maybe like Tiago you see the trick coming. We will apply the principle of linked lists to our ordering process. I'll start by creating the graph as soon as the order is received. To keep the graph consistent, I do it in one shot, i.e. with a single query so that we stay within a single transaction:

```
MATCH (ord:Order{orderId:"20170330-1"})
WITH ord,
     ['Reception','Preparation','Shipping'] as taskNames
FOREACH (n IN RANGE(0, SIZE(taskNames)-1) |
  FOREACH (taskName IN [taskNames[n]] |
    MERGE (task:Task{name:taskName,order:n})-[:IS_ELEMENT_OF]->(ord)))
WITH  ord
MATCH (task:Task)-[:IS_ELEMENT_OF]->(ord)
WITH ord, task ORDER BY task.order
WITH ord, COLLECT(task) AS tasks
FOREACH (n IN RANGE(0, SIZE(tasks)-1) |
  FOREACH (previous IN [tasks[n]] |
    FOREACH (next IN
      CASE n WHEN 0 THEN [tasks[n+1]] END |
        MERGE (previous)-[:CONFIRM_ORDER]->(next))
    FOREACH (next IN
      CASE n WHEN 1 THEN [tasks[n+1]] END |
        MERGE (previous)-[:SEND_ORDER]->(next))))
RETURN ord
```

The team members now resemble a herd of deer staring vacantly into a headlight...

Tiago: That's...kind of...complicated, isn't it?

Iryna: A little, I admit. Let me explain it piece by piece. Starting with the first bloc:

```
MATCH (ord:Order{orderId:"20170330-1"})
```

Nothing very complicated there. I'm getting the order. The next part creates the process tasks associated with the order because, like I said, the order represents the list:

```
WITH ord,
     ['Reception','Preparation','Shipping'] as taskNames
FOREACH (n IN RANGE(0, SIZE(taskNames)-1) |
  FOREACH (taskName IN [taskNames[n]] |
    MERGE (task:Task{name:taskName,order:n})-[:IS_ELEMENT_OF]->(ord)))
```

The two FOREACH instructions allow to retrieve the current index of the task collection so it can be assigned to the order property of the corresponding task node.

The order, acting as a control structure for the list, is in the center of the Figure 1.21, the products are on the right and the process tasks on the bottom.

Figure 1.21 : Generation of process tasks

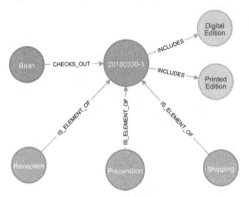

For technical reasons, the rest is a little bit more complicated. I'm trying to link the tasks of the process as I did in the previous example of the linked list. The first FOREACH allows to iterate on tasks (omitting the last element). The second FOREACH finds the current task. The last pair of FOREACH instructions use the next element to create the link:

```
FOREACH (n IN RANGE(0, SIZE(tasks)-1) |
  FOREACH (previous IN [tasks[n]] |
    FOREACH (next IN
      CASE n WHEN 0 THEN [tasks[n+1]] END |
        MERGE (previous)-[:CONFIRM_ORDER]->(next))
    FOREACH (next IN
      CASE n WHEN 1 THEN [tasks[n+1]] END |
        MERGE (previous)-[:SEND_ORDER]->(next))))
```

This gives us the following graph:

Figure 1.22 : Related tasks

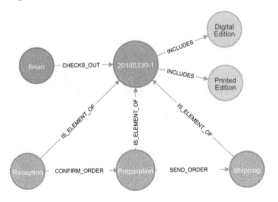

Unlike the earlier example with linked lists, we want the relationship type between tasks to be distinct to make them more meaningful, like CONFIRM_ORDER that links the first task to the second (n=0) or SEND_ORDER linking the second task to the third. Currently CYPHER doesn't have a way to write something like MERGE (previous)-[:relationship_type_variable]->(next)[2], so I had to cobble it together with a double FOREACH and an instruction CASE:

```
FOREACH (next IN
  CASE n WHEN 0 THEN [tasks[n+1]] END |
    MERGE (previous)-[:CONFIRM_ORDER]->(next))
FOREACH (next IN
  CASE n WHEN 1 THEN [tasks[n+1]] END |
    MERGE (previous)-[:SEND_ORDER]->(next))))
```

Finally, we need a FOREACH instruction for each relationship type to be created. That's because the FOREACH instruction is the only one that allows to do conditional processing.

```
next IN CASE n WHEN 0 THEN [tasks[n+1]] END
```

The result of the CASE instruction is stored in the next variable, and can be used in the rest of the instruction scope. The WHEN selector allows to filter on the task index (n), creating the specific relationship according to the position of the task in the list.

Jackie: Okay, it's actually not that difficult. It helps when you explain it.

Iryna: I know it's a little painful at first, but it's a good trick to have in your CYPHER arsenal.

Ashley: But wait, Iryna. Where's the pointer?

Iryna: I was just coming to that!

Ashley: Ah, okay, good, I thought I was lost...

Tiago: Well, Iryna, step on it. We haven't got all day. Brian's already at happy hour in spirit.

Brian: Hey, I'm totally focussed on the beer and now...uh...*here* and now.

Iryna: Better idea...YOU do it. Let's see if you followed!

Jackie: Maybe it will help us to get another perspective!

---

[2]This can be done using the APOC library which is further detailed in the section *APOC procedures and functions*, and left as an exercise for the reader!

Tiago: I smell a trap!

Ashley (laughing): Hey, would we do something like that?!

Tiago: Challenge accepted. So, the customer, on the website, creates an order that we persist in the graph. Then when he confirms his order, we attach a process to it...

Iryna: Solid!

Tiago: Now the process is created and we will point the current state to the first task. The CYPHER should look something like:

```
MATCH (ord:Order{orderId:"20170330-1"})
MATCH (task:Task{name:"Reception"})
MERGE (ord)-[:STEP_IN_PROCESS]->(task)
RETURN ord
```

Given the following graph:

Figure 1.23 : *Step in progress*

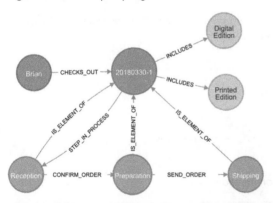

And I can find the task in progress by running the following CYPHER query:

```
MATCH (ord:Order{orderId:"20170330-1"})-[:STEP_IN_PROCESS]->(task:Task)
RETURN ord.orderId AS Order, task.name AS Progress
```

We get the following result that shows the customer where the status of the order:

Table 1.11 : *Order–progress*

Order	Task
20170330-1	Reception

But in the workflow done at ACME Publishing, each department must be able to view their assigned tasks. For example, the department in charge of validating orders (checking the availability of copies, etc.) could use the following to provide a display with the essential information:

```
MATCH (ord:Order{orderId:"20170330-1"})-[:STEP_IN_PROCESS]->(task:Task)
RETURN ord.orderId AS Order, task.name AS Progress
```

which returns:

Table 1.12 : Order—dashboard

Order	Client	E-Mail	ISBNs
20170330-1	Brian	brian@graphits.tech	[9782822703826, 9782822702591]

Once a user completes a task, he would then click a button, executing the following CYPHER query and advancing the process:

```
MATCH (ord:Order{orderId:'20170330-1'})
MATCH (ord)-[r:STEP_IN_PROCESS]->(task:Task)
MATCH (task)-[status]->(nextTask:Task)
DELETE r
MERGE (ord)-[:STEP_IN_PROCESS]->(nextTask)
RETURN 'The step '+task.name+' is done. '
       + 'The process has status ' + nextTask.name
       AS Confirmation
```

Thus, the user would have get a confirmation:

```
Confirmation
-------------
The step Reception is done.
The process has the status: Preparation.
```

Now the graph would look like this:

Figure **1.24** : Next step

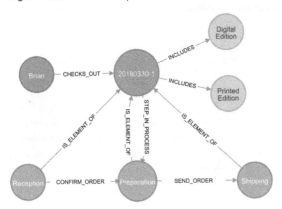

Finally, if the department in charge of processing the next task notices that something has gone wrong, for example a product is out of stock, they could send it back to the first team so they could notify the customer. The CYPHER query would be something like this:

```
MATCH (ord:Order{orderId:"20170330-1"})
MATCH (order)-[r:STEP_IN_PROCESS]->(task:Task)
MATCH (task)<-[]-(previousTask:Task)
DELETE r
MERGE (ord)-[:STEP_IN_PROCESS]->(previousTask)
RETURN "The step "+task.name
       +" is cancelled.  The order reverts to the task : "
       +previousTask.name AS Confirmation
```

```
Confirmation
-------------
The step Preparation is cancelled.
The order reverts to the task : Reception
```

Iryna: Bravo! That's perfect. You did exactly what I had imagined.

Tiago (proud of himself): Well, that's what I do.

Jackie: That's really clear, flexible and easy to set up. I imagine that you wanted to simplify the example as much as possible in order to highlight the procedure without going into the nitty-gritty data details.

Iryna: Right. In fact, we ignored a lot. For example, digital and printed editions are so far being treated in the same way. We might imagine a global process for ordering, then sub-processes for each of the products contained in that order. Moreover, every time a task is started it should be time-stamped, so we can support an audit of the order pipeline. We might want to register comments when moving to a new task, etc.

Jackie: Is that it for this part?

Iryna: Yes, that's it for processes without procedure (or with implicit procedure).

Process with procedure

Iryna: Now, we just saw how we could implement a process with Neo4j. However, the template for this process (which we're defining as the "procedure") was hard coded in CYPHER. Now let's see how we can define a graph representing the procedure as well, and to create instances of this template. With this, we can dynamically create the task at runtime, during the execution of the process. Here is an example of what our order management procedure might look like (Note that I added a cancellation step to the order process we have seen previously):

Figure 1.25 : How to process an order

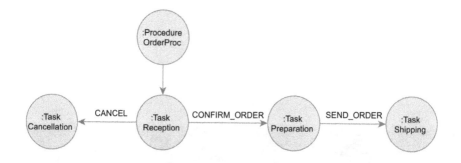

This procedure will be described as an unrelated subgraph, meaning it will not be directly connected to our previous data. First, I'll create an index with a uniqueness constraint for the procedure:

```
CREATE CONSTRAINT ON (proc:Procedure) ASSERT proc.name IS UNIQUE
```

as well as an index for the tasks:

```
CREATE INDEX ON :Task(name)
```

Now I'll delete references to the previous processes:

```
MATCH (t:Task)
DETACH DELETE t
```

Next, I'll create the subgraph that represents the procedure in Neo4j:

```
MERGE (proc:Procedure{name:"OrderProc"})
MERGE (reception:Task{name:"Reception"})
MERGE (prep:Task{name:"Preparation"})
MERGE (shipping:Task{name:"Shipping"})
MERGE (cancel:Task{name:"Cancellation"})
MERGE (proc)-[:START]->(reception)
MERGE (reception)-[:CONFIRM_ORDER]->(prep)
MERGE (reception)-[:CANCEL]->(cancel)
MERGE (prep)-[:SEND_ORDER]->(shipping)
RETURN proc
```

So, I have defined a procedure composed of four tasks as well as the path that will be taken by the order, the object this procedure operates on. The exact path depends on the decisions taken at each step. The possible decisions are indicated by the names of the outgoing relationships of each node (START, CONFIRM_ORDER, SEND_ORDER and CANCEL).

Figure 1.26 : Order management procedure in Neo4j

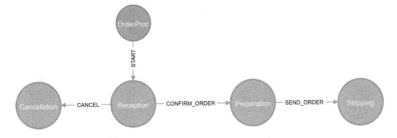

Now let's take another look at the order that Brian placed in the order process graph seen above. Previously this order was confirmed and arrived in our system. At this point, we created the whole process. Now, instead of doing that, we can query the procedure to determine the first step of this process, then create a copy of the first node and finally attach the order just received using a pointer.

Jackie: Hey, Usain Bolt. You're going a little too fast...

Iryna: Sorry, I skipped a few steps. Let me back up a bit. We want to use the procedure to determine how the process starts for this order. The plan is to create a Process node that will link together the order, the procedure, and the task instances. The query creating this node might look like this:

```
MATCH (proc:Procedure{name:"OrderProc"})
MATCH (ord:Order{orderId:"20170330-1"})
MERGE (process:Process{key:"Process "+ ord.orderId})
  <-[:IS_MANAGED_BY]-(ord)
MERGE (process)-[:IS_INSTANCE_OF]->(proc)
RETURN process
```

And then the graph looks like this:

Figure 1.27 : *Process resulting from a procedure*

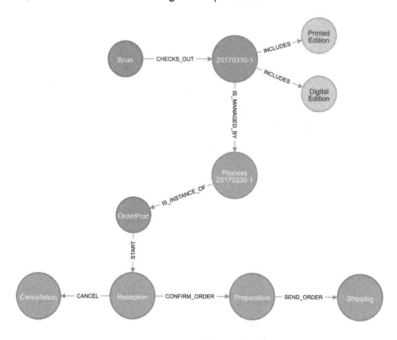

Please note: the bottom part of the diagram is the procedure named order and the top part of the diagram is the order itself. In between is our new node: the Process (which is an instance of the procedure).

Jackie: Okay, better. I guess at some point we'll see TaskInstance nodes connecting to the Process node ?

Iryna: Right, exactly! Instead of creating all the task instances upfront, we'll create them on the fly as the process executes. First, we need to find the starting task. For that we call the procedure and create a corresponding instance for the relevant process:

```
MATCH (ord:Order{orderId:"20170330-1"})
MATCH (process:Process)<-[:IS_MANAGED_BY]-(order)
MATCH (process)-[:IS_INSTANCE_OF]->(proc:Procedure)
MATCH (proc)-[:START]->(task:Task)
MERGE (taskInstance:TaskInstance{key:task.name+" : "+ ord.orderId})
  -[:IS_ELEMENT_OF]->(process)
ON CREATE SET
  taskInstance = task,
  taskInstance.key=task.name+" : "+ ord.orderId
MERGE (process)-[:STEP_IN_PROCESS]->(taskInstance)
RETURN process, taskInstance
```

I start with the order to find its process. From there we can get the procedure from which that process is taken. Finally I lookup in the procedure for the first task to create. Notice that I positioned a pointer on this first instance of a task. That's very similar to what we've seen before.

Figure 1.28 : *First instance of task*

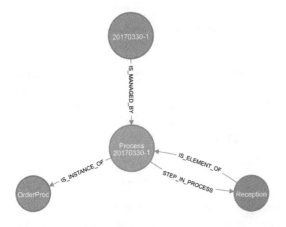

Brian: Wow, you do some weird voodoo incantation when you create your task instance. What's the deal with this "ON CREATE SET taskInstance = task" stuff?

Iryna: So, you *should have* noticed that on the Process and TaskInstance nodes, there is a key composed of the order identifier and the task name. It guarantees that the node (and maybe an associated relationship) is generated only once.

Brian: Uh, yeah...well, no...maybe...wait, what was the question?

Iryna: It appears we could have a more detailed discussion about the MERGE instruction...

FURTHER DETAIL: Conditional writing with MERGE

A `MERGE` clause creates elements if they do not exist, or finds them (using the properties passed) if they do exist.

The `MERGE` clause can be used for both nodes and relationships. If, like in the previous query, the `MERGE` is used on a pattern, then it will not use partially existing patterns. It will attempt to match the entire pattern and create the entire pattern if missing. See this detailed blog post [http://d-booker.jo.my/neo4j-cypher-merge] for in-depth explanation.

The usefulness of the `MERGE` clause lies mainly in its ability to execute `ON CREATE` events (when the graph element does not exist and should therefore be created) and `ON MATCH` events (when the graph element exists and is found). With these, we can do some specific actions when the graph element exists or when it does not exist.

Brian: Well... So... But that doesn't explain weird properties you pass to your task instance.

Iryna: In practice, we can easily imagine that a task in the procedure could have different properties, such as notification information in case we want to send an email when it done, for example. We can imagine a lot of things leading to a bunch of properties for a task. Anyway, we have to copy all the task properties into the task instance by using the `SET taskInstance = task`. It's a copy of the contents of the node.

Brian: But why do you specify the `key` property with the code `SET taskInstance = task, taskInstance.key = task.name+" : "+ ord.orderId`? Don't we already know the key?

Iryna: Because when you pass an object to a node you replace all its properties, thereby deleting the previous ones (like the `key` property in the `MERGE` instruction). So we have to reset the key property.

Jackie: Brian, we have to move on—time is flying fast. We can review all this stuff later. Iryna, can you show us how we make this new process evolve?

Iryna: Sure. We are now at the moment when the order is placed by the customer and the task of *Receiving the account* is opened. I imagine myself in the shoes of the person responsible for receiving orders for the account. Once I've done some checks and maybe entered some data (like a comment, for instance), the following screen appears. At this point I can decide if I should cancel this order or validate it.

Figure 1.29 : Advancing the process

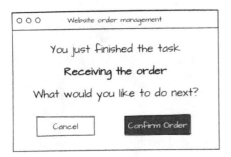

You might note that we can build this screen using the procedure node, with a small CYPHER query.

```
MATCH (proc:Procedure{name:"OrderProc"})
MATCH (proc)-[*]->(task:Task{name:"Reception"})
MATCH (task)-[r]->(nextTask:Task)
RETURN task.name AS `Step in process`, type(r) AS Action
```

which returns:

Table 1.13 : Procedure—actions available from a task

Step in process	Action
Reception	CONFIRM_ORDER
Reception	CANCEL

Brian: Hang on, sorry, I know it's late, Jackie, but I'm having a little trouble understanding this part: `(proc)-[*]->(task:Task{name:"Reception"})`

Iryna: Let me explain, Brian. The idea is to write a generic query, not a query that is only valid for this process. If I were to make it configurable it would have this form:

```
MATCH (proc:Procedure{name:$theProcedure})
MATCH (proc)-[*]->(task:Task{name:$theTaskStep})
MATCH (task)-[r]->(nextTask:Task)
RETURN task.name AS `Step in process`, type(r) AS Action
```

We must set up CYPHER queries with parameters, because by doing so the query interpreter doesn't have to rebuild them every time. It also allows them to be cached (where only the parameter values change). The * character in the relationship essentially means that I am looking for the task that has a specific name and belongs to a given procedure regardless of how many relationships separate the procedure node from the task node. This is known as a *variable length relationship*.

Brian: OK, I think I can buy that.

Iryna: Now I can click one of the buttons on the UI and move the process forward. Technically, this action should be done in the same transaction, but for clarity, I will complete it as I go. It includes three steps:

1. Find the next task in the procedure.

2. Create an instance for this task in our process and link this instance to the previous one (to create a path).

3. Move the pointer to point to the new task instance.

To find the current task in the procedure, I'm going to start from the order for the action CONFIRM_ORDER:

```
// find next task
MATCH (ord:Order{orderId:"20170330-1"})
MATCH (process:Process)<-[:IS_MANAGED_BY]-(ord)
MATCH (process)-[:IS_INSTANCE_OF]->(proc:Procedure)
MATCH (proc)-[*]->(task:Task{name:"Reception"})
MATCH (task)-[e]->(nextTask)
WHERE type(e)="CONFIRM_ORDER"
RETURN nextTask
```

Then I create an instance of that task:

```
// find next task
MATCH (ord:Order{orderId:"20170330-1"})
MATCH (process:Process)<-[:IS_MANAGED_BY]-(ord)
MATCH (process)-[:IS_INSTANCE_OF]->(proc:Procedure)
MATCH (proc)-[*]->(task:Task{name:"Reception"})
MATCH (task)-[e]->(nextTask)
WHERE type(e)="CONFIRM_ORDER"

// Create the task instance
MATCH (process)-[pointer:STEP_IN_PROCESS]-
>(instanceInProgress:TaskInstance)
MERGE (nextInstance:TaskInstance{key: nextTask.name+' : '+ ord.orderId})
  -[:IS_ELEMENT_OF]->(process)
ON CREATE
  SET
    nextInstance = nextTask,
    nextInstance.key=nextTask.name+' : '+ ord.orderId
MERGE (instanceInProgress)-[:TO{action:'CONFIRM_ORDER'}]->(nextInstance)
RETURN instanceInProgress, nextInstance
```

And finally move the pointer:

```
// find next task
MATCH (ord:Order{orderId:"20170330-1"})
MATCH (process:Process)<-[:IS_MANAGED_BY]-(ord)
MATCH (process)-[:IS_INSTANCE_OF]->(proc:Procedure)
MATCH (proc)-[*]->(task:Task{name:"Reception"})
MATCH (task)-[e]->(nextTask)
WHERE type(e)="CONFIRM_ORDER"

// Create the task instance
MATCH (process)-[pointer:STEP_IN_PROCESS]-
>(instanceInProgress:TaskInstance)
MERGE (nextInstance:TaskInstance{key: nextTask.name+' : '+ ord.orderId})
  -[:IS_ELEMENT_OF]->(process)
ON CREATE
  SET
    nextInstance = nextTask,
    nextInstance.key=nextTask.name+' : '+ ord.orderId
MERGE (instanceInProgress)-[:TO{action:'CONFIRM_ORDER'}]->(nextInstance)

// Move the pointer
DELETE pointer
MERGE (process)-[:STEP_IN_PROCESS]->(nextInstance)
RETURN process, nextInstance
```

And, Expecto Patronum, I've pulled the rabbit out of the hat! The query looks complex but it is actually a combination of the different examples we already seen.

Figure 1.30 : The process has progressed!

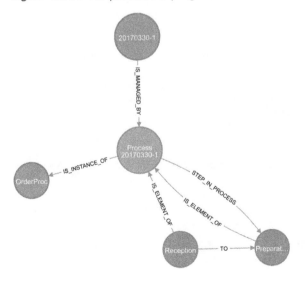

And those are the basic principles of process manipulation in Neo4j. Everybody happy?

Ashley: Hmmm, it's cool you can change the steps of the workflow. Processes that haven't yet reached the new steps will go through them, while existing processes will keep using the old workflow.

Iryna: It's quite dynamic, and you raise a point which leads to other questions. We may want to modify the procedure for all processes. In that case we would make the procedure public. We can also make sure that the procedure the process started with is the same as the one that it finishes with. Or, in other cases, a process can have its own copy of the procedure, and the instance could modify the process according to special business rules. In that case, this copy would be considered a private procedure. As you can see, we're just scratching the surface of what is possible.

Jackie: I don't mean to be a party pooper, but I think we already have what we need for the moment.

1.4. Debriefing

Varsha brings the entire Acme project team together to review the progress of the project, or more precisely, the progress of the proof of concept.

Varsha: Hello everyone. I'm sure that all of you have thought long and hard about how to approach this project. How about sharing your progress with me?

Jackie: Several ideas came up. We've thought through some of them, and we think we're on the right track.

Varsha: Okay. From what I gather, your intention was to broadly guesstimate our client's needs.

Jackie: That's right. Roughly speaking, we see two graphs emerging from our analysis, the *Catalog* graph and the *Order Process* graph.

Varsha: Okay, fill me in.

Jackie: The *Catalog* graph appears to be standard data storage. As such, we were able to use graph development method, which is:

- If you need to *list the business domain object entities*, they should be nodes in our graph.
- *Find the relationships* that these objects maintain with one another and design the metagraph.

- *Define the uniquely identifying properties*, i.e. the properties used to find these objects. These properties will be used to create the indexes and the constraints.
- *Check with sample data*, enter data, write sample business CYPHER queries to evaluate the suitability of the graph, then optimize the queries.

We ended up with a good basis for the *Catalog* graph, and moreover solved some additional unexpected technicalities, like managing the current catalog.

Varsha: Sounds elegant! You can show me the details later. Now let's talk about the part that worries me most, this dreaded order process...

Jackie: Here again, we came up with some ideas. The order process is obviously a little more complex, but once we broke it down into pieces, we can propose some nifty solutions which uses the graph in all its glory. As a result, we have addressed the following points:

- *Definition of domain objects*, that is, objects that are not directly used to manage the process itself. These are business objects such as the object Order.
- *Study on linked lists*, we introduced the concept of a pointer and how certain types of relationships can change.
- *Study on processes*, a matter of combining the first two points, i.e. constructing a life cycle for the domain objects.
- *Study on processes with procedures*, or how to define an order procedure as another (unrelated) subgraph. This subgraph essentially serves as a template of orders lifecycle.

Varsha: So I can stop worrying now?

Jackie: We don't want you to worry, but you can be sure other problems will come up. Let's go with you should be vigilantly relaxed, or maybe calmly nervous. We'll need to talk further with the client to focus in on the best solution for their environment.

Varsha: That's good news. Well done, good job. So what's next?

Jackie: We'll gradually get into the more technical details. We'll need to study the possible facets of interfacing with Neo4j because there is a strong likelihood that we will need to integrate some tools or customer data.

Varsha: That sounds awesome. Thanks everyone, and I'll check in again later when you're further along.

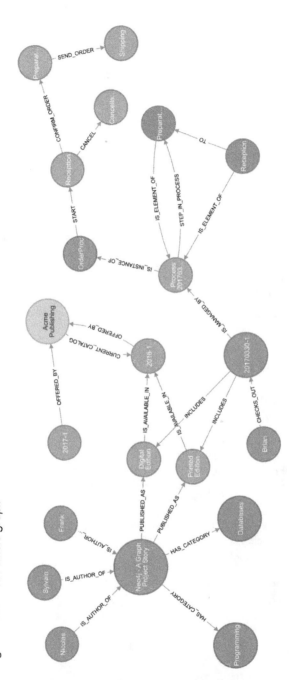

Figure 1.31 : The whole graph

2
Interact with Neo4j

Modern applications are rarely developed around a single system. Solutions often have several modules, each with a well-defined responsibility. To help address these modularity requirements, out-of-the-box Neo4j provides tools and suggested techniques to help users integrate with existing and/or heterogeneous systems. We will see how external systems as well as Neo4j itself can interact with Neo4j.

2.1. Briefing

Jackie, Tiago, Iryna, Ashley and Brian get together to review the different interfaces Neo4j offers.

Jackie: Who's going to get us started?

Iryna: Let's begin by separating our study into two pieces. First, what Neo4j offers to enable interaction with other systems and then, protocols that allow an external system to work with Neo4j.

Jackie: That sounds pretty good to me.

Iryna: Of course any interaction with Neo4j starts with CYPHER...

Brian: Not CYPHER again. I'm getting kinda sick of...

Iryna: But as we're getting to know CYPHER pretty well, now we'll focus more on CYPHER functions and procedures, which offer a flexible and elegant way to extend Neo4j.

Brian: I know I'm going to hate myself for asking, but what is a CYPHER procedure?

Iryna: Glad you asked. Let me explain.

2.2. CYPHER procedures and functions

Iryna: Procedures and functions can be thought of as extensions to CYPHER. Procedures are called from CYPHER to perform processing on the Neo4j server. This processing will return values to be used in the CYPHER query that made the original call.

Brian: And now I truly hate myself. But I guess I'm past the point of no return now. Might as well take the bull by the tail and face the situation. Can you explain, gently, the difference between a procedure and a function?

Iryna: Functions are mainly intended to perform simple calculations or transformations on data within the CYPHER query. Functions return a single value. They can also play the role of predicates, also known as filter criteria.

Brian: So these are like ordinary functions, such as `count()` for example?

Iryna: Yes, and they are used like the built-in CYPHER functions. In contrast, procedures will usually be used for more complex processing, and return a stream of results. A procedure also might perform asynchronously.

Brian: Procedures sound way more complicated. Is there an advantage to using procedures?

Tiago: Sure. We've seen something like this before. Remember when we were looking at a scenario in which some queries were taking a long time to write data? With procedures we could centralize the code, ultimately resulting with a query that is much easier to read and maintain.

Iryna: Right.

General information on procedures

Iryna: As I said before we can think of procedures as an extension of the CYPHER language. While some procedures are integrated into Neo4j server (*built-in procedures*), others are distributed as plugins. And of course, you're free to write your own plugins (using a JVM based language such as Java, Scala or Kotlin for example).

REMINDER: Install a plugin

To add a plugin to Neo4j, follow the following steps:

1. Place the `.jar` file in the `[NEO4J_HOME]/plugins` folder of the Neo4j server.
2. Restart the Neo4j server.
3. Check the Neo4j logs to make sure no errors have occurred.

Tiago: You neglected to mention how to trigger a procedure:

```
CALL procedure.name

CALL procedure.name() YIELD property1

CALL procedure.name() YIELD property1, property2, ..., propertyN
```

Caution › *There should be no space between the procedure name and the parentheses.*

The `CALL` statement is followed by the name of the procedure. The name of the procedure may be hierarchical, in which case each part will be separated by a dot. For example, the procedure to create a user in the Neo4j system is named: `dbms.security.createUser`.

Iryna: You really should explain the `YIELD` instruction.

Tiago: Yeah, I was just getting to that point...

Iryna: Never mind, I'll do it...

Tiago: Hey, step off, Dude. I'll take this!

Ashley: While you guys bicker, *I'll* explain. The `YIELD`, which could be interpreted as meaning that the procedure returns results, allows the CYPHER query that executed the `CALL` to use the values returned by the procedure. The YIELD instruction is followed by a comma delimited list of properties output by the procedure. We have to use the property names defined by the procedure signature. We refer to the documentation of the procedure to get these properties.

Tiago: Word for word what I was going to say.

Iryna: Wha-tevah!

Integrated procedures (Built-in)

Iryna: Neo4j provides several integrated procedures out of the box, not requiring any plugin addition. These are known as *built-in procedures*. To list all the procedures (both integrated and plugin), simply use CYPHER to call the following...what else?...procedure:

```
// Listing procedures
CALL dbms.procedures()
```

As you can see, the listing procedure was called by `CALL`, just like any other procedure.

The built-in procedure names beginning with `db.*` are operations relating to the graph schema (i.e., labels, properties, relationship types, indexes, constraints). Procedures starting with `dbms.*` relate to the management of the Neo4j system. First I'll show you what the `dbms.procedures()` procedure returns, and then I'll explain how to read the signature of any given procedure.

Table 2.1 : List of built-in procedures

Name (name)	Signature (signature)
Description (description)	
db.awaitIndex	db.awaitIndex (index :: STRING?, timeOutSeconds = 300 :: INTEGER?) :: VOID
Waits for any given index availability (example: CALL db.awaitIndex(":Person(name)"))	

Name (name)	Signature (signature)
Description (description)	
`db.constraints`	`db.constraints() ::` `(description :: STRING?)`
Lists all constraints set on the graph database	

`db.indexes`	`db.indexes() ::`
	`(description :: STRING?,`
	`  state :: STRING?,`
	`  type :: STRING?)`

Lists all indexes of the graph database	
`db.labels`	`db.labels() ::` `(label :: STRING?)`
Lists all labels in the graph database	
`db.propertyKeys`	`db.propertyKeys() ::` `(propertyKey :: STRING?)`
Lists all properties in the graph database	
`db.relationshipTypes`	`db.relationshipTypes() ::` `(relationshipType :: STRING?)`
Lists all relationship types in the graph database	

`db.resampleIndex`	`db.resampleIndex`
	`(index :: STRING?)`
	`:: VOID`

Plans the reindexing of a given index (example: `CALL   db.resampleIndex(":Person(name)")`)	
`db.resampleOutdatedIndexes`	`db.resampleOutdatedIndexes()` `:: VOID`
Plans the reindexing of obsolete indexes	

`db.schema`	`db.schema() ::`
	`(nodes :: LIST? OF NODE?,`
	`  relationships :: LIST? OF`
	`  RELATIONSHIP?)`

Lists node labels (types) as well as relationship types	

Name (name)	Signature (signature)
Description (description)	
`dbms.components`	``` dbms.components() :: (name :: STRING?, versions :: LIST? OF STRING?, edition :: STRING?) ```
Lists Neo4j components and respective versions	
`dbms.functions`	``` dbms.functions() :: (name :: STRING?, signature :: STRING?, description :: STRING?) ```
Lists user functions	
`dbms.procedures`	``` dbms.procedures() :: (name :: STRING?, signature :: STRING?, description :: STRING?) ```
Lists all Neo4j procedures	
`dbms.queryJmx`	``` dbms.queryJmx (query :: STRING?) :: (name :: STRING?, description :: STRING?, attributes :: MAP?) ```
Query JMX management data by domain and name(currently "org.neo4j:*")	
`dbms.security.changePassword`	``` dbms.security.changePassword (password :: STRING?) :: VOID ```
Change password for connected user	
`dbms.security.createUser`	``` dbms.security.createUser (username :: STRING?, password :: STRING?, requirePasswordChange = true :: BOOLEAN?) :: VOID ```
Create new user	

Name (name)	Signature (signature)
Description (description)	

`dbms.security.deleteUser`	`dbms.security.deleteUser`
	`(username :: STRING?)`
	`:: VOID`

Delete user	

`dbms.security.listUsers`	`dbms.security.listUsers() ::`
	`(username :: STRING?,`
	` flags :: LIST? OF STRING?)`

Lists all (local) users	

`dbms.security`
`.showCurrentUser`
	`dbms.security.showCurrentUser() ::`
	`(username :: STRING?,`
	`flags :: LIST? OF STRING?)`

Displays current connected user	

Brian (sighing): Sheesh. This stuff is painful reading.

Iryna: Hence the explanation. So, as for the procedure name, Tiago has already explained how it works. For example, if I want to call the procedure that shows the current user, I would simply write:

```
CALL dbms.security.showCurrentUser
```

Which returns:

Table 2.2 : *CALL dbms.security.showCurrentUser*

name	flags
neo4j	`["admin"]`

The signature of this procedure is:

```
dbms.security.showCurrentUser() ::
    (username :: STRING?,
     flags :: LIST? OF STRING?)
```

To understand this, you need to realize that the characters : : separate the name from the type of the returned value, and that the ? suffix designates a native Neo4j type. Hence:

- dbms.security.showCurrentUser() returns a qualified object with two properties (username and flags);
- username returns a string value (STRING?);
- flags returns a list of strings value, i.e. a collection (LIST? OF STRING?).

Does that help?

Brian: Yeah, the pain is only like a dull toothache now, instead of like a stubbed toe.

Iryna: Now we can use the return value of the procedure with YIELD as Ashley kindly explained a couple of minutes ago. For example, if I want to use the name of the current user within a CYPHER query, I can write something like:

```
CALL dbms.security.showCurrentUser() YIELD username
RETURN "Current user is: " + username AS User
```

Table 2.3 : Using YIELD

User
Current user is: neo4j

Here's another example. Suppose I want to count the number of procedures available in Neo4j. How do we do this?

Brian: I'm looking at the description of the dbms.procedures procedure to get its signature:

```
dbms.procedures() ::
(name :: STRING?,
signature :: STRING?,
description :: STRING?)
```

Seems to me this procedure returns one or more objects each having three properties: name, signature and description. All three are string values.

Iryna: Right. So how do you count the number of Neo4j procedures?

Brian: Could I count them by name? Like this:

```
CALL dbms.procedures() YIELD name
RETURN count(name) AS `Number of available CYPHER procedures`
```

Table 2.4 : *Using YIELD*

Number of available CYPHER procedures
19

Iryna: Sweet, that's nothing short of perfect! The built-in procedures in the namespace db.* are useful in recovering information about the graph data. For example, we might list all the labels used in the graph to check to see if any nodes are poorly qualified:

```
CALL db.labels() YIELD label
RETURN count(label) AS `Number of labels`, COLLECT(label) AS Labels
```

Table 2.5 : *db.labels() procedure*

Number of labels	Labels
11	[Person, Book, Category, Product, Catalog, Publisher, Order, Task, Procedure, InstanceTask, Process]

It works the same with properties, relationship types, indexes and constraints. Even more interesting, one of these procedures returns a metagraph (starting with Neo4j version 3.1):

```
CALL db.schema()
```

I think understanding this makes this diagram fairly clear:

Figure 2.1 : *Metagraph obtained by* db.schema() *procedure*

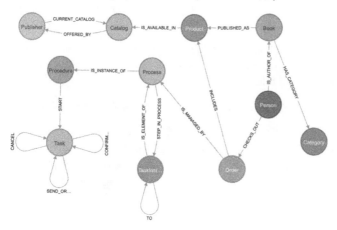

Note that some procedures have restricted access and can only be executed if the user has the permissions to do so. We can remove these restrictions by modifying the neo4j.conf file using the parameter dbms.security.procedures.unrestricted [217]. More on this when we get to the security aspects.

So much for the basics. We won't bother to list all these procedures, as this catalog differs a bit between Neo4j versions. The main thing is that you remember this catalog exists and generally how it can be used.

Jackie: Wait! How about those famous APOC procedures? Can you tell us a little about them?

Iryna: I'd describe them as more awesome than famous, but whatever! Along with being the name of a character in the film series *The Matrix* (who is coincidentally killed by CYPHER), APOC is also an acronym for *Awesome Procedures On Cypher!*

Jackie: What makes APOC such a big deal?

Iryna: Allow me to demonstrate what this plug-in can do for us.

APOC procedures and functions

Iryna: The APOC plug-in combines a large number of very useful CYPHER procedures and functions. They come from contributions provided by the Neo4j community (as well as from members of the Neo4j, Inc. team). Therefore, they are not truly official, insofar as they are not validated by the team which works on the Neo4j core. However, they are widely used and they are quite useful.

Brian: How can we distinguish them from built-in procedures?

Iryna: First of all, they are not installed by default. You have to download the apoc-[version].jar file which corresponds to the Neo4j version you are using. Then you place this jar file in the /plugins folder as we discussed earlier.

Tiago: Oh, so APOC procedures are not necessarily compatible with every Neo4j version?

Iryna: That's right. They use native Neo4j functions, so you have to be careful to check that the version of the APOC procedures is compatible with the version of Neo4j on which they will run. In my opinion, this is the main danger in using them. By the way, another danger is that, in not being an official part of Neo4j, there is no official support or release schedule.

APOC procedures: Documentation and downloads

APOC procedures are grouped on the neo4j-apoc-procedures GitHub repository [http://d-booker.jo.my/neo4j-apoc-github]. Here you can download them and check out the latest compatibility information. Full documentation is also available [http://d-booker.jo.my/neo4j-apoc-doc].

Table 2.6 : Compatibility matrix

APOC version	Neo4j version
3.5.0.1	3.5.0 (3.5.x)
3.4.0.4	3.4.10 (3.4.x)
3.3.0.4	3.3.6 (3.3.x)
3.2.3.5	3.2.3 (3.2.x)
3.2.0.4	3.2.2
3.2.0.3	3.2.0
3.1.3.9	3.1.6 (3.1.x)
3.1.3.8	3.1.5
3.1.3.7	3.1.4
3.1.2.5	3.1.2
3.1.0.4	3.1.0 - 3.1.1
3.0.8.4	3.0.8 (3.0.x)
3.0.4.3	3.0.4 (3.0.x)
1.1.0	3.0.0 - 3.0.3
1.0.0	3.0.0 - 3.0.3

Iryna: Now that I have installed them, we can check their availability using the following CYPHER query:

```
CALL dbms.procedures()
```

This time, the APOC procedures are present, and located with the apoc.* namespace. Another way to get help with these additional procedures is by simply calling the APOC help procedure:

```
CALL apoc.help('apoc')
```

This procedure also tells us the type of extension, i.e., whether it is a function or a procedure. For example with the following command:

```
CALL apoc.help('help')
```

we get the following result:

Table 2.7 : apoc.help() procedure

type	name	signature
text		
procedure	apoc.help	apoc.help (proc :: STRING?) :: (type :: STRING?, name :: STRING?, text :: STRING?, signature :: STRING?, roles :: LIST? OF STRING?, writes :: BOOLEAN?)
Provides descriptions of available procedures. To narrow the results, supply a search string. To also search in the description text, append + to the end of the search string.		

Notice the *type* column, which in this case says that the extension type is procedure. Alternatively I could submit the query:

```
CALL apoc.help('text.replace')
```

This time, I see that the apoc.text.replace extension is a function:

Table 2.8 : Procedure apoc.help()

type	name	signature
text		
function	apoc.text.replace	apoc.text.replace (text :: STRING?, regex :: STRING?, replacement :: STRING?) :: (STRING?)
apoc.text.replace(text, regex, replacement) - replace each substring of the given string that matches the given regular expression with the given replacement.		

And while we're talking about functions, remember that there is a `dbms` (i.e., built-in) procedure that allows us to list them:

```
// Listing functions
CALL dbms.functions()
```

Table 2.9 : Sample APOC functions

Name	Signature	Description
apoc.coll.avg	apoc.coll.avg (numbers :: LIST? OF NUMBER?) :: (FLOAT?)	apoc.coll.avg([0.5,1,2.3]) This returns the average of all the values in the list.
apoc.col- l.contains	apoc.coll.contains (coll :: LIST? OF ANY?, value :: ANY?) :: (BOOLEAN?)	apoc.coll.contains(coll, value) optimized contains operation (using a HashSet) (returns single row or not)
[...]	[...]	[...]

Reiterating what I mentioned before, for those who might not have followed (NOT looking at you Brian, so just chill), the functions return only one value and are used as a standard CYPHER operation. Here is an example of how the `apoc.text.replace` function could be used:

```
WITH apoc.text.replace("iryna","i","I") AS name
RETURN name
```

In this example the lower case `"i"` in "iryna" is replaced by a capital `"I"`.

Table 2.10 : Procedure apoc.text.replace()

name
Iryna

Tiago: Okay, I think we've got it now. But what kind of stuff can be found in these APOC procedures and functions?

Iryna: Here is a summary of what you get with APOC:

Table 2.11 : APOC procedures and functions

Domain	Description
apoc.algo	Algorithms (A*, Cliques, etc.)
apoc.bolt	Interactions with other Neo4j databases
apoc.coll	Operations on collections
apoc.config	Operations on configuration
apoc.convert	Type conversion utilities
apoc.couchbase	Interactions with CouchBase database
apoc.create	Operations related to creating/changing elements in the graph (properties, labels, etc.)
apoc.cypher	Operations related to the execution of CYPHER commands (executing them in parallel, for example)
apoc.date	Date and node expiration handling (TTL)
apoc.es	Operations related to ElasticSearch
apoc.export	Operations to export the graph database using various formats
apoc.generate	Operations to generate random graphs
apoc.gephi	Interactions with Gephi
apoc.graph	Operations to manipulate virtual nodes
apoc.import	Import operations (GraphML)
apoc.index	Operations on indexes
apoc.load	Operations to import data coming from other formats (JDBC, JSON, XML, etc.)
apoc.lock	Locking operations (nodes, relationships)
apoc.map	Operations on associative arrays
apoc.meta	Operations related to graph metadata
apoc.mongodb	Interactions with MongoDB
apoc.monitor	Access internal Neo4j information (DB size, kernel info)
apoc.nodes	Operations on nodes (get degree, collapsing, etc.)
apoc.path	Operations on paths
apoc.periodic	Operations related to asynchronous tasks
apoc.refactor	Operations to do graph refactoring

Domain	Description
apoc.search	Parallel search queries using indexes
apoc.spatial	Operations involving geolocation data
apoc.static	For handling in-memory configuration values
apoc.text	Handling strings
apoc.util	Various utility functions

So that's the essence of APOC. Oh wait, I almost forgot something! Some procedures, especially those which have external connectors require additional parameters. These parameters are configured in the Neo4j general configuration file:[NEO4J_HOME]/conf/ neo4j.conf:

Table 2.12 : Additional configuration

Parameter	Description
apoc.trigger.enabled	*[true|false]* false by default. Activates the triggers.
apoc.ttl.enabled	*[true|false]* false by default. Enables expiration of nodes (Time To Live).
apoc.ttl.schedule	*[digital integer]* default value: 60 (expressed in seconds). Sets the frequency for the background task that checks the expiration of nodes.
apoc.import.file.enabled	*[true|false]* false by default. Allows local files to be read.
apoc.export.file.enabled	*[true|false]* false by default. Allows local files to be written.
apoc.jdbc.<key>.url	*[jdbc-url-with-credentials]* Associates an arbitrarily defined key (<key> parameter) with a JDBC connection URL.
apoc.es.<key>.uri	*[es-url-with-credentials]* Associates an arbitrarily defined key (<key> parameter) with an ElasticSearch connection URI.
apoc.mongodb.<key>.uri	*[mongodb-url-with-credentials]* Associates an arbitrarily defined key (<key> parameter) with a MongoDB connection URI.
apoc.couchbase.<key>.uri	*[couchbase-url-with-credentials]* Associates an arbitrarily defined key (<key> parameter) with a Couchbase connection URI.

Obviously, these parameters are not mandatory. For example, it is quite possible to connect to a MongoDB database without adding to the general configuration. However, *passing authentication information or a host name in a CYPHER query is not recommended*. Hence these configuration options are provided.

Jackie: Okay, but practically speaking, Iryna, how do APOC extensions help us meet our current requirements?

Iryna: Well, some of these procedures are rather technical. They allow us to do what cannot be done with plain vanilla CYPHER.

Jackie: I'm not sure what you mean.

Iryna: For example, CYPHER does not allow us to dynamically set a label on a node, so it is not possible to pass a node type as a parameter of a CYPHER query. So if we were to attempt the following query:

```
WITH ['MyLabel'] as DynLabels
CREATE (n:DynLabels[0])
RETURN n
```

we would get the following error:

```
Invalid input '[': expected an identifier character,
whitespace, NodeLabel, a property map, ')' or a relationship pattern
(line 1, column 51 (offset: 50))
"WITH ['MyLabel'] as DynLabels CREATE (n:DynLabels[0]) RETURN n"
```

CYPHER expects a literal value for the label defined for a node. However, by using the following `apoc.create.setLabels` APOC procedure, we can create a node with labels which are provided in the parameters (the parameters are replaced by a collection of strings).

```
CREATE (n)
WITH n,['MyLabel'] as DynLabels
CALL apoc.create.setLabels(n,DynLabels) YIELD node
RETURN node
```

Jackie: If I understand you correctly, you're essentially saying that APOC procedures provide us with tools to augment the CYPHER arsenal?

Iryna: Right. I also think in the design phase it's likely that mistakes will be made. APOC can help us refactor without resorting to deleting the whole graph. For example, the `apoc.refactor` procedures allow us to reverse the direction of a relationship or to merge distinct nodes. This can come in very handy.

Jackie: Okay, you mean we are dealing with technical utilities.

Iryna: Well..yes and no. If you don't mind, I'd like to describe a business use case by talking about node expiration.

Jackie: I'm not sure what you're talking about.

Iryna: Let's take our `Order` node as an example. Suppose we want to persist a user's shopping cart even if they haven't yet confirmed their order. So we will create the `Order` node in our system without linking it to a process. Later we can find this user's cart and let them complete their order without losing any of the selected items.

Jackie: Ok, so far so good.

Iryna: We might also decide to add a time limit. After all, if the order was started two months ago, it would probably be preferable for the user to to start all over with an empty shopping cart.

Jackie: Right.

Iryna: This is called node expiration: a node becomes invalid and is removed from the graph after a specified time period.

Jackie: Hey, that is actually pretty cool.

Iryna: To set up node expiration (also known as *TTL* for *Time To Live*), we need to:

- configure the TTL in `[NEO4J_HOME]/conf/neo4j.conf`;
- manually activate the TTL for a given node via a CYPHER query;
- or use one of the two APOC procedures provided for this purpose.

For example, this node will live only ten seconds:

```
CREATE (example:Extra:TTL{ttl:timestamp() + 10000})
RETURN example
```

If 20 seconds later we look for this node in the graph:

```
MATCH (example:Extra)
RETURN example
```

and, viola, nothing is returned...

Brian: You mean voila, which is French for something like "here it is". A viola is a musical instrument. I may not know much about programming, but I kill at French. I spent a year there between high school and college studying l'architecture francaise, la cuisine francaise, les filles francaises...

Jackie: I'm sure you did, Brian. Anyway, Iryna, I think that's very cool! I think we have seen the essentials of procedures and functions. How about we move on?

APOC procedures: Node Expiration (TTL)

Configure the TTL in the `[NEO4J_HOME]/conf/neo4j.conf` file : Two properties should be added to the general configuration file (this is mandatory):

- `apoc.ttl.enabled=true` to enable the background checking task for expired nodes;
- `apoc.ttl.schedule=5` to determine the frequency at which the background task is started (expressed in seconds).

Manually activate the TTL for a node via a CYPHER command : A background task checks eligible nodes, and a node will be deleted (by a `DETACH DELETE`) if the time to live has expired. To be eligible for expiration, a node must meet the following criteria:

- have the `:TTL` label;
- have a `ttl` property indicating its expiration date.

For example:

```
MATCH (n:Lambda)
SET n:TTL, n.ttl = timestamp () + 10000
```

Activate TTL with APOC procedures : There are two ways to configure a node to be eligible for expiration:

- `apoc.date.expire.in(node,delay,unit-time)` configures a node to expire after a time delay;
- `apoc.date.expire(node,date,unit-time)` configures a node with a date on which to expire.

2.3. Integration from Neo4j to other systems

Iryna: The next step is to study how to interact with other systems from Neo4j.

Jackie: By the way I'm not saying that this will be immediately useful to us, but I suspect our client will have a few surprises in store for us. We haven't really yet heard the full story.

RDBMS

Iryna: It is possible to communicate with a relational database management system (RDB-MS) from Neo4j. Once again, APOC helps us achieve this by providing the two following procedures:

- `apoc.load.jdbc(jdbc :: STRING?, tableOrSql :: STRING?) :: (row :: MAP?)`

- `apoc.load.jdbcParams(jdbc :: STRING?, sql :: STRING?, params :: LIST? OF ANY?) :: (row :: MAP?)`

Ashley: Oh ok, so it uses JDBC?

Iryna: Exactly.

REMINDER: JDBC

JDBC stands for *Java DataBase Connectivity*, which, as the name implies, provides connectivity between Java and databases. JDBC is defined as an interface in the Java programming language, and implementations of this interface allow any database to be connected as long as a JDBC driver is provided.

To get a JDBC connection, the Java program has to:

- load the JDBC driver: this driver (which is a Java class provided in the library, i.e., a `.jar`) must be accessible from the program's *classpath* (basically, the classpath designates the physical location from which classes are loaded);

- provide an URL to access the database: the format of this URL depends on the type of database. For a MySQL database, for example, it looks like:`jdbc:mysql://localhost:3306/my_database?user=root&password=secret`.

Iryna: The first `apoc.load.jdbc` procedure allows us to query a remote database via a simple SQL statement. The second, `apoc.load.jdbcParams`, does pretty much the same thing, except that it uses parameterized queries.

Ashley: But I'll bet you have to provide the driver that matches the system you want to connect to, right?

Iryna: Yes, you do, and for that we need to download the JDBC connector, a `.jar` file, provided by the database vendor. Then we will drop this jar file in the `[NEO4J_HOME]/plugins` folder of the Neo4j server, because this folder is part of the Neo4j classpath. Then we restart my Neo4j server, which reloads the classes.

Ashley: Can we check to make sure the driver is now accessible?

Iryna: Yes, good idea! First of all, restart Neo4j and then, load the driver from CYPHER:

```
CALL apoc.load.driver('com.mysql.jdbc.Driver')
```

Ashley: Hmmm, something doesn't feel quite right...

Iryna: Oh yeah. Oops. If CYPHER responds with something like `No suitable driver found for...` it's because something went wrong. I think I forgot to restart Neo4j...

Ashley: Well, let's move it... time is running short...

Iryna: I know. Ok, the server has restarted, and now I can try my CYPHER query again... Right, nothing is returned this time, which is a good thing. That means that the driver has been loaded.

Ashley: Okay, that's progress.

Iryna: And let's take it for a spin: we'll create a small `persons` table in our example MySQL RDBMS:

```
CREATE TABLE `neo4j`.`persons` (
`id` INT NOT NULL AUTO_INCREMENT,
`name` VARCHAR(45) NULL,
`email` VARCHAR(45) NULL,
PRIMARY KEY (`id`));
```

And then insert some data into this table:

```
INSERT INTO `persons`
VALUES
```

```
(1,'Tiago','tiago@graphits.tech'),
(2,'Ashley','ashley@graphits.tech');
```

Now all we have to do now is enter a CYPHER query that will read this table:

```
WITH "jdbc:mysql://localhost:3306/neo4j?user=root&password=secret" as
url
CALL apoc.load.jdbc(url,"persons") YIELD row
RETURN row.name AS name, row.email AS email
```

Bam! There it is!

Table 2.13 : Query a RDBMS

name	email
Tiago	tiago@graphits.tech
Ashley	ashley@graphits.tech

Ashley: Hey, that's not hard at all. Is there a way to pass an actual SQL query?

Iryna: Sure! The second argument of the apoc.load.jdbc procedure corresponds either to a table name or to a SQL query. So we could just as well write our query this way:

```
WITH "jdbc:mysql://localhost:3306/neo4j?user=root&password=secret" as
url
CALL apoc.load.jdbc(url,"SELECT * FROM persons") YIELD row
RETURN row.name AS name, row.email AS email
```

And we get the same results. Now let's insert these people in our graph database:

```
WITH "jdbc:mysql://localhost:3306/neo4j?user=root&password=secret"
as url
CALL apoc.load.jdbc(url,"SELECT * FROM persons") YIELD row
MERGE (p:Person{name:row.name,email:row.email}) RETURN p
```

And now these new people are accessible from our graph database!

Jackie: Have we covered everything we need about Neo4j's interactions with RDBMS?

Iryna: Almost. Just one more thing: it is strongly recommended that the connection strings live in the [NEO4J_HOME]/conf/neo4j.conf file, which is done by adding the apoc.jdbc.<key>.url (where key is an arbitrary name). For example apoc.jdbc.mysqlDatabase.url=jdbc:mysql://localhost:3306/neo4j?

`user=root&password=secret`. Of course you'll have to restart Neo4j after changing the configuration. It's simple to use this configuration. We just replace the URL by the key:

```
CALL apoc.load.jdbc("mysqlDatabase","SELECT * FROM persons") YIELD row
RETURN row.name AS name, row.email AS email
```

And I think that's it.

Jackie: Perfect. What's next?

Elasticsearch

Brian: What in heaven's name is *Elasticsearch*?

Iryna: Patience, Brian, chill pill time. I'm getting there. Ok, so we will study how Neo4j might interact with *Elasticsearch*.

Brian: Ok, you've started... I repeat... What is Elasticsearch?

Iryna: Elasticsearch is sometimes called a search engine...

Brian: Really? Never heard of them. Where can I find documentation?

Iryna (ignoring Brian): ...but I prefer the term *indexing engine* so as not to confuse it with websites used to find other web pages. That said, search engines all use an indexing engine, which allows us to find approximate matches in the search. Elasticsearch is a scalable system based on the Java *Apache Lucene* indexing library, and is designed for indexing and searching for text.

Brian: You lost me.

Iryna: Think of it as a database management system which specializes in text search. You enter text (called documents) into this system. The document is indexed and prepared for search using one or more keywords (a query). The keyword(s) can be either completely or partially matched, and Elasticsearch calculates a relevance score on each document for the query. Elasticsearch can also make suggestions if the keyword is poorly or incorrectly written, and can do useful tricks like highlighting the search words in the text, etc. It provides a pretty useful set of features revolving around text analysis.

Brian: Ah, okay.

Iryna: Like before, the APOC extension gives us the hook to query Elasticsearch. The simple call:

```
CALL apoc.help('apoc.es')
```

will return the list of APOC procedures which have been provided to interact with Elasticsearch.

Table 2.14 : APOC and Elasticsearch

Name	Description
apoc.es.get	Performs a GET operation
apoc.es.getRaw	Performs a GET operation with full path
apoc.es.post	Performs a POST operation
apoc.es.postRaw	Performs a POST operation with full path
apoc.es.put	Performs a PUT operation
apoc.es.query	Performs a SEARCH operation
apoc.es.stats	Returns Elasticsearch statistics

Iryna: I'll tell you right now, we're not going to dive too deeply into all the procedures listed here. Their use requires a fair amount of knowledge of the Elasticsearch system. We'll just run a query on Elasticsearch and inject data into our graph as we did before for relational databases.

Jackie: What datasets are available to us in Elasticsearch?

Iryna: Well, in preparation for this exercise we went to the Web and imported some data from Wikipedia [https://en.wikipedia.org] into our Elasticsearch. Our documents are stored into an Elasticsearch index called wikipediaIndex, using a document type wikipediaDocType and structured as follows:

```
{
title:[document title],
content: [web page text content],
reference: [web page link]
}
```

So now we'll look for data on the ICIJ, the famous International Consortium of Investigative Journalists. We will use the following CYPHER query, using the `apoc.es.query()` APOC procedure. It looks like this:

```
CALL apoc.es.query("127.0.0.1:9200","wikipediaIndex",
   "wikipediaDocType",null,{from:0,size:100,
    query:{term:{content:"icij"}}}) YIELD value
UNWIND value.hits.hits as hits
RETURN hits._source.title, hits._source.reference
```

And the query returns:

Table 2.15 : Query Elasticsearch

hits._source.title hits._source.reference

International Consortium of Investigative Journalists – Wikipedia
`https://en.wikipedia.org/wiki/International_Consortium_of_Investigative_`
`Journalists`

List of people named in the Panama Papers - Wikipedia `https://en.wikipedia.org/wiki/List_of_people_named_in_the_Panama_Papers`
Panama Papers - Wikipedia `https://en.wikipedia.org/wiki/Panama_Papers`
Investigative journalism - Wikipedia `https://en.wikipedia.org/wiki/Investigative_journalist`
Reactions to the Panama Papers - Wikipedia `https://en.wikipedia.org/wiki/Reactions_to_the_Panama_Papers`
John Doe (Panama Papers' whistleblower) - Wikipedia `https://en.wikipedia.org/wiki/John_Doe_(Panama_Papers%27_whistleblower)`

Organized Crime and Corruption Reporting Project - Wikipedia
`https://en.wikipedia.org/wiki/Organized_Crime_and_Corruption_`
`Reporting_Project`

David Leigh (journalist) - Wikipedia `https://en.wikipedia.org/wiki/David_Leigh_(journalist)`

Brian: Ouch, your query is stomping on my brain cells.

Iryna: Okay, it'll help to break it down a bit. First let's get the method signature using help:

```
CALL apoc.help("apoc.es.query") YIELD signature
```

Table 2.16 : apoc.es.query signature

signature
apoc.es.query(host :: STRING?, index :: STRING?, type :: STRING?, query :: ANY?, payload :: ANY?) :: (value :: MAP?)

This signature tells us that method parameters are:

* *host*, the address of the Elasticsearch server (on HTTP port);

* *index*, the name of the queried Elasticsearch index;

* *type*, the type of document concerned (Elasticsearch documents are typed);

* *query*, a query to be sent to Elasticsearch;

* *payload*, and/or structured parameters in JSON format.

Iryna: Clearer, Brian?

Brian: A little, I guess...if I squint and tilt my head a bit.

Iryna: So we can now inject this data into our graph database:

```
WITH "icij" AS queryStr
MERGE (queryNode:QUERY{query:queryStr})
WITH queryStr, queryNode
CALL apoc.es.query("127.0.0.1:9200","wikipediaIndex",
  "wikipediaDocType",null,{from:0,
    size:100,query:{term:{content:queryStr}}}) YIELD value
UNWIND value.hits.hits as hits
WITH queryNode, hits
MERGE (queryNode)-[:YIELDS]->(result:RESULT{title:hits._source.title,
  reference:hits._source.reference, score:hits._score})
RETURN queryNode,result
```

And this graph model represents the Elasticsearch query and its results, as stored in the graph.

Figure 2.2 : Elasticsearch–ICIJ query

Brian (looking at Figure 2): That's a really cool figure. Could we pause while I take it in? A couple of years should suffice.

Iryna: Be brave, Brian. These are the most complicated procedures. The others are much easier to use.

MongoDB

Brian (confused, still): Uh...so...

Iryna: Something on your mind, Brian?

Brian: Forget about it. I'll wait for you to explain.

Iryna: Ok, *that* was weird. Anyway, next we'll see how to interact with MongoDB. Before you ask me, Brian, MongoDB is a document oriented NoSQL database system. Mongo uses structured JSON documents. Here is the list of APOC procedures for communication with MongoDB:

```
CALL apoc.help("mongo")
```

Table 2.17 : APOC and MongoDB

Name	Description
apoc.mongodb.count	Performs a count() operation
apoc.mongodb.delete	Deletes a document
apoc.mongodb.find	Make a query to find documents
apoc.mongodb.first	Returns the first element of a query result
apoc.mongodb.get	Make a query to find documents
apoc.mongodb.insert	Insert a document
apoc.mongodb.update	Update a document

To use these, first you need to add some Java libraries to the[NEO4J_HOME]/plugins folder, because MongoDB drivers are not bundled with the APOC library.

MongoDB Drivers

The following Java libraries should be installed in the[NEO4J_HOME]/plugins folder. A Neo4j restart is needed for Neo4j to see them.

Table 2.18 : MongoDB Drivers

Library name	Download link
bson-3.4.2.jar	http://d-booker.jo.my/neo4j-bson

Library name	Download link
`mongo-java-dri-ver-3.4.2.jar`	http://d-booker.jo.my/neo4j-mongodb-driver
`mongodb-dri-ver-3.4.2.jar`	
`mongodb-dri-ver-core-3.4.2.jar`	

Iryna: Now I restart Neo4j and enter my first query:

```
CALL apoc.mongodb.get(
  "localhost",
  "myMongoDatabase",
  "blog",
  {reference:"https://neo4j.com/blog/fraud-prevention-neo4j-5-minute-
overview/"})
YIELD value
RETURN value.reference, value.description
```

Our dataset stored in MongoDB corresponds to several dozen pages of the official Neo4j blog. This query returns the following document:

Table 2.19 : APOC—*apoc.mongodb.get*

value.reference	https://neo4j.com/blog/fraud-prevention-neo4j-5-minute-overview/
value.description	Learn how to harness Neo4j for operationalized fraud prevention designed to detect and deter complex fraud patterns that traditional technology can't match.

Brian: I understood literally nothing whatsoever about what you just said. In fact, I think I got confused about some things that I had previously understood.

Iryna: Okay, let's address it bit by bit, starting at the beginning. First, we use `apoc.help` to look at the signature of this procedure:

```
CALL apoc.help("apoc.mongodb.get") YIELD signature
```

Table 2.20 : apoc.mongodb.get *signature*

signature
apoc.mongodb.get(host :: STRING?, db :: STRING?, collection :: STRING?, query :: MAP?) :: (value :: MAP?)

So the parameters of this procedure are:

- *host*, the address of the MongoDB server (if the port is not specified, the default port, 27017, is used);
- *db*, the name of the MongoDB database that is used;
- *collection*, the collection of documents used (in MongoDB, documents are stored in *collections*);
- *query*, a JSON object representing the query.

The query I sent to MongoDB is the following:

```
{reference:"https://neo4j.com/blog/fraud-prevention-neo4j-5-minute-
overview/"}
```

It means: *Give me all the documents whose* reference *field has for value* "https://neo4j.com/blog/fraud-prevention-neo4j-5-minute-overview/". In MongoDB, as in Neo4j, there are no real schemas. The structure of a document is thus stored with its data at write time. My sample documents have the following structure:

```
{
  reference: blog page url
  description: short description of the page
  referrer: url of the parent page
}
```

However we need to be careful. In MongoDB, there are no relations or transactions. Now, the nodes are provided with a parent URL (*referrer*), i.e. a web link from one web page to another, so we can create a small graph of the site like this:

```
// sending query to MongoDB
CALL apoc.mongodb.get("localhost",
 "myMongoDatabase",
 "blog",{}) YIELD value

// creating nodes corresponding to blog posts
MERGE (m:Mongo{reference:value.reference})
ON CREATE SET m.description=value.description, m.referrer=value.referrer

// collect nodes, this allows us to wait until all nodes are created
 before connecting with them
WITH COLLECT (m) as ms

// converting the 'ms' table into lines of results
UNWIND ms AS m

// looking for parent node
```

```
MATCH (parent:Mongo{reference:m.referrer})

// creating the relationship
CREATE (m)-[:IS_CHILD_OF]->(parent)
RETURN parent.reference as reference,  parent.referrer as parent
```

This time my MongoDB query is empty, just {}. This means *Return to me all the documents in the "blog" collection.* This will build a graph which looks like this:

Figure 2.3 : *Neo4j Blog*

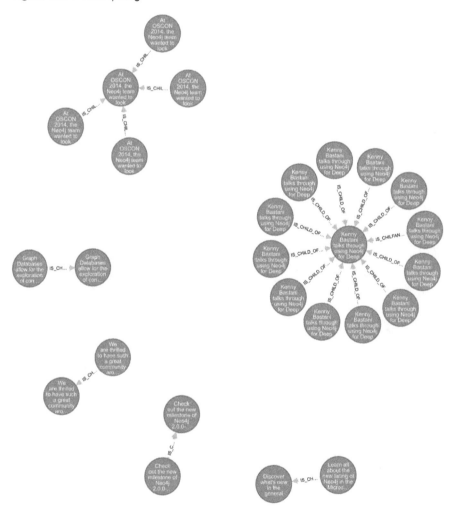

As you can see, there are several unrelated components. This is an artifact of our data set being incomplete. Now, as we did for JDBC, you should set the connection parameters in the neo4j.conf file, using similar keys:

```
apoc.mongodb.<key>.uri = mongodb://localhost:27017
```

That's enough for MongoDB.

And the others...

Iryna: Yes, and there are others! Because obviously that isn't all there is.

Ashley: What do you mean?

Iryna: There are procedures to work with another document-oriented NoSQL system named CouchBase [https://www.couchbase.com]:

```
CALL apoc.help('apoc.couchbase')
```

Table 2.21 : APOC and CouchBase

Name	Description
apoc.couchbase.append	apoc.couchbase.append(nodes, bucket, documentId, jsonDocument) yield id, expiry, cas, mutationToken, content – add a JSON document to an already existing document.
apoc.couchbase.exists	apoc.couchbase.exists(nodes, bucket, documentId) yield value – test if document with documentId code already exists.
apoc.couchbase.get	apoc.couchbase.get(nodes, bucket, documentId) yield id, expiry, cas, mutationToken, content – find a document from its documentId.
apoc.couchbase.insert	apoc.couchbase.insert(nodes, bucket, documentId, jsonDocument) yield id, expiry, cas, mutationToken, content – insert a document with a specified documentId.
apoc.couchbase .namedParamsQuery	apoc.couchbase.namedParamsQuery(nodes, bucket, statement, paramNames, paramValues) yield queryResult – executes a N1QL query with named parameters.
apoc.couchbase .posParamsQuery	apoc.couchbase.posParamsQuery(nodes, bucket, statement, params) yield queryResult – executes a N1QL query with indexed parameters.

Name	Description
apoc.couchbase.prepend	apoc.couchbase.prepend(nodes, bucket, documentId, jsonDocument) yield id, expiry, cas, mutationToken, content - prefix a JSON document by another existing one.
apoc.couchbase.query	apoc.couchbase.query(nodes, bucket, statement) yield queryResult - executes a non-parametered N1QL query.
apoc.couchbase.remove	apoc.couchbase.remove(nodes, bucket, documentId) yield id, expiry, cas, mutationToken, content - remove a JSON document identified by its documentId.
apoc.couchbase.replace	apoc.couchbase.replace(nodes, bucket, documentId, jsonDocument) yield id, expiry, cas, mutationToken, content - replace the content of a given document.
apoc.couchbase.upsert	apoc.couchbase.upsert(nodes, bucket, documentId, jsonDocument) yield id, expiry, cas, mutationToken, content - insert or update a document.

We've already looked at MongoDB, so we won't go any deeper into CouchBase.

Beyond that, there are also procedures that load data in JSON format:

```
CALL apoc.help('apoc.load.json')
```

Table 2.22 : APOC and JSON

Name	Description
apoc.load.json	apoc.load.json('url') YIELD value - JSON import (JSON feed or unitary JSON document).
apoc.load.jsonArray	apoc.load.jsonArray('url') YIELD value - load a given JSON feed from a URL.
apoc.load.jsonParams	apoc.load.jsonParams('url',{header:value},payload) YIELD value - load a JSON feed from a URL while passing a particular HTTP header and/or request body.

Likewise, we can also load data in XML format:

```
CALL apoc.help('apoc.load.xml')
```

Table 2.23 : APOC and XML

Name	Description
`apoc.load.xml`	`apoc.load.xml('http://example.com/test.xml')` `YIELD value as doc CREATE (p:Person) SET p.name =` `doc.name` – loads an XML feed from a URL and imports it into a single integrated object (map) whose fields are JSON attributes and `_type`, `_text` and `_children`.
`apoc.load.xmlSimple`	`apoc.load.xmlSimple('http://exemple.com/` `test.xml') YIELD value as doc CREATE (p:Person)` `SET p.name = doc.name` – loads an XML feed from a URL and imports it into a single integrated object (map) whose fields are JSON attributes and `_type`, `_text` and a collection of `<childtype>` for each type of child.

There are procedures for geolocation:

```
CALL apoc.help('apoc.spatial')
```

Table 2.24 : APOC and Spatial

Name	Description
`apoc.spatial.geocode`	`apoc.spatial.geocode('address') YIELD location,` `latitude, longitude, description, osmData` – searches for a geographic address using the OpenStreetMap service.
`apoc.spatial` `.sortByDistance`	`apoc.spatial.sortByDistance(List<Path>)` – sort the given paths based on the geo information (lat/long) in ascending order.

Ashley: That's right. I just tested this query:

```
CALL apoc.spatial.geocode('1600 Pennsylvania Avenue, Washington, D. C.,
   United States') YIELD location
RETURN location.latitude, location.longitude
```

and sure enough it returned a latitude and longitude:

Table 2.25 : APOC—apoc.spatial.geocode

location.latitude	location.longitude
38.8977	-77.0365

Iryna: Yes, and we can go even further because these procedures are quite customizable.

Jackie: That's right, we could propose to show our client a distribution of their customers geographically on a map.

Iryna: We totally could. I'll conclude by saying that APOC procedures present a very nice tool to simplify interactions from Neo4j to other systems. Some are more difficult to understand than others, but as far as I'm concerned it's essential to study this extension. The Neo4j community is always there to support us if we run into issues.

Jackie: The value of using the APOC extension seems pretty obvious now that you've shown how much it offers.

Iryna: It's valuable for data import, graph refactoring, graph algorithms, asynchronous processing, and more...

2.4. From other systems to Neo4j

Iryna: Let's go through the looking glass and see how we can interact with our graph database from a third party application.

Jackie: We know Neo4j exposes a HTTP API. Can't we just use that?

Iryna: We could, but because the HTTP protocol is relatively slow, that method isn't preferred if we have a large volume of data. In many cases the Bolt Protocol could be more efficient. Neo4j is also accessible via a JDBC driver and the communication protocol can be both Bolt and HTTP. So let's review the different ways to access the Neo4j graph database.

Neo4j and HTTP

Iryna: We already know the HTTP API pretty well, so I'm not going to spend much time on it. Just a little booster shot.

We can execute a CYPHER query using the `/db/data/transaction/commit` URL, to execute the query in an auto-commit transaction (because Neo4j HTTP API is definitely transactional!):

```
POST http://localhost:7474/db/data/transaction/commit
Accept: application/json; charset=UTF-8
Content-Type: application/json
Body :
{
```

```
    "statements" : [
      {"statement" : "MATCH (n:Catalog) RETURN n"}
    ]
  }
```

```
{
  "results":[{
  "columns":["n"],
  "data":[
    {
      "row":[{"reference":"2016-1","year":2016}],
      "meta":[{"id":8,"type":"node","deleted":false}]
    },
    {
      "row":[{"reference":"2017-1","year":2017}],
      "meta":[{"id":9,"type":"node","deleted":false}]
    }]
  }],
  "errors":[]
}
```

You can find all the details of this API in the Neo4j *HTTP API reference* [http://d-booker.jo.my/neo4j-http-reference].

Jackie: Perfect, so let's focus on something we don't already know.

Neo4j and Bolt

Iryna: Bolt is a TCP-based communication protocol, which transmits information much faster than HTTP. The transported data is in binary form and the serialization is defined in the Bolt protocol [http://d-booker.jo.my/neo4j-bolt] specification. Here's a list of the different officially supported Bolt client implementations:

Table 2.26 : Bolt—implementations

Implementation	Description
Neo4j Java Driver	Java Driver (with additional tools like Neo4j-OGM for object/graph mapping, and Spring Data Neo4j to integrate with the Spring ecosystem). Officially supported
Neo4j Javascript Driver	JavaScript Driver. Officially supported
Neo4j .NET Driver	Microsoft .NET Driver. Officially supported
Neo4j Python Driver	Python Driver. Officially supported
Neo4j Go Driver	Go Driver. Officially supported
cypher-shell	Command line interface (CLI)/client shell

But there are also many other drivers and clients for other languages developed and supported by the community: GraphAware PHP client, libneo4j-client (C/C++ Driver), Neo4j.rb (Ruby driver), R, Erlang/Elixir, Perl, Haskell, cypher-stream (Flow-based JavaScript API), py2neo (Python toolbox), neomodel (Python ORM).

We'll use a short example written in Java, our preferred language. However, Bolt's general principles apply to all customers regardless of the technology that is used.

Bolt: Java Driver

Driver (MAVEN):

```
<dependency>
  <groupId>org.neo4j.driver</groupId>
  <artifactId>neo4j-java-driver</artifactId>
  <version>1.7.2</version>
</dependency>
```

General information

Tiago: Okay, Iryna, can you give us the principles for using the BOLT protocol?

Iryna: Gladly. Let me start by explaining the four key concepts handled by any Bolt client:

*   *Driver:* Bolt session creation model. It maintains the link between the client program and an instance of a Neo4j server as well as a pool of Session objects (and therefore connections). We need to instantiate it only once;

*   *Session:* the logical context which interacts with the graph database. This object gives the illusion of locally manipulating the graph, even though the graph is actually remote;

*   *Transaction:* this is known in the RDBMS as a logical work unit. In Neo4j, transactions are ACID and are obtained from the Session object;

*   *Statement Result:* results and metadata flow. This is received when a CYPHER query is sent via either the `Session` or the `Transaction` object.

Connection

Tiago: Why don't we begin at beginning, for a change? How do you connect to a Neo4j graph using the Bolt protocol?

Iryna: No big surprises here. We need a login URL and a Neo4j username and password. Those are the parameters. The first step is getting an instance of the Bolt driver, for which we write:

```
AuthToken token = AuthTokens.basic(USERNAME, PASSWORD);
Driver driver = GraphDatabase.driver("bolt://localhost:7687", token);
```

This driver will be closed once all operations have been performed or before closing application by using:

```
driver.close ()
```

By default, the Neo4j server exposes the Bolt connector on port 7687. This port number can be changed, along with other parameters concerning Bolt, in the [NEO4J_HOME]/conf/neo4j.conf file. You will need to update the following keys:

```
# Bolt connector
dbms.connector.bolt.enabled=true
dbms.connector.bolt.listen_address=0.0.0.0:7687
#dbms.connector.bolt.tls_level=OPTIONAL
```

After getting the driver instance, we can get an instance of the org.neo4j.driver.v1.Session object (Everybody defines their own special "session" object—be careful not to confuse this session object with the org.neo4j.ogm.session.Session object of the API neo4j-ogm, or any of the plethora of other session objects that roam the coding Serengeti!):

```
try(Session boltSession = driver.session()){

}
```

Tiago: Okay, so do I ask for a Session object for every query I want to execute?

Iryna: Not necessarily! Logically, we would group our operations per transactions, so in this case you should only use one Session object for the duration of your transaction.

Operations: read/write

Iryna: Before we delve into transactions, first let's see how to run a CYPHER query through Bolt:

```
try(Session boltSession = driver.session()){
```

```
boltSession.run( "MERGE (p:Person {name: $name})",
    Values.parameters( "name", "Nicolas" ) );
}
```

The `Session` object has a `run()` method that takes a CYPHER query and parameters as input. We can see that this is a parameterized query. The parameter, whose value will be replaced at runtime, is identified by a name prefixed with $ symbol, that is to say: $name (this replaces the {name} expression used in previous versions of Neo4j). The value for this parameter is defined by the second argument of the `run()` method. This argument is an object through which we can make key-value associations, such as an object of type `java.util.Map` or, as shown in the example above, an object of type `org.neo4j.driver.v1.Value`. While we're talking about the `Value` class, we'll mention that it is used both as an input parameter and an output value. For example, for a read operation we'd use:

```
try(Session boltSession = driver.session()){
  final StatementResult sr =
    boltSession.run(
       "MATCH (p:Person {name: $name}) RETURN p",
       Values.parameters( "name", "Nicolas" ) );

  while (sr.hasNext()){
    Record line = sr.next();
    Value columnP = line.get("p");
    Node node = columnP.asNode();
    Value value = node.get("name");
    System.out.println(value.asString());
  }
}
```

There's really nothing new here—we're just iterating on a data result. Each time we loop through the `while` instruction we get a new result line. This result contains a table which creates a correspondence between a column name, the RETURN p of our CYPHER query and the associated value.

Tiago: Easy for you to say that there's *nothing new*! For the rest of us it's not so old. For example, this `Value` object appears in the code snippet above twice. Why are we encapsulating the data in this value object?

Iryna: Because the `Value` object is very useful. It tries to handle type conversions when possible. For example, rather than getting a `Node` object we might prefer a `java.util.Map` object, as follows:

```
Map node = columnP.asMap();
```

Tiago: Ah, ok, I see. Actually, that's a pretty cool feature.

Iryna: I'll jump in as we're talking about type conversions. The types are classified into two categories. Basic types:

- Boolean;
- Integer;
- Float;
- String;
- ByteArray;
- Date / Time / LocalTime / DateTime / LocalDateTime / Duration;
- Point;
- List;
- Map.

And the graph types:

- Node;
- Relationship;
- Path.

Iryna: In Java the type matches are shown in the following table:

Table 2.27 : Bolt–type match for Java

Neo4j Type	Java Type
Null	null
Boolean	java.lang.Boolean
Integer	java.lang.Long
Float	java.lang.Double
String	java.lang.String
ByteArray	byte[]
Date	java.time.LocalDate
Time	java.time.OffsetTime
LocalTime	java.time.LocalTime
DateTime	java.time.ZonedDateTime

Neo4j Type	Java Type
`LocalDateTime`	`java.time.LocalDateTime`
`Duration`	`org.neo4j.driver.v1.types.IsoDuration`
`Point`	`org.neo4j.driver.v1.types.Point`
`List`	`java.util.List<T>`
`Map`	`java.util.Map<K,V>`
`Node`	`org.neo4j.driver.v1.types.Node`
`Relationship`	`org.neo4j.driver.v1.types.Relationship`
`Path`	`org.neo4j.driver.v1.types.Path`

Transactions

Tiago: How do the transactions work?

Iryna: There are three types of transactions:

- auto-commit transactions;
- explicit transactions;
- transactional functions.

Tiago: I think I know how the first two work, but go through them anyway. Start with the first type, the *auto-commit* transaction.

Iryna: The call to the `run()` method opens a transaction called *auto-commit*, i.e. it is managed internally by Neo4j and we don't have to write any further code. If the query works, the operation is validated (*commit*), otherwise it is cancelled (*rollback*). The auto-commit transaction does not allow for automatically replaying the request if it fails, nor can it participate in a *causal chain* (basically, it can't participate in a transaction involving a *causal* cluster).

Tiago: In that case I suppose we need to open an explicit transaction in the code?

Iryna: That's exactly right. We will ask the `Session` object to provide us with a transaction of type `org.neo4j.driver.v1.Transaction`:

```
try(Session boltSession = driver.session()){
  try (Transaction tx = boltSession.beginTransaction()){
    tx.run( "MERGE (p:Person {name: $name})",
      parameters("name", "Nicolas") );
```

```
      tx.success();
  }
}
```

This transaction pattern is similar to what is usually done for other transactional systems. However, Neo4j teams recommend that you use transactional functions.

Tiago: I'm not familiar with *transactional functions*.

Iryna: The purpose of transactional functions is to separate the graph query logic from the application logic. The basic idea is this: we tell the `Session` object what transaction type we want to use, and then supply it with an object which contains the task to be performed. There are two types of transactional functions:

- **read type:** `boltSession.readTransaction();`
- **write type:** `boltSession.writeTransaction()`.

Tiago: What's the point of distinguishing between the read and write operations?

Ashley: If I may jump in here, as we will see when we study the implementation of a causal cluster, some Neo4j servers will play the role of primary servers (*Core Servers*), while other servers will have the role of replica servers (*Read Replicas*), i.e. datasets available for reading (we'll need more servers for these operations). For this reason it is necessary to specify the type of transaction that we wish to carry out so that the internal routing done by the Bolt protocol can route the query to the server best adapted to the processing.

Tiago: Okay, I can see what you're getting at. Separating the read and write operations makes the Neo4j server perform better in a causal cluster.

Iryna: That's right. So, let's continue. We pass a unit of work to the transaction in the form of an object whose class implements the `org.neo4j.driver.v1.TransactionWork` interface, such as this one:

```
TransactionWork<Node> unit = new TransactionWork<Node>() {
  @Override
  public Node execute(Transaction tx){
    Node node = null;
    StatementResult sr = tx.run("MATCH (p:Person {name: $name}) RETURN
p",
      parameters("name", name) );
    if (sr.hasNext()){
      node = sr.next().get("p").asNode();
    }
    return node;
  }
```

```
    });
```

As we can see, the work unit contains all the query logic of the graph. And then we just need to wrap it with the appropriate transaction:

```
try(Session boltSession = driver.session()){
  Node node = boltSession.readTransaction(unit);
  System.out.println(node.get("name").asString());
}
```

Tiago: That is majorly elegant!

Iryna: Cool, right? This may be a bit more complicated to write in simple systems, but in a distributed transaction it reduces the lines of code needed because the Bolt API manages some of the complexity associated with using transaction in clustered Neo4j servers. Moreover, it manages the automatic *retry* (i.e., executing the instruction again) in case of failure. This feature is configured at driver instantiation:

```
Driver driver = GraphDatabase.driver( uri, auths,
Config.build().withMaxTransactionRetryTime( 15, SECONDS ).toConfig() );
```

Bolt and Neo4j cluster

Iryna: Hey Ashley, to finish up with Bolt, can you please say a few words about using Bolt within a causal cluster?

Ashley: It'd be my pleasure. I'm not going to completely explain the causal cluster [157] right now. Just understand for now that a causal cluster is a network of several Neo4j servers (enterprise edition only). One of the tricky parts of this type of architecture is the replication of data on each Neo4j server. But a Neo4j cluster handles that and guarantees that a transaction done on one server is propagated on other servers to ensure data consistency.

Tiago: Hate to say, but that's closer to the clarity of mud than of crystal.

Ashley: Let me try a different approach. Tiago, imagine you're the client program using the Bolt protocol. And to talk with Bolt, we provided a connection string like:

```
"bolt://localhost:7687"
```

So, now, what happens if this Neo4j instance crashes?

Tiago: I'd obviously lose the connection, right?

Ashley: Precisely! This scenario is known as a *single point of failure*. To handle this problem we'd need to set up a *failover* mechanism, i.e. an automatic fallback to another server that *is* accessible. Some applications publish multiple server addresses that a client program can issue queries to. The way of doing this with Bolt is the use of the "bolt +routing" protocol:

```
"bolt+routing://localhost:7687"
```

The server address is the primary server. When the Bolt driver first connects, the server it connects to sends a routing table from the Neo4J cluster. Upon failure, the Bolt driver uses this table to route the query to another available server. This is how Bolt implements failover.

Tiago: Interesting. So in fact, we don't have much configuration to do on the client side, do we?

Ashley: Yeah, and the *bolt+routing* protocol can embed other parameters to perform even more complex routing operations (*such as Multi-Data Center Support*). But that's enough for the moment. Let's now take a look at transactions and the *bookmark* notion.

Tiago: What about it?! What's new about this?

Ashley: Let's say you write something in Neo4j and immediately afterwards you want to read it.

Tiago: Easy. What's the problem?

Ashley: The problem is you will write your data on the primary server in the Neo4j cluster (*Core Server*). But then you'll read your data on a replica, and because of the replication latency, there is no guarantee that your new data is available yet on any given replica server.

Tiago: Oh, yeah, I see...

Ashley: To address this scenario, we will use a bookmark. You get a bookmark returned to you when writing, and you provide the bookmark in your read operation. Without going into the implementation details, if you write data in a transaction, and then try to read this new data within another transaction using this same identifying bookmark, the Neo4j cluster will only route your Bolt client to a replica that has already processed the previous transaction bearing this bookmark (or the server will wait until it has an up to date version of the data). Consequently, you are guaranteed to read *at least* your own writes (that is, you might miss data that another client has written). The bookmark has to be fetched when writing data:

```
String bookmark = boltSession.lastBookmark();
```

And then, before starting the next transaction, passed in at Bolt session creation time:

```
try(Session boltSession = driver.session(bookmark)){

}
```

Iryna: Thanks for this additional information, Ashley. I think we now have a good idea of how to work with Bolt.

Jackie: Ok, let's move on...

Neo4j and JDBC

Iryna: We already talked about JDBC, when we wanted to query a SQL database from Neo4j. Now, we have to do the opposite–from a program using JDBC, we will connect to a Neo4j server. That way, a Java program could work with JDBC without having to add Neo4j dependencies to its classpath.

Tiago: Moreover, products that are compatible only with JDBC can still use the graph data.

Iryna: Absolutely. Except that queries used are CYPHER rather than SQL, so if our client has an automatic report built on SQL queries, they will have to rewrite all those. Apart from that, you're right, tools working with JDBC, like, for example, JasperReports [http://d-booker.jo.my/neo4j-jasperReports] or QlikView [http://d-booker.jo.my/neo4j-qlikview] will be able to read graph data. I recommend looking at the official documentation [http://d-booker.jo.my/neo4j-jdbc-doc].

Tiago: So, Iryna, how do we set this up?

Iryna: Well, Tiago, we start by choosing the communication protocol that we'll use with the JDBC interface, either HTTP or Bolt. The latter will undoubtedly bake faster.

Brian (giggling): Pretty funny how you're talking like you're on a TV cooking show! Anybody want some of these brownies I got from a booth at the *Hooray For Hippies* festival? By the way, I just wanted to say this stuff is getting utterly fascinating!!! Is it really only 2:15? It seems like it should be past 6!

Iryna: Maybe later, Brian, and you might want to put those brownies away until after work. Anyway, the JDBC interface that uses the Bolt protocol is based on the Java Neo4j driver which we saw before. The interface that uses the HTTP protocol relies on an internal HTTP client based on *Apache Commons httpclient* for communication and *Jackson* for JSON serialization.

JDBC Neo4j: Drivers (MAVEN)

Official documentation: http://d-booker.jo.my/neo4j-jdbc-doc

All drivers:

```
<dependency>
    <groupId>org.neo4j</groupId>
    <artifactId>neo4j-jdbc-driver</artifactId>
    <version>3.1.0</version>
</dependency>
```

HTTP driver:

```
<dependency>
    <groupId>org.neo4j</groupId>
    <artifactId>neo4j-jdbc-http</artifactId>
    <version>3.1.0</version>
</dependency>
```

Bolt driver:

```
<dependency>
    <groupId>org.neo4j</groupId>
    <artifactId>neo4j-jdbc-bolt</artifactId>
    <version>3.1.0</version>
</dependency>
```

Tiago: Hey, Iryna, I have a quick question: are all JDBC features implemented in this Neo4j JDBC driver?

Iryna: That's a really pertinent question, Tiago. The team that owns the Neo4J JDBC driver development tells us that the only following features are guaranteed:

* automatic registering of the JDBC driver in the JVM (no need to code `DriverManager.registerDriver()`)
* obtaining connections in `autocommit` mode or in `explicit commit` mode;
* management of transactions;

- read and write queries;

- prepared queries, including parameters ordered by the ? character or by the position given according to a string of the type: ${1};

- results of all columns returned as a string. Native objects and types may require the use of type converters.

However, it must be taken into account that this driver continues to evolve and that its functionalities could be extended in the future.

JDBC login URL

- Bolt driver

  ```
  jdbc:neo4j:bolt://host:port/?username=neo4j,password=xxxx
  ```

- HTTP Driver

  ```
  jdbc:neo4j:http://host:port/?username=neo4j,password=xxxx
  ```

Iryna: Now, having said that, we'll connect to Neo4j via a client program using JDBC:

```
try (Connection con = DriverManager.getConnection("jdbc:neo4j:bolt://
localhost", "neo4j", "neo4j")) {

}
catch (SQLException e) {
    e.printStackTrace();
}
```

Tiago: This time we are really close to the JDBC standard.

Iryna: Exactly! Moreover, there will never be any explicit reference to a Neo4j dependency for this program. If we wish to introduce a new person in our graph, using a parameterized query, we can use the java.sql.PreparedStatement object. As I said earlier in the introduction, we write our query in CYPHER rather than SQL:

```
final String writeQuery = "MERGE (p:Person {name: {1}})";

try (Connection con = DriverManager.getConnection(JDBC_Bolt_URL, USER,
PASSWORD)) {
```

```
PreparedStatement pstmt = con.prepareStatement(writeQuery);
pstmt.setString(1, "Jackie");
pstmt.executeUpdate();

}
catch (SQLException e) {
    e.printStackTrace();
}
```

Again, it's 100% pure JDBC even though the query is written in CYPHER.

Tiago: How about for reading? I'd imagine you can't find nodes and relationships objects directly from the JDBC interface, can you?

Iryna: Well, yes and no. In general using CYPHER, we don't recommend returning complete objects, or pieces of graph. Doing so can be inefficient for large volumes of data. But it's also true that it's sometimes useful to return complete objects. First let's look at a simple query that returns property values from nodes:

```
final String readQuery ="MATCH (p:Person {name:{1}}) RETURN p.name AS
  name";

try (Connection con = DriverManager.getConnection(JDBC_Bolt_URL, USER,
  PASSWORD)) {

    PreparedStatement pstmt = con.prepareStatement(readQuery);
    pstmt.setString(1, "Jackie");

    try (ResultSet rs = pstmt.executeQuery()) {
        while (rs.next()) {
            System.out.println("Person: "+rs.getString("name"));
        }
    }
    catch (SQLException err) {
        err.printStackTrace();
        Assert.fail(err.getMessage());
    }
}
```

First we run the CYPHER query via the executeQuery() method. Then we get a cursor as a java.sql.ResultSet object. Finally, we go through the list of results, and for each result, we get the value of the *name* column that corresponds to the alias specified in the RETURN clause of our CYPHER query. In short, nothing particularly fancy here.

Tiago: Now for graph objects?

Iryna: Well, if you really need to do this, here are two solutions. The first is to use the getObject() method of the java.sql.ResultSet object. This object is in fact an array of key/value pairs of a java.util.Map: object

```
final String readQuery ="MATCH (p:Person {name:{1}}) RETURN p";
[...]
try (ResultSet rs = pstmt.executeQuery()) {
    while (rs.next()) {
        Map<String,Object> node = (Map<String,Object>)
 rs.getObject("p");
        System.out.println("Person object : "+node);
    }
}
```

Tiago: Not bad. Not bad at all!

Iryna: And if you want you can go further and build a `Person` object:

```
public class Person{
    private Long _id;
    private List<String> _labels;
    private String name;

    // Accessors and mutators (get, set)
    [...]
}
```

The trick here is to transform the result node of type `java.util.Map` into an object of type `tech.graphits.catalog.Person`. We could match the properties manually, fetching the property values from the initial object and inserting them into the `Person` object. But there's an easier way: we get the Jackson API to do the work for us. To get it working, we add the following MAVEN dependency to our program:

```
<dependency>
    <groupId>com.fasterxml.jackson.core</groupId>
    <artifactId>jackson-databind</artifactId>
    <version>2.8.9</version>
</dependency>
```

And then all we have to do is let *Jackson* do the mapping job:

```
final ObjectMapper MAPPER = new ObjectMapper();

final String readQuery ="MATCH (p:Person {name:{1}}) RETURN p";

[...]

try (ResultSet rs = pstmt.executeQuery()) {
    while (rs.next()) {
```

```
        Map<String,Object> node = (Map<String,Object>)
    rs.getObject("p");
        Person person = MAPPER.convertValue(node, Person.class);
        System.out.println("Person object : "+person.getName()+"
    labels :"+person.get_labels());
    }
}
```

The `Jackson` object in the code is of type `com.fasterxml.jackson.databind.Ob-jectMapper` which has a very useful `convertValue()` method that converts our node object into a Person object.

Tiago: Very nice! Does it also manage the relationships? Does it understand the links between nodes?

Iryna: No, sorry, it can't go that far. That you'll have to do manually. However, we are inching closer to the work done by an ORM, or maybe I should say a OGM. I'll tell you a bit about ORM because I think we've seen enough of the basics as far as JDBC is concerned.

Neo4j and ORM

Brian: Feel free to laugh as I ask "What the hell is an ORM"?

Tiago: ORM stands for *Object Relational Mapper*. A clumsy definition would be a *Relational Object-Base Correspondence*. An ORM makes it possible to transform SQL query results into Java objects (or objects in some other technology–ORMs are not specific to Java). We can also go the other direction. Obviously, working with a graph is a bit more complex, but this type of tool also exists for Neo4j.

Iryna: Right. Actually, we no longer really talk about ORM, but instead about OGM for *Object Graph Mapper*, or *Object-Graph Correspondence*. Here is a non-exhaustive list of existing OGMs for Neo4j:

Table 2.28 : OGM implementations

Name	Technology	Description
`neo4j-ogm`	Java	OGM for Java (not to be confused with *Hibernate OGM* project)
`spring-data-neo4j`	Java	Spring Data for Neo4j, based on neo4j-ogm
`neo4j-php-ogm`	PHP	OGM for PhP
`neomodel`	Python	OGM for Python
`datanucleus-neo4j`	Java	Neo4j plugin for DataNucleus platform

Iryna: I'll send you a link to some documentation on `neo4j-ogm` and `spring-data-neo4j`.

The reader can find a presentation of these two subjects in the appendix [223].

Jackie: Ah! I see Varsha lurking about, wanting an update. I think it's time to wrap things up and fill her in on what we've been studying.

2.5. Debriefing

Varsha: So, what've you guys been busying yourselves with?

Jackie: We've had a really productive session! With what we've seen, I think we're prepared to deal with just about any eventuality!

Varsha: Well, I know it's not easy because our customer hasn't sent us the functional specifications yet. No doubt we'll get some nasty surprises when they do. They're working on it, I suspect, but nothing concrete has come to me yet. How did you proceed without this information?

Jackie: Well, our study was based on the notion that the fewer functional details we have, the more we need to know and review the multitude of available tools that will allow us respond to any unexpected client request. For this we focused on various ways to interact with Neo4j.

Varsha: You mean, like how our client's existing system will interact with Neo4j?

Jackie: That, but not only that: we also reviewed the reverse, how Neo4j could interact with our client's existing system.

Varsha: Okay, so you thought about the other direction, too. Can you summarize things for me?

Jackie: We started by studying CYPHER functions and procedures [60]. These are provided from Neo4j's version 3.0.0, and they allow us to perform some basic operations (metagraph, administration, etc.). From there, we went through the APOC extension [68] which will allow to:

- simplify the writing of our CYPHER queries;
- simplify updating operations of the graph still under development (update labels, relationships, etc.);
- connect to external systems (Elasticsearch, MongoDB, SQL databases);
- use graph algorithms (shortest path, community detection, etc.).

And so on...these are the kinds of extension we might need. Then we reviewed how a Neo4j graph could be queried from an external system:

- with the HTTP API;
- with the Bolt TCP protocol;
- with JDBC.

We can integrate all of these with our client's system, both from Neo4j to an external system and from an external system to Neo4j, with no roadblocks.

Varsha: So yes, Neo4j will rarely act alone, and obviously the development teams and the Neo4j community understand this. What topic do you want to tackle next?

Jackie: We thought we'd study data import and export techniques, because sooner or later we will have to deal with our client's legacy data.

Varsha: Yes, there's no way to escape that. Wake Brian up, go forth, and study...

3
Data Import/Export

As noted earlier, a project often has pre-existing conditions, the legacy data. This data will sometimes need to be imported into a Neo4j database from an existing application reading the legacy data store. Conversely, it might be useful to export data present in Neo4j to an outside data store. In this chapter we will show how to use the different data import and export tools available in Neo4j. The tools differ in their format, their volume and the external processes which launch the import and export commands.

3.1. Briefing

Jackie, Tiago, Iryna, Ashley and Brian would like to settle on a set of best practices for importing and exporting data.

Jackie: We already have legacy data on catalog, orders and events. How should we import this data into our new storage format? I'm all ears for ideas on how to get started.

Brian: Coffee. We should start with coffee. Definitely, coffee. Brian needs coffee.

Jackie: Solid contribution there, Brian. By the way, the molecular structure of the components of coffee can be described as a graph. We'll wait for you to get the coffee. Then can we start?

Brian: Yes, sir...uh, maam! I'm all set. I think you were saying something about data import?

Jackie: Right, we need to import the existing catalog, orders and events into our graph database. How are we gonna do that?

Iryna: I can see three possible situations, with different data models and different volumes of data. For example, the catalog contains at most a few thousand records. On the other hand, the order processing system is quite a bit larger.

Brian: Just use the `LOAD CSV` command to import data. Done!

Iryna: Not done. It'd be crazy to use the `LOAD CSV` command in some cases...

Ashley: Right! In fact, in some cases the `neo4j-admin` administration tool would be preferable.

Tiago: There are situations where the CYPHER `LOAD CSV` command would perform poorly and the `neo4j-admin` tool, though efficient, nonetheless has some limitations. So...

Iryna: ... so you may need to write roll-your-own code using `BatchInserter`!

Jackie: Ok then, let's study these different import techniques in detail together. Then we can move on to data export. For the first data source, we can look at how it works with CSV import. Afterwards we'll discuss whether or not we should use another technique for larger graphs.

3.2. Loading data with LOAD CSV

REVIEW: LOAD CSV

The CYPHER LOAD CSV command imports medium sized data structured in CSV (Comma Separated Values) into Neo4j. This command requires good quality data sets with correct character encoding, proper escaping and line breaks, etc.

Data import is performed with the LOAD CSV command which literally integrates the data file into the query. This command is then completed by other CYPHER create or update commands. Example below:

```
LOAD CSV FROM 'file:///persons.csv' AS line
CREATE (:Person { name: line[1], email: line[2]})
```

If the first line of the CSV file is headers identifying the name of the columns, we can use the header column names directly instead of referring to the indices by using the keyword WITH HEADERS:

```
LOAD CSV WITH HEADERS FROM 'file:///persons.csv' AS line
CREATE (:Person { name: line.name, email: line.email})
```

We can also batch transactions by using the USING PERIODIC COMMIT clause:

```
USING PERIODIC COMMIT 10000
LOAD CSV  WITH HEADERS  FROM 'file:///persons.csv' AS line
CREATE (:Person { name: line.name, email: line.email})
```

The example above will commit data into the database every 10000 updates (default is 1000).

The FIELDTERMINATOR instruction enables you to specify the separator character for CSV fields:

```
LOAD CSV FROM 'file:///persons.csv' AS line
FIELDTERMINATOR ','
CREATE (:Person { name: line[1], email: line[2]})
```

Ashley: I guess we should start with the catalog, reusing the catalog data model already defined during the method and analysis phase.

Iryna: If I could interrupt...

Ashley: Yes?

Iryna: Before rushing into importing our catalog data, I think we should talk a little more about the LOAD CSV method!

Tiago: What's to talk about? LOAD CSV is really, really simple!

Iryna: I'd just like to point out that we'd be better off to use two separate input data files: one set of files for importing the entities, and another set of files for importing the relationships.

Brian: Really? Why not do everything at once?

Iryna: You can... but this introduces an undesirable amount of complexity into the CYPHER query... For example, if we create nodes and relationships in the same query, we'd have to make sure that the nodes exist before creating the relationships.

Tiago: Yep, you're right Iryna. It's too complex to solve the problem with a single CYPHER query. I really don't want to try to lift Thor's hammer. Thanks for making this essential point. We'll have to deal with this.

Iryna: So let's distinguish the input data for the nodes from the input data for the relationships. Here is our catalog data model:

Figure 3.1 : Book, Product, Author, Catalog and Publisher

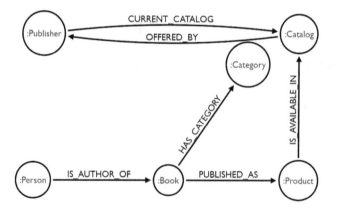

Iryna: If the existing relational database defines each entity (book, product, author, catalog, publisher) as a specific table, then each table of books, products, authors, catalogs, and publishers can be exported as separate CSV files. The relationships between the entities, which would be in join tables of the relational database, are also exported as individual CSV files.

Figure 3.2 : Relational model with joins

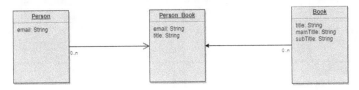

Ashley: Well, let's now imagine we have a CSV file books.csv. Each line contains:

* the title property of the Book;
* the mainTitle property of the Book;
* the subTitle property of the Book;

Table 3.1 : Catalog–CSV file of books to be imported

title	mainTitle	subTitle
Neo4j - A Graph Project Story	Neo4j	A Graph Project Story
Neo4j - Discover	Neo4j	Discover Neo4j
...	...	...

Iryna: If we expect to export the list of authors from the relational database, then we'd need another file like authors.csv file, with the email address and the name fields.

Table 3.2 : Catalog–CSV file of authors to be imported

email	name
sylvain@graphits.tech	Sylvain
frank@graphits.tech	Frank
nicolas.mervaillie@graphits.tech	Nicolas Mervaillie
nicolas.rouyer@graphits.tech	Nicolas Rouyer
...	...

Iryna: Finally, the join table which establishes the relationships between authors and books written by these authors contains the title field and the email field.

Table 3.3 : *Catalog—CSV file of relationships between authors and books*

email	title
sylvain@graphits.tech	Neo4j - A Graph Project Story
frank@graphits.tech	Neo4j - A Graph Project Story
nicolas.mervaillie@graphits.tech	Neo4j - A Graph Project Story
nicolas.rouyer@graphits.tech	Neo4j - A Graph Project Story
sylvain@graphits.tech	Neo4j - Discover
nicolas.rouyer@graphits.tech	Neo4j - Discover
...	...

Brian: So we load these CSV files one by one with the CYPHER LOAD CSV instruction, right?

Iryna: Yes, exactly.

Jackie: Very nice. Can you give us more detail about this LOAD CSV instruction?

Iryna: Sure. First we'll load the authors (label: Person).

Tiago: There should be only one field (the email address) in the CSV file, so there is no need to specify the delimiter of the CSV file.

Iryna: If that's the case, here is the CYPHER query we are going to execute:

```
LOAD CSV WITH HEADERS FROM "file:///authors.csv" AS author
MERGE (person:Person {email: author.email})
```

Tiago: Hold on a second! We also have the name field!

Iryna: No worries. Happy you told me that fast... Here we are:

```
LOAD CSV WITH HEADERS FROM "file:///authors.csv" AS author
MERGE (person:Person {email: author.email, name: author.name})
```

Tiago: You haven't specified the delimiter!

Iryna: Default delimiter is a comma, so that also works. The same idea applies to load books into our graph database (label: Book).

Tiago: This time let's make the delimiter explicit. Our CSV file contains three fields: title, mainTitle, subTitle.

Iryna: Sure! That would give the following CYPHER query with a comma delimiter:

```
LOAD CSV WITH HEADERS FROM "file:///books.csv" AS bookitem
FIELDTERMINATOR ','
MERGE (book:Book
{
    title: bookitem.title,
    mainTitle: bookitem.mainTitle,
    subTitle: bookitem.subTitle
})
```

Finally, let's create the :IS_AUTHOR_OF relationships between authors and books...

Tiago: ...by using the `authors_books.csv` join file.

Iryna: Yes, and that gives us:

```
LOAD CSV WITH HEADERS FROM "file:///authors_books.csv" AS authorbook
FIELDTERMINATOR ','
MATCH (person:Person {email: authorbook.email})
MATCH (book:Book {title: authorbook.title})
MERGE (person)-[:IS_AUTHOR_OF]->(book)
```

Jackie: Can we already see the results in the graph database? With the two labels `Person` and `Book` and the relationship :IS_AUTHOR_OF?

Tiago: We sure can. I'm working on the query:

```
MATCH (p:Person)-[r:IS_AUTHOR_OF]->(b:Book)
RETURN p, b
```

We see the following in the Neo4j browser:

Figure 3.3 : *Import–result in the graph database*

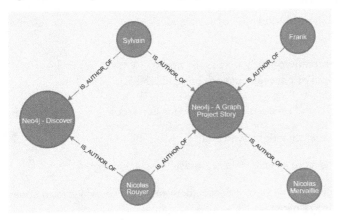

Or, in tabular form:

```
MATCH (p:Person)-[r:IS_AUTHOR_OF]->(l:Book)
RETURN p.email, type(r), l.title
```

Figure 3.4 : *Import-export—result in tabular form*

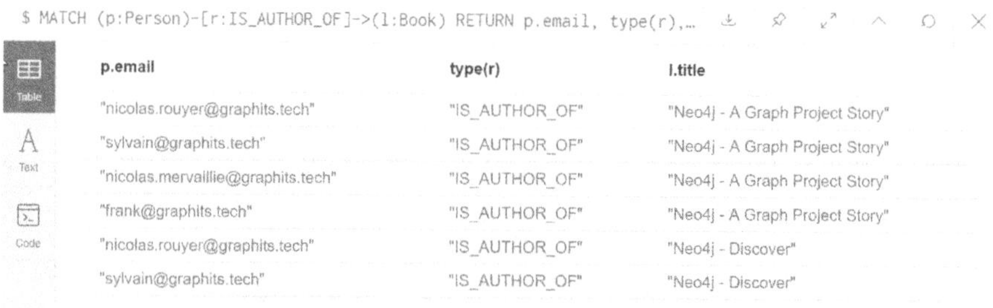

```
$ MATCH (p:Person)-[r:IS_AUTHOR_OF]->(l:Book) RETURN p.email, type(r),…      ⤓   ⌂   ↗   ∧   ○   ✕
```

p.email	type(r)	l.title
"nicolas.rouyer@graphits.tech"	"IS_AUTHOR_OF"	"Neo4j - A Graph Project Story"
"sylvain@graphits.tech"	"IS_AUTHOR_OF"	"Neo4j - A Graph Project Story"
"nicolas.mervaillie@graphits.tech"	"IS_AUTHOR_OF"	"Neo4j - A Graph Project Story"
"frank@graphits.tech"	"IS_AUTHOR_OF"	"Neo4j - A Graph Project Story"
"nicolas.rouyer@graphits.tech"	"IS_AUTHOR_OF"	"Neo4j - Discover"
"sylvain@graphits.tech"	"IS_AUTHOR_OF"	"Neo4j - Discover"

Jackie: That's really sweet! And I bet we can use the same strategy loading the remaining data of the catalog?

Iryna: Absolutely. Let's start by listing what we still have to create in our graph catalog:

- `Book` nodes (already loaded), `Category` nodes, `:HAS_CATEGORY` relationships between books and categories;

- `Book` nodes (already loaded), `Product` nodes, `:PUBLISHED_AS` relationships between books and products;

- `Product` nodes (already loaded), `Catalog` nodes, `:IS_AVAILABLE_IN` relationships between products and catalogs;

  `Catalog` nodes (already loaded), `Publisher` nodes, `:OFFERED_BY` and `:CURRENT_CATALOG` relationships between catalogs and publishers.

To create all these nodes and relationships, we need the corresponding CSV input files.

Tiago: Don't forget the brilliant insight Iryna had!

Jackie: You'll need to be more specific. Which particular brilliant insight?

Tiago: We have to continue to make a distinction between CSV files which load nodes and CSV files which load relationships!

Iryna: Here are the said files:

books and categories

```
title,matching,category
Neo4j - Discover,1,Database
Neo4j - Discover,0.3,Programming
Neo4j - A Graph Project Story,1,Database
Neo4j - A Graph Project Story,0.3,Programming
Neo4j - A Graph Project Story,0.7,Operations
```

books and products

```
title,isbn,module
Neo4j - Discover,9782822704182,Printed Edition
Neo4j - Discover,9782822704373,Digital Edition
Neo4j - A Graph Project Story,9782822703826,Printed Edition
Neo4j - A Graph Project Story,9782822702591,Digital Edition
```

products and catalogs

```
isbn,module,reference,year
9782822704182,Printed Edition,2017-1,2017
9782822704373,Digital Edition,2017-1,2017
9782822703826,Printed Edition,2018-1,2018
9782822702591,Digital Edition,2018-1,2018
```

catalogs and publishers

```
reference,year,id,name,active_catalog
2017-1,2017,AcmeId,Acme Publishing,NO
2018-1,2018,AcmeId,Acme Publishing,YES
```

And here are the CYPHER queries which load these relationships:

```
// Load :HAS_CATEGORY relationships between books and categories
LOAD CSV WITH HEADERS FROM "file:///books_categories.csv" AS
 bookcategory
FIELDTERMINATOR ','
MATCH (book:Book {title: bookcategory.title})
MERGE (category:Category {title: bookcategory.category})
MERGE (book)-[:HAS_CATEGORY {matching:
 bookcategory.matching}]->(category)

// Load :PUBLISHED_AS relationships between books and products
```

```
LOAD CSV WITH HEADERS FROM "file:///books_products.csv" AS bookproduct
FIELDTERMINATOR ','
MATCH (book:Book {title: bookproduct.title})
MERGE (product:Product {isbn: bookproduct.isbn, module:
 bookproduct.module})
MERGE (book)-[:PUBLISHED_AS]->(product)

// Load :IS_AVAILABLE_IN relationships between products and catalogs
LOAD CSV WITH HEADERS FROM "file:///products_catalogs.csv" AS
 productcatalog
FIELDTERMINATOR ','
MATCH (product:Product {isbn: productcatalog.isbn})
MERGE (catalog:Catalog {reference: productcatalog.reference, year:
 toInt(productcatalog.year)})
MERGE (product)-[:IS_AVAILABLE_IN]->(catalog)


// Load :OFFERED_BY and :CURRENT_CATALOG between catalogs and publishers
LOAD CSV WITH HEADERS FROM "file:///catalogs_publishers.csv" AS
 catalogpublisher
FIELDTERMINATOR ','
MATCH (catalog:Catalog {reference: catalogpublisher.reference})
MERGE (publisher:Publisher {id: catalogpublisher.id, name:
 catalogpublisher.name})
MERGE (catalog)-[:OFFERED_BY]->(publisher)
FOREACH(n IN (CASE WHEN catalogpublisher.active_catalog IN ["YES"] THEN
 [1] else [] END) | MERGE (publisher)-[:CURRENT_CATALOG]->(catalog)
    )
```

Jackie: Great work! Is our catalog now available and complete?

Ashley: It is. Look and be amazed:

```
MATCH (n)-[r]->()
RETURN n, r
```

Figure 3.5 : CSV import—the exhaustive catalog graph

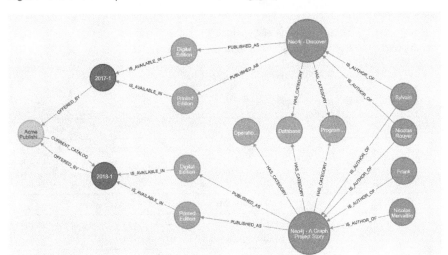

3.3. The big fat graph

Jackie continues the discussion.

Jackie: All right gentle persons, I now understand LOAD CSV...

Iryna, Tiago: But?

Ashley: Always a "but" in this imperfect world.

Jackie: But I don't see how this works for a big fat graph! My point is how do we proceed for a very large graph, especially when importing data into an empty graph database.

Iryna: I see two alternatives...

Tiago: First, the ever popular neo4j-admin import administration tool!

Iryna: And second, custom development!

Ashley: Let's start by looking at the neo4j-admin administration tool:

TECHNICAL: neo4j-admin

neo4j-admin is a command line utility which executes graph database administration commands. It is only available in the enterprise edition.

neo4j-admin can use host system environment variables:

Table 3.4 : neo4j-admin—options

Variable	Description
NEO4J_DEBUG	Activates debug mode on standard output (example:NEO4J_DE-BUG=true)
NEO4J_HOME	Path for Neo4j instance installation directory
NEO4J_CONF	Path of the directory that contains neo4j.conf file
HEAP_SIZE	Specifies the JVM memory size to use when executing a command (2GB is a reasonable value to start with, HEAP_SIZE=2G)

Available commands are as follows:

- backup: hot backup of the graph database;
- check-consistency: check consistency of the graph database;
- dump: graph database backup under single archive file;
- help: display neo4j-admin help;
- import: import a CSV file or a database whose version is prior to 3.0;
- load: load a database from an archive file created with the dump command;
- memrec: provides memory settings recommendations for the neo4j instance;
- report: builds a zip containing valuable information on the graph database, often used for remote assessment;
- restore: restore a database that was hot-backuped;
- set-default-admin: creates default administrator user when no role has been defined;
- set-initial-password: set the initial administrator user password ('neo4j');
- store-info: provides information on store format version;
- unbind: deletes cluster status information from the database.

Iryna: In this case we want to use `neo4j-admin import` command because it is tailored to load a large amount of data. This command requires 1) an empty database and 2) a particular input format. If we revisit the example of people and authors, the file format was:

Table 3.5 : Catalog—CSV file to import books

title	mainTitle	subTitle
Neo4j - Discover	Neo4j	Discover Neo4j
Neo4j - A Graph Project Story	Neo4j	A Graph Project Story
...	...	...

While loading data with `neo4j-admin import`, we will have instead:

Table 3.6 : Catalog—CSV file to import books

bookId:ID	title	mainTitle	subTitle
book0001	Neo4j - Discover	Neo4j	Discover Neo4j
book0002	Neo4j - A Graph Project Story	Neo4j	A Graph Project Story
...	...	...	...

And the same goes for loading the authors:

Table 3.7 : Catalog—CSV file to import authors

authorId:ID	email	name
author0001	sylvain@graphits.tech	Sylvain
author0002	frank@graphits.tech	Frank
author0003	nicolas.mervaillie@graphits.tech	Nicolas Mervaillie
author0004	nicolas.rouyer@graphits.tech	Nicolas Rouyer
...	...	...

Tiago: Basically, you've just added identifiers for books and authors...

Iryna: Right, for these ID columns we've suffixed the header with `:ID`. Later we'll use these identifiers in the :IS_AUTHOR_OF relationship file which binds authors to books.

Table 3.8 : Catalog—CSV file to load relationships between authors and books

:START_ID	:END_ID
author0001	book0001
author0004	book0001

:START_ID	:END_ID
author0001	book0002
author0002	book0002
author0003	book0002
author0004	book0002
...	...

Iryna: Finally we launch the command!

Brian: You mean like "Three, two, one, we have ignition!"

Iryna: Almost as simple... Watch. Let's navigate to the `bin` directory and run the following command:

```
[NEO4J_HOME]/bin$>./neo4j-admin import
--mode=csv
--database=databasename.db
--report-file=reportfilename.report
--nodes:Book=/path/to/books.csv
--nodes:Person=/path/to/authors.csv
--relationships:IS_AUTHOR_OF=/path/to/authors_books.csv
```

Tiago: And does that really work?

Iryna: Darn straight it does! The standard output gives us the following information:

```
Neo4j version: 3.5.1
Importing the contents of these files into /path/to/graph.db:
Nodes:
  :Book
  /path/to/import/import_books.csv

  :Person
  /path/to/import/import_authors.csv
Relationships:
  :IS_AUTHOR_OF
  /path/to/import/import_authors_books.csv

Available resources:
  Total machine memory: 15.88 GB
  Free machine memory: 8.41 GB
  Max heap memory : 3.53 GB
  Processors: 4
  Configured max memory: 11.12 GB
  High-IO: false
```

```
Import starting 2019-03-09 01:20:25.190+0100
  Estimated number of nodes: 6.00
  Estimated number of node properties: 20.00
  Estimated number of relationships: 6.00
  Estimated number of relationship properties: 0.00
  Estimated disk space usage: 1.05 kB
  Estimated required memory usage: 1020.01 MB

InteractiveReporterInteractions command list (end with ENTER):
  c: Print more detailed information about current stage
  i: Print more detailed information

(1/4) Node import 2019-03-09 01:20:25.681+0100
  Estimated number of nodes: 6.00
  Estimated disk space usage: 875.00 B
  Estimated required memory usage: 1020.01 MB
-......... .......... .......... .......... ..........   5% â100ms
.......... .......... .......... .......... ..........  10% â3ms
(...)
.......... .......... .......... .......... .......... 100% â5ms

(2/4) Relationship import 2019-03-09 01:20:25.895+0100
  Estimated number of relationships: 6.00
  Estimated disk space usage: 204.00 B
  Estimated required memory usage: 1.00 GB
.......... .......... .......... .......... ..........   5% â314ms
.......... .......... .......... .......... ..........  10% â1ms
(...)
.......... .......... .......... .......... .......... 100% â2ms

(3/4) Relationship linking 2019-03-09 01:20:26.229+0100
  Estimated required memory usage: 1020.01 MB
-......... .......... .......... .......... ..........   5% â217ms
.......... .......... .......... .......... ..........  10% â1ms
(...)
.......... .......... .......... .......... .......... 100% â0ms

(4/4) Post processing 2019-03-09 01:20:26.698+0100
  Estimated required memory usage: 1020.01 MB
-......... .......... .......... .......... ..........   5% â289ms
.......... .......... .......... .......... ..........  10% â2ms
(...)
.......... .......... .......... .......... .......... 100% â2ms


IMPORT DONE in 2s 674ms.
Imported:
  6 nodes
  6 relationships
  20 properties
Peak memory usage: 1.00 GB
```

Tiago: After database restart, we can show everything, including the relationships, was loaded with a small CYPHER query MATCH (n) RETURN n in the Neo4j web browser. See, everything has been imported, including the relationships:

Figure 3.6 : Books and authors after import

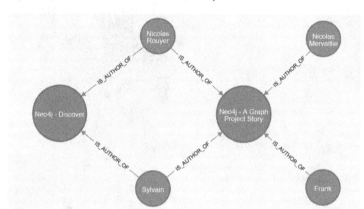

As another sanity check, we can also display the IS_AUTHOR_OF relationships with a CYPHER query that returns relationships in tabular form:

```
MATCH (p:Person)-[r:IS_AUTHOR_OF]->(b:Book)
RETURN p.email AS email, type(r) AS relationship, b.title AS title
```

Table 3.9 : neo4j-admin—authors and books now loaded

email	relationship	title
"nicolas.rouyer@graphits.tech"	"IS_AUTHOR_OF"	"Neo4j - Discover"
"sylvain@graphits.tech"	"IS_AUTHOR_OF"	"Neo4j - Discover"
"nicolas.rouyer@graphits.tech"	"IS_AUTHOR_OF"	"Neo4j - A Graph Project Story"
"nicolas.mervaillie@graphits.tech"	"IS_AUTHOR_OF"	"Neo4j - A Graph Project Story"
"frank@graphits.tech"	"IS_AUTHOR_OF"	"Neo4j - A Graph Project Story"
"sylvain@graphits.tech"	"IS_AUTHOR_OF"	"Neo4j - A Graph Project Story"

Caution › *But...empty database! neo4j-admin import can only be used for an empty database. Therefore, this tool cannot be used on an existing database. If we need to insert nodes and relationships efficiently into an existing database, we'll have to build a custom tool. We'll see how to do that in the next section.*

3.4. Coding your own insertion system

Tiago: Seriously? We get to write some code? Do developers even do that anymore?

Iryna: We don't really have a choice in this situation. We want to insert data quickly into an existing graph database, hence we need custom insertion code.

Brian: Wait...what? We're gonna code? FROM SCRATCH!? I'm a bit rusty...I have a headache...my computer is acting flaky...

Iryna: Deep breaths, Brian. Remember your "Hitchhiker's Guide to the Galaxy"...DON'T PANIC. We're not starting from scratch. We have a Neo4j library...

Tiago: ...which is called `BatchInserter`!

Iryna: We will use the same example as before, but this time we'll add new data to the existing database.

BatchInserter

`BatchInserter` is a Java interface which is part of the `org.neo4j.unsafe` library.

BatchInserter, is a batch insertion process that prioritizes insertion speed over trans-actions and concurrent access (*multithreading*). To support multithreading and run several insertion processes simultaneously, then each process (i.e. each thread) must synchronize with the others.

Regarding transactions, it is vital to invoke the `shutdown()` method so that the Neo4j database can reach a consistent state. In case of a crash, before the `shutdown()` method can be invoked, you have to start data insertion all over from the beginning.

Using BatchInserter operationally consists of running a standalone program that will work directly with the Neo4j database file system without interacting with a Neo4j server. To perform this operation, the graph database must be writable (meaning, the Neo4j server accessing the graph database must be stopped).

It is wise to backup the graph database before performing the batch insertion.

The two Java libraries that you'll need to compile and run the insert program are (shown here as MAVEN dependencies):

```xml
<dependency>
    <groupId>org.neo4j</groupId>
    <artifactId>neo4j-kernel</artifactId>
    <version>3.3.0</version>
</dependency>

<dependency>
    <groupId>org.neo4j</groupId>
    <artifactId>neo4j-lucene-index</artifactId>
    <version>3.3.0</version>
</dependency>
```

Tiago: Here is the code for our custom insertion. We begin by describing our data model as Java classes. Thus, we will create a Book class and an Author class:

```java
package tech.graphits.inserter;

public class Book {
    private String title;
    private String mainTitle;
    private String subTitle;

    public Book (String title, String mainTitle, String subTitle) {
        super();
        this.title = title;
        this.mainTitle = mainTitle;
        this.subTitle = subTitle;
    }

    public String getTitle() {
        return title;
    }

    public String getMainTitle() {
        return mainTitle;
    }

    public String getSubTitle() {
        return subTitle;
    }

    public void setTitle (String title) {
        this.title = title;
    }

    public void setMainTitle (String mainTitle) {
        this.mainTitle = mainTitle;
    }

    public void setSubTitle (String subTitle) {
        this.subTitle = subTitle;
```

```
    }

    @Override
    public String toString() {
        return "Book [title=" + title + ", mainTitle=" + mainTitle + ",
 subTitle=" + subTitle + "]";
    }

}


package tech.graphits.inserter;

public class Author {
    private String email;
    private String name;

    public Author (String email, String name) {
        super();
        this.email = email;
        this.name = name;
    }

    public String getEmail() {
        return email;
    }

    public String getName() {
        return name;
    }

    public void setEmail(String email) {
        this.email = email;
    }

    public void setName(String name) {
        this.name = name;
    }

}
```

Once we have defined the `Author` and `Book` classes, we can move on to our main program, i.e. the insertion code. To do this, we can create a `BookInserter` class with an `execute` method that triggers the following workflow:

```
public void execute() throws IOException {

    // Initialize BatchInserter Neo4j object
    this.initializeBatchInserter();

    // Load books from CSV file
    this.loadBooks();
```

```
        // Load authors from CSV file
        this.loadAuthors();

        // Initiates insertion treatment
        this.insert();

        // Stops the insertion program correctly
        this.shutdown();
    }
```

The initializeBatchInserter method will initialize the Neo4j BatchInserter object as its name suggests. This object is responsible for handling data from the graph database:

```
    private void initializeBatchInserter () throws IOException{
        File importedData = new File( pathToGraphDB );
        batchInserter = BatchInserters.inserter(pathToGraphDBRepository);
    }
```

The loadBooks() and loadAuthors() methods simply load CSV files and transform this data into Java Book and Author objects. Only then do we start inserting data by calling the insert() method:

```
    private void insert () throws UnsupportedEncodingException,
      FileNotFoundException, IOException{

      // Create labels
      Label authorLabel = Label.label("Person");
      Label bookLabel = Label.label("Book");
      batchInserter.createDeferredSchemaIndex(authorLabel).on("email")
    .create();
      batchInserter.createDeferredSchemaIndex(bookLabel).on("title")
    .create();

      // Create IS_AUTHOR_OF relationship type
      RelationshipType isAuthor =
      RelationshipType.withName("IS_AUTHOR_OF");

      // Create Author nodes
      for (Author author : authors.values()) {
         long node = batchInserter.createNode(authorToProperty(author),
      authorLabel);
         authorNodes.put(author.getEmail(), node);

      }

      // Create Book nodes
      for (Book book : books.values()) {
         long node = batchInserter.createNode(bookToProperty(book),
      bookLabel);
         bookNodes.put(book.getTitle(), node);
```

```
    }
    // Create author => book relationship (IS_AUTHOR_OF)
    BufferedReader fileReader = new BufferedReader(
      new InputStreamReader(

ClassLoader.getSystemResourceAsStream("authors_books.csv"), "UTF8"));
    // Read the file line by line
    String line ="";
    while ((line = fileReader.readLine()) != null)
    {
      // We take every available token
      String[] authorbook = line.split(";", -1);

      String email = authorbook[0];
      String title = authorbook[1];

      if ( authorNodes.containsKey(email) ) {
        if ( bookNodes.containsKey(title) ) {
      // Create IS_AUTHOR_OF relationship
      Map<String, Object> isAuthorProperties = new HashMap<String,
Object>();
        batchInserter.createRelationship(
        authorNodes.get(email),
        bookNodes.get(title),
        isAuthor,
        isAuthorProperties);
        }
      }
    }
    System.out.println("Insertions completed");

  }
```

Simply put, the *BatchInserter* object is responsible for creating nodes and relationships in the graph database. Each node created has its Neo4j identifier stored in a map (Map). Then the CSV file containing the relationships is loaded. We reuse previously stored identifiers in order to ask the BatchInserter to create the relationships in the graph database:

```
batchInserter.createRelationship(
    authorNodes.get(email),
    bookNodes.get(title),
    isAuthor,
    isAuthorProperties);
```

And just like that, and we end up with the same results as with LOAD CSV!

Tiago: Perfect, even if you don't have here a large data set...

Iryna: Yeah, this isn't really a representative example–it's tiny. But this approach would be a good, performant way to import a massive amount of data.

3.5. Neo4j data export

Jackie's brings the team together.

Jackie: Our business activities may also require exporting our catalog. Is this possible? And, if so, what formats are possible?

Iryna: We have several ways to export our graph database. In particular, using APOC procedures we can export data in output formats accessible by our partners. For example, if a partner wants a CSV format, we can provide one.

Tiago: Alternatively, if a partner wants the catalog data in JSON, XML or SQL format, we can also generate those...

Jackie: How about in CYPHER?

Tiago: You mean, for another company that would use a graph database?

Jackie: Yes, such companies do exist!

Ashley: CYPHER export can also be used for operational processes, managing backups, rebuilding a crashed database...

Iryna: But we'll come back to the operations stories later.

Tiago: Finally, you can export data from the graph to other database products...

Jackie: Nice assortment of possibilities! Where shall we start? CSV?

Tiago: Why not? To export in CSV format, we'll reuse nearly the same query we used before to export the authors and books:

```
MATCH (p:Person)-[r:IS_AUTHOR_OF]->(b:Book)
RETURN p.email AS email, b.title AS title
```

To export the results in CSV format, we use the `apoc.export.csv.query` stored procedure.

```
CALL apoc.export.csv.query("MATCH (p:Person)-[r:IS_AUTHOR_OF]->(b:Book)
RETURN p.email AS email, b.title AS title","authors_books.csv", {})
```

We expect to find the content of the CSV file will contain the email address of the authors and the title of the book they wrote.

```
"email","title"
"nicolas.rouyer@graphits.tech","Neo4j - A Graph Project Story"
"sylvain@graphits.tech","Neo4j - A Graph Project Story"
"nicolas.mervaillie@graphits.tech","Neo4j - A Graph Project Story"
"frank@graphits.tech","Neo4j - A Graph Project Story"
"nicolas.rouyer@graphits.tech","Neo4j - Discover"
"sylvain@graphits.tech","Neo4j - Discover"
```

To export the entire graph database (i.e the nodes and relationships), we can use the `apoc.export.csv.all` stored procedure.

```
CALL apoc.export.csv.all('all.csv', {})
YIELD file, source, format, nodes, properties, time, rows, relationships
RETURN *
```

Which gives:

Table 3.10 : APOC–Export CSV ALL

"file"	"format"	"nodes"	"prop-erties"	"rela-tionships"	"rows"	"source"	"time"
"all.csv"	"csv"	21	46	30	0	"database: nodes(21), rels(30)"	38

Here is the content of the output CSV file:

```
"_id","_labels","email","name","subTitle","mainTitle","title","module",
"isbn","reference","year","id","orderId","text","order","subTitle",
"_start","_end","_type","matching"
"0",":Person","nicolas.mervaillie@graphits.tech","Nicolas
Mervaillie","","","","","","","","","","","","",,,,
"1",":Person","frank@graphits.tech","Frank","","","","","","","","","","","","",,,,
"2",":Book","","","A Graph Project Story","Neo4j","Neo4j - A Graph
Project Story","","","","","","","","","",,,,
"4",":Category","","","","","Programming","","","","","","","","","",,,,
"5",":Product","","","","","","Printed
Edition","9782822703826","","","","","","","",,,,
"6",":Product","","","","","","Digital
Edition","9782822702591","","","","","","","",,,,
"7",":Catalog","","","","","","","","","2017-1","2017","","","","",,,,
"8",":Catalog","","","","","","","","","2018-1","2018","","","","",,,,
"9",":Publisher","","Acme
Publishing","","","","","","","","AcmeId","","","","",,,,
"20",":Person","sylvain@graphits.tech","Sylvain","","","","","","","","","","","","",,,,
```

```
"84",":Person","nicolas.rouyer@graphits.tech","Nicolas
Rouyer","","","","","","","","","","","",""
"104",":Book","","","Discover Neo4j","Neo4j","Neo4j -
Discover","","","","","","","","","A Graph Project Story",,,,
"124",":Category","","","","","Database","","","","","","","","","","",,,,
"125",":Category","","","","","Operations","","","","","","","","","","",,,,
"127",":Product","","","","","","Printed
Edition","9782822704182","","","","","","",,,,
"128",":Product","","","","","","Digital
Edition","9782822704373","","","","","","",,,,
,,,,,,,,,,,,,,,"7","9","OFFERED_BY",""
,,,,,,,,,,,,,,,"8","9","OFFERED_BY",""
,,,,,,,,,,,,,,,"9","8","CURRENT_CATALOG",""
,,,,,,,,,,,,,,,"127","7","IS_AVAILABLE_IN",""
,,,,,,,,,,,,,,,"128","7","IS_AVAILABLE_IN",""
,,,,,,,,,,,,,,,"84","2","IS_AUTHOR_OF",""
,,,,,,,,,,,,,,,"0","2","IS_AUTHOR_OF",""
,,,,,,,,,,,,,,,"1","2","IS_AUTHOR_OF",""
,,,,,,,,,,,,,,,"20","2","IS_AUTHOR_OF",""
,,,,,,,,,,,,,,,"84","104","IS_AUTHOR_OF",""
,,,,,,,,,,,,,,,"20","104","IS_AUTHOR_OF",""
,,,,,,,,,,,,,,,"104","124","HAS_CATEGORY","1"
,,,,,,,,,,,,,,,"104","4","HAS_CATEGORY","0.3"
,,,,,,,,,,,,,,,"2","124","HAS_CATEGORY","1"
,,,,,,,,,,,,,,,"2","4","HAS_CATEGORY","0.3"
,,,,,,,,,,,,,,,"2","125","HAS_CATEGORY","0.7"
,,,,,,,,,,,,,,,"2","6","PUBLISHED_AS",""
,,,,,,,,,,,,,,,"2","5","PUBLISHED_AS",""
,,,,,,,,,,,,,,,"104","128","PUBLISHED_AS",""
,,,,,,,,,,,,,,,"104","127","PUBLISHED_AS",""
,,,,,,,,,,,,,,,"5","8","IS_AVAILABLE_IN",""
,,,,,,,,,,,,,,,"6","8","IS_AVAILABLE_IN",""
```

Iryna: For CYPHER format, you can export the entire database using the `apoc.export.cypher.all` APOC procedure. The first argument of this procedure takes the full name of the file containing the exported data (created on the fly). The second argument describes the configuration of this export. In this example, we configure the `format` which can take three values:

- `cypher-shell` — exports the CYPHER script in a syntax intended to be manipulated with the `cypher-shell` tool;

- `plain` — merely exports CYPHER queries;

- `neo4j-shell` — exports the CYPHER script in a syntax intended to be manipulated with the now deprecated `neo4j-shell` tool.

Let's run our export query:

```
CALL apoc.export.cypher.all("export.cypher", {format:'cypher-shell'})
```

Here is the result of the executed procedure:

```
:begin
CREATE (:`Person`:`UNIQUE IMPORT LABEL`
 {`email`:"nicolas.mervaillie@graphits.tech", `name`:"Nicolas
 Mervaillie", `UNIQUE IMPORT ID`:0});
CREATE (:`Person`:`UNIQUE IMPORT LABEL` {`email`:"frank@graphits.tech",
 `name`:"Frank", `UNIQUE IMPORT ID`:1});
CREATE (:`Book` {`mainTitle`:"Neo4j", `subTitle`:"A Graph Project
 Story", `title`:"Neo4j - A Graph Project Story"});
CREATE (:`Category` {`title`:"Programming"});
CREATE (:`Product` {`isbn`:"9782822703826", `module`:"Printed
 Edition"});
CREATE (:`Product` {`isbn`:"9782822702591", `module`:"Digital
 Edition"});
CREATE (:`Catalog` {`reference`:"2017-1", `year`:2017});
CREATE (:`Catalog` {`reference`:"2018-1", `year`:2018});
CREATE (:`Publisher` {`id`:"AcmeId", `name`:"Acme Publishing"});
CREATE (:`Person`:`UNIQUE IMPORT LABEL`
 {`email`:"sylvain@graphits.tech", `name`:"Sylvain", `UNIQUE IMPORT
 ID`:20});
CREATE (:`Person`:`UNIQUE IMPORT LABEL`
 {`email`:"nicolas.rouyer@graphits.tech", `name`:"Nicolas Rouyer",
 `UNIQUE IMPORT ID`:84});
CREATE (:`Book` {`mainTitle`:"Neo4j", `subTitle`:"Discover Neo4j",
 `subTitle`:"A Graph Project Story", `title`:"Neo4j - Discover"});
CREATE (:`Category` {`title`:"Database"});
CREATE (:`Category` {`title`:"Operations"});
CREATE (:`Product` {`isbn`:"9782822704182", `module`:"Printed
 Edition"});
CREATE (:`Product` {`isbn`:"9782822704373", `module`:"Digital
 Edition"});
:commit
:begin
CREATE INDEX ON :`Publisher`(`name`);
CREATE INDEX ON :`Product`(`module`);
CREATE INDEX ON :`Book`(`subTitle`);
CREATE INDEX ON :`Book`(`mainTitle`);
CREATE INDEX ON :`TTL`(`ttl`);
CREATE CONSTRAINT ON (node:`Category`) ASSERT node.`title` IS UNIQUE;
CREATE CONSTRAINT ON (node:`Book`) ASSERT node.`title` IS UNIQUE;
CREATE CONSTRAINT ON (node:`Product`) ASSERT node.`isbn` IS UNIQUE;
CREATE CONSTRAINT ON (node:`Catalog`) ASSERT node.`reference` IS UNIQUE;
CREATE CONSTRAINT ON (node:`Publisher`) ASSERT node.`id` IS UNIQUE;
CREATE CONSTRAINT ON (node:`UNIQUE IMPORT LABEL`) ASSERT node.`UNIQUE
 IMPORT ID` IS UNIQUE;
:commit
CALL db.awaitIndex(':`TTL`(`ttl`)');
CALL db.awaitIndex(':`Book`(`mainTitle`)');
CALL db.awaitIndex(':`Book`(`subTitle`)');
CALL db.awaitIndex(':`Product`(`module`)');
CALL db.awaitIndex(':`Publisher`(`name`)');
CALL db.awaitIndex(':`Category`(`title`)');
CALL db.awaitIndex(':`Book`(`title`)');
CALL db.awaitIndex(':`Product`(`isbn`)');
```

```
CALL db.awaitIndex(':`Catalog`(`reference`)');
CALL db.awaitIndex(':`Publisher`(`id`)');
:begin
MATCH (n1:`Catalog`{`reference`:"2017-1"}),
 (n2:`Publisher`{`id`:"AcmeId"}) CREATE (n1)-[r:`OFFERED_BY`]->(n2);
MATCH (n1:`Catalog`{`reference`:"2018-1"}),
 (n2:`Publisher`{`id`:"AcmeId"}) CREATE (n1)-[r:`OFFERED_BY`]->(n2);
MATCH (n1:`Publisher`{`id`:"AcmeId"}),
 (n2:`Catalog`{`reference`:"2018-1"}) CREATE (n1)-[r:`CURRENT_CATALOG`]-
>(n2);
MATCH (n1:`Product`{`isbn`:"9782822704182"}),
 (n2:`Catalog`{`reference`:"2017-1"}) CREATE (n1)-[r:`IS_AVAILABLE_IN`]-
>(n2);
MATCH (n1:`Product`{`isbn`:"9782822704373"}),
 (n2:`Catalog`{`reference`:"2017-1"}) CREATE (n1)-[r:`IS_AVAILABLE_IN`]-
>(n2);
MATCH (n1:`UNIQUE IMPORT LABEL`{`UNIQUE IMPORT ID`:84}),
 (n2:`Book`{`title`:"Neo4j - A Graph Project Story"}) CREATE (n1)-
[r:`IS_AUTHOR_OF`]->(n2);
MATCH (n1:`UNIQUE IMPORT LABEL`{`UNIQUE IMPORT ID`:0}),
 (n2:`Book`{`title`:"Neo4j - A Graph Project Story"}) CREATE (n1)-
[r:`IS_AUTHOR_OF`]->(n2);
MATCH (n1:`UNIQUE IMPORT LABEL`{`UNIQUE IMPORT ID`:1}),
 (n2:`Book`{`title`:"Neo4j - A Graph Project Story"}) CREATE (n1)-
[r:`IS_AUTHOR_OF`]->(n2);
MATCH (n1:`UNIQUE IMPORT LABEL`{`UNIQUE IMPORT ID`:20}),
 (n2:`Book`{`title`:"Neo4j - A Graph Project Story"}) CREATE (n1)-
[r:`IS_AUTHOR_OF`]->(n2);
MATCH (n1:`UNIQUE IMPORT LABEL`{`UNIQUE IMPORT ID`:84}),
 (n2:`Book`{`title`:"Neo4j - Discover"}) CREATE (n1)-[r:`IS_AUTHOR_OF`]-
>(n2);
MATCH (n1:`UNIQUE IMPORT LABEL`{`UNIQUE IMPORT ID`:20}),
 (n2:`Book`{`title`:"Neo4j - Discover"}) CREATE (n1)-[r:`IS_AUTHOR_OF`]-
>(n2);
MATCH (n1:`Book`{`title`:"Neo4j - Discover"}),
 (n2:`Category`{`title`:"Database"}) CREATE (n1)-[r:`HAS_CATEGORY`
{`matching`:"1"}]->(n2);
MATCH (n1:`Book`{`title`:"Neo4j - Discover"}),
 (n2:`Category`{`title`:"Programming"}) CREATE (n1)-[r:`HAS_CATEGORY`
{`matching`:"0.3"}]->(n2);
MATCH (n1:`Book`{`title`:"Neo4j - A Graph Project Story"}),
 (n2:`Category`{`title`:"Database"}) CREATE (n1)-[r:`HAS_CATEGORY`
{`matching`:"1"}]->(n2);
MATCH (n1:`Book`{`title`:"Neo4j - A Graph Project Story"}),
 (n2:`Category`{`title`:"Programming"}) CREATE (n1)-[r:`HAS_CATEGORY`
{`matching`:"0.3"}]->(n2);
MATCH (n1:`Book`{`title`:"Neo4j - A Graph Project Story"}),
 (n2:`Category`{`title`:"Operations"}) CREATE (n1)-[r:`HAS_CATEGORY`
{`matching`:"0.7"}]->(n2);
MATCH (n1:`Book`{`title`:"Neo4j - A Graph Project Story"}),
 (n2:`Product`{`isbn`:"9782822702591"}) CREATE (n1)-[r:`PUBLISHED_AS`]-
>(n2);
MATCH (n1:`Book`{`title`:"Neo4j - A Graph Project Story"}),
 (n2:`Product`{`isbn`:"9782822703826"}) CREATE (n1)-[r:`PUBLISHED_AS`]-
>(n2);
```

```
MATCH (n1:`Book`{`title`:"Neo4j - Discover"}),
 (n2:`Product`{`isbn`:"9782822704373"}) CREATE (n1)-[r:`PUBLISHED_AS`]-
>(n2);
MATCH (n1:`Book`{`title`:"Neo4j - Discover"}),
 (n2:`Product`{`isbn`:"9782822704182"}) CREATE (n1)-[r:`PUBLISHED_AS`]-
>(n2);
MATCH (n1:`Product`{`isbn`:"9782822703826"}),
 (n2:`Catalog`{`reference`:"2018-1"}) CREATE (n1)-[r:`IS_AVAILABLE_IN`]-
>(n2);
MATCH (n1:`Product`{`isbn`:"9782822702591"}),
 (n2:`Catalog`{`reference`:"2018-1"}) CREATE (n1)-[r:`IS_AVAILABLE_IN`]-
>(n2);
:commit
:begin
MATCH (n:`UNIQUE IMPORT LABEL`)  WITH n LIMIT 20000 REMOVE n:`UNIQUE
 IMPORT LABEL` REMOVE n.`UNIQUE IMPORT ID`;
:commit
:begin
DROP CONSTRAINT ON (node:`UNIQUE IMPORT LABEL`) ASSERT node.`UNIQUE
 IMPORT ID` IS UNIQUE;
:commit
```

You can then replay this entire CYPHER script (making sure the `:begin` and `:commit` are lower case!) to recreate the data in another graph database instance.

Brian: What if we only want to export some specific elements?

Iryna: In that case, we use the `apoc.export.cypher.query` procedure. For example:

```
CALL apoc.export.cypher.query("MATCH (p:Person)-[r:IS_AUTHOR_OF]-
>(b:Book)
RETURN p, r, b","authors_books.cypher", {format:'cypher-shell'})
```

Using this query, only `Author` and `Book` nodes are exported, along with the IS_AU-THOR_OF relationships! Here is the CYPHER content of the export file:

```
:begin
CREATE (:`Person`:`UNIQUE IMPORT LABEL`
 {`email`:"nicolas.mervaillie@graphits.tech", `name`:"Nicolas
 Mervaillie", `UNIQUE IMPORT ID`:0});
CREATE (:`Person`:`UNIQUE IMPORT LABEL` {`email`:"frank@graphits.tech",
 `name`:"Frank", `UNIQUE IMPORT ID`:1});
CREATE (:`Book` {`mainTitle`:"Neo4j", `subTitle`:"A Graph Project
 Story", `title`:"Neo4j - A Graph Project Story"});
CREATE (:`Person`:`UNIQUE IMPORT LABEL`
 {`email`:"sylvain@graphits.tech", `name`:"Sylvain", `UNIQUE IMPORT
 ID`:20});
CREATE (:`Person`:`UNIQUE IMPORT LABEL`
 {`email`:"nicolas.rouyer@graphits.tech", `name`:"Nicolas Rouyer",
 `UNIQUE IMPORT ID`:84});
CREATE (:`Book` {`mainTitle`:"Neo4j", `subTitle`:"Discover Neo4j",
 `subTitle`:"A Graph Project Story", `title`:"Neo4j - Discover"});
```

```
:commit
:begin
CREATE INDEX ON :`Book`(`subTitle`);
CREATE INDEX ON :`Book`(`mainTitle`);
CREATE CONSTRAINT ON (node:`Book`) ASSERT node.`title` IS UNIQUE;
CREATE CONSTRAINT ON (node:`UNIQUE IMPORT LABEL`) ASSERT node.`UNIQUE
 IMPORT ID` IS UNIQUE;
:commit
CALL db.awaitIndex(':`Book`(`title`)');
CALL db.awaitIndex(':`Book`(`mainTitle`)');
CALL db.awaitIndex(':`Book`(`subTitle`)');
:begin
MATCH (n1:`UNIQUE IMPORT LABEL`{`UNIQUE IMPORT ID`:84}),
 (n2:`Book`{`title`:"Neo4j - A Graph Project Story"}) CREATE (n1)-
[r:`IS_AUTHOR_OF`]->(n2);
MATCH (n1:`UNIQUE IMPORT LABEL`{`UNIQUE IMPORT ID`:0}),
 (n2:`Book`{`title`:"Neo4j - A Graph Project Story"}) CREATE (n1)-
[r:`IS_AUTHOR_OF`]->(n2);
MATCH (n1:`UNIQUE IMPORT LABEL`{`UNIQUE IMPORT ID`:1}),
 (n2:`Book`{`title`:"Neo4j - A Graph Project Story"}) CREATE (n1)-
[r:`IS_AUTHOR_OF`]->(n2);
MATCH (n1:`UNIQUE IMPORT LABEL`{`UNIQUE IMPORT ID`:20}),
 (n2:`Book`{`title`:"Neo4j - A Graph Project Story"}) CREATE (n1)-
[r:`IS_AUTHOR_OF`]->(n2);
MATCH (n1:`UNIQUE IMPORT LABEL`{`UNIQUE IMPORT ID`:84}),
 (n2:`Book`{`title`:"Neo4j - Discover"}) CREATE (n1)-[r:`IS_AUTHOR_OF`]-
>(n2);
MATCH (n1:`UNIQUE IMPORT LABEL`{`UNIQUE IMPORT ID`:20}),
 (n2:`Book`{`title`:"Neo4j - Discover"}) CREATE (n1)-[r:`IS_AUTHOR_OF`]-
>(n2);
:commit
:begin
MATCH (n:`UNIQUE IMPORT LABEL`)  WITH n LIMIT 20000 REMOVE n:`UNIQUE
 IMPORT LABEL` REMOVE n.`UNIQUE IMPORT ID`;
:commit
:begin
DROP CONSTRAINT ON (node:`UNIQUE IMPORT LABEL`) ASSERT node.`UNIQUE
 IMPORT ID` IS UNIQUE;
:commit
```

To import this data, we just need to run the following command:

```
[NEO4J_HOME]$>cat authors_books.cypher | cypher-shell -u neo4j -p neo4j
--format plain
```

If your Neo4j server is ran with Docker, you can use the following command line:

```
docker exec compose_neo4j_1 bash -c "cat authors_books.cypher | /var/
lib/neo4j/bin/cypher-shell -u neo4j -p neo4j --format plain"
```

Jackie: Very good, I think we have an understanding of the export tools.

Iryna: For JSON formatted data, the simplest way to export it is to use Neo4j's HTTP API. We'll need the authorization header if the Neo4j database is in secure mode (parameter `dbms.security.auth_enabled=true` in the `neo4j.conf` configuration file.)

```
curl -X POST -o authors_books.json
-H Authorization:'Basic smVeNGr6bm2jbx=='
-H Accept:application/json
-H Content-Type:application/json
--data '{"statements" :
    [{"statement":"MATCH (p:Person)-[:IS_AUTHOR_OF]->(b:Book) RETURN
p.email+\",\"+b.title AS CSVline"}]}'
http://localhost:17474/db/data/transaction/commit
```

And we'll see our exported authors and books in JSON format:

```
{
    "errors": [],
    "results": [
      {
        "columns": ["CSVline"],
        "data": [
          {"meta": [null], "row": ["nicolas.rouyer@graphits.tech,Neo4j -
A Graph Project Story"]},
          {"meta": [null], "row": ["sylvain@graphits.tech,Neo4j - A
Graph Project Story"]},
          {"meta": [null], "row":
["nicolas.mervaillie@graphits.tech,Neo4j - A Graph Project Story"]},
          {"meta": [null], "row": ["frank@graphits.tech,Neo4j - A Graph
Project Story"]},
          {"meta": [null], "row": ["nicolas.rouyer@graphits.tech,Neo4j -
Discover"]},
          {"meta": [null],"row": ["sylvain@graphits.tech,Neo4j -
Discover"]}
        ]
      }
    ]
}
```

We'd get the same result using the Neo4j browser, by clicking on the CODE icon in the CYPHER results block.

Figure 3.7 : *JSON export from Neo4j browser*

Tiago: It works, and it wasn't even too hard!

Iryna: I'm pragmatic. We could have written a procedure, but by the time it's done, we can do thousands of API calls...

Jackie: Well, that's fine if you want to go that route. But this works, and that's what we're after. Hats off to you Tiago!

Tiago: Regarding SQL, I suggest we use existing procedures! Let's talk about prerequisites. Obviously we need to have a relational database, for example MySQL, which is up and running and contains a schema, either with existing or non-existing tables. For our example, I'll start by creating an `authors_books` table in a schema already present in the relational database:

```
CALL apoc.load.jdbcUpdate('jdbc:mysql://localhost:3306/library?
zeroDateTimeBehavior=CONVERT_TO_NULL&serverTimezone=UTC&user=root&password=nico',
 'CREATE TABLE authors_books (email VARCHAR(40) NOT NULL, title
 VARCHAR(100) NOT NULL, PRIMARY KEY(email, title))')
YIELD row
RETURN row
```

Iryna: Can we do a sanity check to make sure the table has been created?

Tiago: Sure, look!

Figure 3.8 : Create a MYSQL table from Neo4j

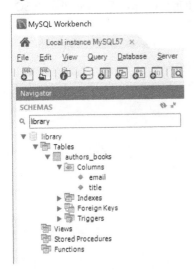

Tiago: The second step consists of inserting the authors and their books into the relational database. To do this, we just run the following CYPHER query:

```
MATCH (p:Person)-[r:IS_AUTHOR_OF]->(b:Book)
WITH p.email AS email, b.title AS title
CALL apoc.load.jdbcUpdate('jdbc:mysql://localhost:3306/library?
zeroDateTimeBehavior=CONVERT_TO_NULL&serverTimezone=UTC&user=root&password=nico',
'insert into authors_books values(?, ?)',[email, title])
YIELD row
RETURN row;
```

Brian: I'm going to need some more explanation about this one.

Tiago: Okay. The first two lines of the CYPHER query extract the authors and books from the Neo4j graph database. The `CALL` instruction lets you use the `apoc.load.jdbcUpdate` APOC procedure. This procedure requires two parameters. The first is the relational database server address. The second is the SQL query that updates the database.

Brian: But why does the SQL query contain those question marks?

Tiago: Because the query uses parameters. And these parameters (`email`, `title`), are precisely those that we extracted from the CYPHER query!

Brian: Does your query even work? I don't think it works. I don't think anything works. Are we about done?

Tiago: Ok, Mr. Skeptic von Pessimist, we'll check it in two ways. First with the MySQL Workbench tool:

Figure 3.9 : *MySQL table content loaded from Neo4j*

Jackie: That's pretty conclusive! What about the other way to do it?

Tiago: Just go directly to our Neo4j graph database...

Iryna: But this time we'll use the APOC procedure to *read* from the relational database!

Tiago: Right, we do this with the `apoc.load.jdbc` APOC procedure. Thusly:

```
CALL apoc.load.jdbc('jdbc:mysql://localhost:3306/library?
zeroDateTimeBehavior=CONVERT_TO_NULL&serverTimezone=UTC&user=root
&password=nico','SELECT * FROM authors_books')
YIELD row
RETURN row.email as email, row.title as title
```

Caution › *We strongly recommend placing the connection strings in the [NEO4J_HOME]/conf/ neo4j.conf file by adding the key* **apoc.jdbc.<key>.url** *(where* **key** *is an arbitrary name). For example* **apoc.jdbc.neo4j.url=jdbc:mysql://192.168.1.30:3306/neo4j? user=root&password=nico.**

Here is the result in the Neo4j browser:

Figure 3.10 : View relational database content from Neo4j

Started streaming 6 records after 2 ms and completed after 18 ms.

Jackie: Okay, very good, but what if we need to apply more complex transformations or business rules on data we import or export?

Tiago: Well, in that case I'd suggest to use a full fledged ETL tool that support advanced transformations and complex import workflows. There are several off the shelf products, like Talend, Kettle or GraphAware DataBridge.

Jackie: Let's keep it for later if we need it. I think we have a complete analysis now. Shall we debrief on data import-export?

3.6. Debriefing

Varsha: Hi! Our customer is looking forward to hearing about our data import-export study... in particular, they'd like to know if they can keep their relational databases! What did you come up with?

Jackie: We've identified a critical tool, the CYPHER LOAD CSV instruction, which will be useful in creating an import model of our customer data.

Varsha: Is that your final answer?

Jackie: It depends on the volume of data to be migrated and how frequently the data migration occurs between the current system and the graph database. If we have a ton of data, as we would, for example, with the ordering process, we will use a more suitable tool, like the neo4j-admin tool which is powerful as long as we have well structured data to be imported...

Tiago: And if we don't have well structured data, then we write our own import tool, using the Neo4j BatchInserter library.

Jackie: The first two solutions require our customer data to be exported in CSV format.

Varsha: Isn't there a more direct way?

Jackie: Yes, there is. Using APOC stored procedures, data can be imported directly from a relational database into our graph database.

Varsha: I suppose we could go the other way as well? Say we have a business partner who wants to access the content of our catalog, or who would be in charge of a part of the ordering process?

Jackie: Neo4j data can be exported into relational databases (always with APOC procedures), but it can also be exported in other formats, such as CSV, JSON, etc.

Varsha: Awesome! So, what's next?

Brian: Maybe talk about this to the client, and do some tests on real data?

Jackie: Absolutely, let's test with the client! That's the only way to be sure we've found the right tool for the job. We have a wide range of import-export alternatives, and at least one of them will work...

4
Operating Neo4j

Need to improve the overall performance of your graph database? Make it more reliable? Learn how to monitor it? In this section, we will describe ways of correctly operating a production Neo4j graph database.

4.1. Briefing

Jackie: Let's talk about to setup Neo4j in production, how the servers behave and how we go about ensuring maximum availability. Ashley, it seems to me that you are the expert on these questions, aren't you?

Ashley: Well, yes, I think as much as anyone. I'll try to share what I have learned with you.

Jackie: Do you have a roadmap or something like that?

Ashley: Yes, of course, we will learn to:

- set up a Neo4j - HA (high availability) cluster;
- set up a Neo4j causal cluster;
- prepare for disaster recovery (backup, recovery);
- set up Neo4j logging;
- adapt our system to the resources we have (memory);
- update our system to limit technical debt.

Jackie: Yet another long agenda means another busy day! Well, guess we should get started...

Ashley: First, a little prologue: I will use *Neo4j server* and *Neo4j instance* interchangeably to designate any Neo4j installation. When I want to talk about the actual physical server, I will use term *machine*. Sound ok?

4.2. High Availability Cluster (HA)

Ashley: Where to start? Ok, so let's imagine that we have a Neo4j server, which is working just fine, but the machine that hosts the Neo4j server fails. Definitely sucks. What happens then?

Tiago: Well, every program connected to Neo4j loses its connection to the graph database and can no longer read data from it. Even worse, no application can write to the graph database, creating a high risk of data loss.

Ashley: Exactly! What can we do to solve this problem? And how how can we minimize downtime?

Tiago: We could install another Neo4j server on another machine and ingest data from the last backup...

Iryna: That would certainly result in some lost data (probably at least for the current day, depending on the frequency of the backups). As for the system restart time, I guess it would depend on the volume of data to be loaded...

Tiago: And meanwhile, the applications would still try in vain to write to the graph database, and each time data would vanish into the abyss of error logs...

Iryna: Not to mention that the new machine would have to have the same IP address or host name as the previous machine, unless all the settings for connecting client applications are changed...

Tiago: Yeah, that would be the end of the world...

Jackie: Being a bit of a drama queen, aren't you?

Tiago: Maybe to someone who hasn't experienced something like this.

Ashley: And sadly, this scenario is fairly likely to happen eventually. During a service interruption, we say that the Neo4j server is no longer *available*.

Brian: Hence the importance of *high availability*?

Ashley: Precisely. To avoid this kind of meltdown, we need to execute three actions:

- detect *single points of failure* of the system;
- set up an automatic failover process to an available server, which is triggered by a connection failure on the first server*(failover)*;
- distribute the load to maximize the volume of possible transactions on the network so as not to slow down the system.

Tiago: So we need several Neo4j servers running at the same time.

Ashley: Right, and that's where things get complicated.

Iryna: Because this is more than just a switch to an available Neo4j instance. For consistency, the same data must also be available from any of these servers.

Ashley: Absolutely, we certainly can't tolerate switching to another Neo4j server to result in finding only part of our data. So the Neo4j servers will need to communicate with each other, and the graph data will have to be replicated on each server. We call this a *Neo4j cluster* (a cluster of servers) and a server in the cluster is called a *node*, as in a graph. Funny, right?

Brian: I get it! So we mount two Neo4j servers and we've fixed our high availability issue!

Ashley: Yes, but only temporarily. We still have the *load balancing* problem I mentioned! If one of our two Neo4j instances is no longer accessible, the other will have to absorb the entire load of the first server as well as its own. This will soon lead to performance degradation, and can ultimately end with the second server falling over. So we assert that *a cluster must have at least three nodes*. If one of them becomes unavailable, then the load will be spread over at least two remaining servers.

How a Neo4j HA cluster works

Ashley: A Neo4j cluster has a Neo4j instance called the *master*, intended for read/write use, and zero to many instances called *slaves*, ideally limited to read operations. Each instance has its own local copy of the graph database. Because we decided we need at least three servers, imagine we have one master and two slaves.

Brian: One question, please: why is only one server configured in read/write mode?

Ashley: Several considerations must be taken into account. First, write operations generally take longer than read-only operations. Our goal is to maintain availability on the read-only servers for massive queries, but without reducing the performance of write operations. The second consideration concerns transactions. It is difficult to provide secure ACID transactions on different servers. But, starting with Neo4j v3.2, this exists under the poetic name of *causal cluster* [157]. Let's start by making it simple with HA cluster, then we'll transform it into a causal cluster.

Brian: But are the master and slave Neo4j servers different? I mean, are there different Neo4j operations for a server in an HA cluster as opposed to a causal cluster?

Ashley: No, and let's underscore this–each instance of a Neo4j server is *capable* of reading/writing, and everything that is possible with one Neo4j server is possible with any other. The distinction lies entirely in the role they are given within the Neo4j cluster:

- *master instance:* is responsible for managing transactions and persisting new data;
- *slave instance:* is preferably accessed only for read operations (however it would be possible to query this instance with write operations);
- *arbiter instance:* is a slave instance that does not expose data (no data replication) but which participates in cluster management.

Figure 4.1 : HA Cluster

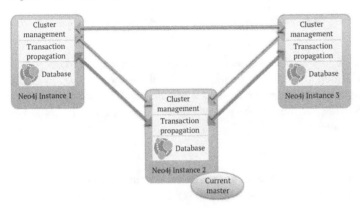

(Source: *Operations Manual*, Neo4j Inc [http://d-booker.jo.my/neo4j-ha-cluster])

Tiago: So how does the Neo4j cluster work? How is data replicated? And what happens if the master goes down?

Ashley: Let's start with the master instance. This instance type is responsible for the propagation of transactions. Here's how it goes: writing directly to the master server works, initially, as if it were not part of a cluster. The transaction is opened, the graph is updated locally, and if successful the write becomes final (*commit*), otherwise it is invalid (*rollback*), then the transaction is closed. If the transaction is successful, the changes will be propagated to some (configurable) number of slaves, which is called the *push*.

Tiago: But the *push* might fail. What then?

Ashley: This is called an *optimistic* operation. If the *push* fails, the master server transaction still remains valid. The slave server(s) would be out-of-date, but will be synchronized with the master instance at the next data replication.

Tiago: What if we try to write on a slave instance?

Ashley: The master server remains responsible for the propagation of transactions but the operation is somewhat different. The first step is the slave server synchronizing its data with the master server. The slave instance data must be updated before any write operation, otherwise it could potentially overwrite data. In the second step, a write to a slave server will be synchronized with the master server, with the transactional locks set on both master and slave instances. The write to the master will be performed and validated first, followed by validation on the slave server.

Election of a new master

Tiago: But you haven't answered the question of the master server becoming unavailable.

Ashley: That depends. We have to live with the possibility that a master may occasionally be unavailable (due to network overload, etc.). But if the unavailability threshold becomes too great, then the cluster should elect a new master. This process itself takes considerable time (a few seconds), which is why it should not be triggered immediately any old time the master falters.

Tiago: Really? A new master is elected?

Ashley: This is called the *quorum* (*that is, the number of members present required in a deliberative assembly for the vote to be valid. This is the dictionary definition.*).

Tiago: And there are election rules, I suppose?

Ashley: It turns out everything is governed! A quorum is reached when more than 50% of the active members of the cluster are still active. If we define n as the number of defaulting masters we can lose but still have a functioning cluster, then a valid cluster will contain $2n + 1$ Neo4j instances.

Brian: Give me a break... equations? Math was never very kind to me...

Ashley: Then I'll say it again in a different way. Let's imagine that we want to absorb the impact of a single Neo4j master instance failure ($n = 1$). To meet this need, our cluster must consist of at least three instances ($2 \times 1 + 1 = 3$). If the initial master server croaks, a new master can be elected because there is still a quorum: the two remaining machines represent more than 50% of the original cluster members. One of the two remaining servers will then be promoted to be the new master. But, if this new master goes down, then election will no longer be possible, because the last standing server would be master of itself.

Brian: Oh, is that all it is? Ok, got it now.

Tiago: How does the cluster decide which Neo4j instance will be the best master?

Ashley: When a master goes down (or during a cold start of the cluster), the slave with the highest (most recent) *transaction identifier* will be elected master. This way the cluster ensures that the new master is the instance with the freshest data. If both slaves are up to date, then the one with the lowest *instance identifier* will be elected master.

Tiago: What's this *instance identifier* thing?

Ashley: Each cluster node is identified by a unique numerical value (some positive integer) that is associated, through the `[NEO4J_HOME]/conf/neo4j.conf` configuration file, with the `ha.server_id` key. This value makes it possible to distinguish between the various server instances.

Using a Neo4j cluster from a Bolt or HTTP client

Ashley: So let's say our cluster is started and now we want to be able to use it from a client program.

Tiago: I guess the question now is: how are we going to ensure *failover*? Does the *bolt +routing* protocol allow routing in case of failure of a cluster node?

Ashley: Unfortunately not, the *bolt+routing* protocol only works with the causal cluster, which we will get to shortly. We have to manage the *failover* ourselves via a *load balancer* [http://d-booker.jo.my/neo4j-load-balancer].

Tiago: Ugh. How do we go about doing that?

Ashley: Well, you need to find a software or hardware tool that performs failover and load balancing tasks. Then configure it by providing our server resources (that is, their addresses, which will constitute the *pool* of servers) and by pointing our Bolt driver to the load balancer address:

```
Driver driver = GraphDatabase.driver("bolt://
load_balancer_ip:load_balancer_port",token);
```

When the driver is defined this way, the load balancer will receive the Bolt requests and find the most available server in the cluster, depending, of course, on its configuration.

Tiago: Can you give an example of a product that performs this kind of work?

Ashley: Sure. HAProxy [http://www.haproxy.org] software specializes in this type of operation. It is also highly configurable and allows routing to be defined according to read/write access. However, configuring HAProxy is beyond the scope of this working session. Instead we will learn how to configure a Neo4j cluster. As you'll see, it's not rocket science.

Configuring an HA cluster

Ashley: We'll start by installing three Neo4j enterprise edition servers on three separate machines. Then, we will edit the `neo4j.conf` file foreach of these servers, setting the following required elements:

- `dbms.mode`: specifies the type of installation for the Neo4j server. The default mode is `dbms.mode=SINGLE`, i.e. a Neo4j instance operating in an isolated and autonomous way. If this Neo4j instance is in a cluster, we must set this parameter to HA: `dbms.mode=HA`.

- `ha.server_id`: we have already mentioned this before. This parameter identifies the Neo4j instance within the cluster. We can, for example, set this parameter to the value: `ha.server_id=1` for the first instance, `ha.server_id=2` for the second instance, `ha.server_id=3` for the third instance.

- `ha.initial_hosts`: the list of addresses of the cluster members who will be a part of a cold start for the cluster. A server address consists of its IP (or host name) followed by port 5001 (i.e. the `ha.host parameter.coordination` default port, which we will see shortly). With the server ids above, we get: `ha.initial_hosts=[ip_server_1]:5001,[ip_server_2]:5001,[ip_server_3]:5001`. This value will be the same for all instances.

Caution › *No spaces are expected before or after the = symbol! If there are spaces, an error will appear in the error logs and your setting will be ignored. Most likely the instance will not start.*

You should realize that other cluster configuration parameters exist. As they have default values, it is not necessary to define them. However, it is useful to know they exist:

- `ha.host.coordination`: the address and port on which a Neo4j instance listens to cluster events (failure of another instance, election of a new master, etc.). The default port is 5001.

- `ha.host.data`: the address and port on which a Neo4j instance listens to transaction events on the cluster master. This port must be separate from that of the `ha.host.coordination` parameter. The default port is 6001.

- `ha.join_timeout`: the time, expressed in seconds, that is the maximum time for the cluster to be formed. This means that all instances specified by the `ha.initial_hosts` parameter must join the cluster within this time, otherwise these instances will stop. The default value is 30 seconds.

Tiago: How do I handle a case in which I need to install the different Neo4j instances on the same machine?

Ashley: You do this by setting the listening ports of the different instances so that none of them try to listen on a port used by another instance. Here is a list of the ports used:

TECHNIQUE: Neo4j listening ports

Table 4.1 : *List of used ports*

Parameter	Default value	Description
dbms.connector.bolt	7687	Bolt connector
dbms.connector.http	7474	HTTP connector
dbms.connector.https	7473	HTTPS connector
ha.host.coordination	5001	HA cluster coordination
ha.host.data	6001	Listening port for transaction events of a given HA cluster
causal_clustering.discovery _listen_address	5000	Listening port for discovery events for a given causal cluster
causal_clustering.transaction _listen_address	6000	Listening port for transaction events of a given causal cluster
causal_clustering.raft_listen _address	7000	Listening port for Raft protocol used in the causal cluster
dbms.backup.address	6362	Listening port for hot backup service (disabled by default)
dbms.jvm.additional=-Dcom.sun .management.jmxremote.port	3637	JMX listening port (disabled by default)
dbms.shell.port	1337	Listening port for neo4j-shell tool (deprecated, disabled by default)

TECHNICAL: Address and port format

The address of the ha.host.data parameter must be assigned to one of the network interfaces of the host machine.

The address of the ha.host.coordination parameter must be assigned to one of the network interfaces of the host machine, or must be set to value 0.0.0.0 which will cause all network interfaces of the host machine to listen.

The address or port can be omitted, in which case the default value will be used. If you wish to specify the port by omitting the address, it is possible to use the following syntax: `ha.host.coordination=:<port_number>`, for instance: `ha.host.coordination=:5001`.

It is possible to specify a range of ports using the `address:first_port-last_port` syntax. Neo4j will test each port in this range and will use the first unused port. However, such use is not permitted when all network interfaces are used (`0.0.0.0`).

Once that's done, I'll start all the servers with a command line:

```
[NEO4J_HOME_1]/bin/neo4j start
[NEO4J_HOME_2]/bin/neo4j start
[NEO4J_HOME_3]/bin/neo4j start
```

I'm looking through the (`[NEO4J_HOME]/logs`) log files on each server to see if there were any problems. I can also check on this by connecting to the HTTP console of one of the servers and run the monitoring command, typing `:sysinfo` in the query field:

Figure 4.2 : :sysinfo Web browser

And we can check the status of the cluster in the CLUSTER block:

Figure 4.3 : Web browser–cluster status

Cluster			
Id	Alive	Available	Is Master
1	true	true	yes
2	true	true	-
3	true	true	-

In this block, we can verify that the cluster consists of three Neo4j instances, with identifiers 1, 2 and 3 respectively. The instance with identifier 1 is currently the cluster master.

Tiago: What else should we check?

Ashley: We should check to make sure that the election of a new master will work. To do so, we simply drop the instance with identifier 1, then connect to a Neo4j web browser to check the status again. I could also check the logs of instance number 2. In case of election of a new master, if the last transaction identifier is equal for the remaining slaves, the rule is that the elected instance is the one with the smallest instance identifier (in our case the instance number 2). We can find some interesting things in this log (I purposely ignored a number of events so I could focus on the main one):

```
INFO [o.n.c.p.c.ClusterConfiguration] Instance 1 is leaving the cluster
INFO [o.n.c.p.c.ClusterConfiguration] Removed role 1 from leaving
 instance coordinator
WARN [o.n.c.p.e.ClusterLeaveReelectionListener] Demoting member 1
 because it left the cluster
INFO [o.n.k.h.HighAvailabilityLogger] Instance 1 has left the cluster
WARN [o.n.k.h.c.m.ObservedClusterMembers] Unknown member with id '1'
 reported unavailable as 'master'
INFO [o.n.k.h.HighAvailabilityLogger] Instance 1 is unavailable as
 master
```

The number 2 instance then notices that the number 1 instance has left the cluster, and thus is no longer an available as a master. Continuing:

```
INFO [o.n.c.p.a.m.c.ElectionContextImpl] Doing elections for role
 coordinator
DEBUG [o.n.c.p.e.ElectionState$2] ElectionState: election-[vote]-
 >election from:cluster://172.18.0.3:5001 conversation-id:2/17#
 payload:VoteRequest{role='coordinator', version=-1}
DEBUG [o.n.c.p.e.ElectionState] cluster://172.18.0.4:5001
 voted VersionedVotedData[role:coordinator, instance:3,
 credentials:DefaultElectionCredentials[serverId=3, latestTxId=66,
 currentWinner=false], version: -1] which i accepted
DEBUG [o.n.c.p.e.ElectionState$2] ElectionState: election-
 [voted]->election from:cluster://172.18.0.4:5001 conversation-
 id:2/17# payload:VersionedVotedData[role:coordinator, instance:3,
 credentials:DefaultElectionCredentials[serverId=3, latestTxId=65,
 currentWinner=false], version: -1]
DEBUG [o.n.c.p.e.ElectionState] cluster://172.18.0.3:5001
 voted VersionedVotedData[role:coordinator, instance:2,
 credentials:DefaultElectionCredentials[serverId=2, latestTxId=66,
 currentWinner=false], version: -1] which i accepted
DEBUG [o.n.c.p.a.m.DefaultWinnerStrategy] Election: received
 votes [2:DefaultElectionCredentials[serverId=2, latestTxId=66,
 currentWinner=false], 3:DefaultElectionCredentials[serverId=3,
 latestTxId=66, currentWinner=false]], eligible votes
 [2:DefaultElectionCredentials[serverId=2, latestTxId=66,
 currentWinner=false], 3:DefaultElectionCredentials[serverId=3,
 latestTxId=66, currentWinner=false]]
DEBUG [o.n.c.p.e.ElectionState] Elected 2 as coordinator
```

The election of a new master occurs, instances 2 and 3 are eligible. Their last transaction ID (*latestTxId*) is 66 for both. The election strategy will therefore rely on the lowest *serverId*. The number 2 instance is elected. Looking further down in the log, we see:

```
INFO [o.n.k.h.HighAvailabilityLogger] Instance 2 (this server)  was
  elected as coordinator
INFO [o.n.k.AvailabilityGuard] Requirement makes database unavailable:
  High Availability member state not ready
INFO [o.n.k.h.HighAvailabilityLogger] Write transactions to database
  disabled
INFO [o.n.k.i.f.GraphDatabaseFacadeFactory] Database is now unavailable
DEBUG [o.n.k.h.c.HighAvailabilityMemberStateMachine] Got
  masterIsElected(2), moved to TO_MASTER from SLAVE. Previous elected
  master is 1
INFO [o.n.k.h.HighAvailabilityLogger] Instance 2 (this server)  is
  unavailable as slave
INFO [o.n.k.h.MasterClient320]
  MasterClient320[1dfd4309b668/172.18.0.2:6001] shutdown
INFO [o.n.k.h.c.SwitchToMaster] I am 2, moving to master
INFO [o.n.k.h.HighAvailabilityLogger] Database available for write
  transactions
INFO [o.n.k.i.f.GraphDatabaseFacadeFactory] Database is now ready
[MemberIsAvailable[ Role: slave, InstanceId: 3, Role
  URI: ha://172.18.0.4:6001?serverId=3, Cluster URI:
  cluster://172.18.0.4:5001], MemberIsAvailable[ Role: master,
  InstanceId: 2, Role URI: ha://22fc9237304b:6001?serverId=2, Cluster
  URI: cluster://172.18.0.3:5001], MemberIsAvailable[ Role: backup,
  InstanceId: 2, Role URI: backup://127.0.0.1:6362, Cluster URI:
  cluster://172.18.0.3:5001]]
INFO [o.n.k.h.HighAvailabilityLogger] Instance 2 (this server)
  is available as backup at backup://127.0.0.1:6362 with
  StoreId{creationTime=1502179473519, randomId=-945597455483335713,
  storeVersion=15813456178476550, upgradeTime=1502179473519, upgradeId=1}
```

In this log, the second instance changes from slave to master (*I am 2, moving to master*), and write transactions are enabled for this instance (*Database available for write transactions*). If we then check the *Cluster* block of either one of the available instances, we'll see that only two cluster members are still available and that the master is the number 2 instance:

Figure 4.4 : Web browser—cluster status (2)

Cluster		
Id	Alive	Available	Is Master
2	true	true	yes
3	true	true	-

So you see, it's pretty straightforward to set up a basic HA cluster (of course you'll need to use other configuration parameters to fine-tune the cluster for a production environment).

4.3. Causal cluster

Ashley: This is good stuff. Let's review all this logic for clustering and *fault tolerance*. It's pretty easy to configure the HA cluster, but are there any known drawbacks?

Tiago: I'd like to underscore that only one instance is in charge of transactions at any given time.

Ashley: Which means?

Tiago: Potentially it means data desynchronization. What happens to the writes that arrive while an election is occurring? Or when a master goes down and the chosen slave has not had enough time to synchronize with the latest master? I doubt that anything good happens.

Ashley: Those are some of the reasons for designing a new type of cluster. To truly ensure data consistency, we must distribute transaction validation. The causal cluster will provide these three main features:

- *availability*: primary (core) servers provide a fault-tolerant platform for transaction processing. These servers remain available for writing as long as a simple majority of these servers are up and running;

- *scaling*: secondary servers (*replica*) (read-only) provide the ability to expand the cluster to handle read requests that involve a high volume of data or complex processing in a large graph database;

- causal *consistency*: guarantees that a client application can read at least what that particular client has written.

In order to comply with the official terminology, going forward I'll use the term core to designate a primary instance, and the term *replica* to designate a secondary server.

The operational point of view

Ashley: From an operational perspective, the Neo4j instances that make up a causal cluster are divided into two types: core servers and replica servers. You need to understand that core servers are the heart of the cluster—that's where it all happens. Replicas are optional, and are not involved in cluster management, unlike HA cluster slave instances. They will simply be used to relieve core servers from read-only work (and processing this type of CYPHER queries).

Figure 4.5 : *Causal cluster*

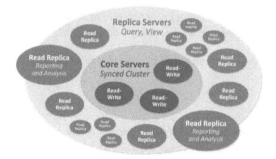

(Source: *Operations Manual*, Neo4j Inc [http://d-booker.jo.my/neo4j-cluster_causal])

Tiago: It seems to me like transactions occur at the core server level, whereas replica servers act as a sort of cache for data.

Ashley: Bam, that's a great way to put it. The hard part of core servers lies in ensuring consistency between transactions. For a transaction to be considered valid, it must be accepted by a majority of the cluster's core servers (Number of instances / 2 + 1). If a majority is not available, then the graph database will become read-only.

Tiago: Doesn't that make transaction processing fairly expensive?

Ashley: Well, there certainly is an overhead cost. And the more servers there are in the cluster, the higher the cost. That's why we'll try to build a cluster core with the minimum number of servers to meet the fault tolerance we want to achieve. We can calculate the number of core instances of our cluster based on the number of core server failures that would be acceptable to us using the following formula: M=2F+1 where M is the total number of core servers needed to absorb F failures.

Brian (moaning): OMG! More equations? What is this? Relativistic quantum mechanics? Please, could you just KMN?

Tiago: Can you give us an example before Brian does something drastic?

Ashley: Okay. Suppose we wanted to stay up for business with a maximum of two core server failures. Then our causal cluster should consist of five core instances (2 × 2 + 1).

Tiago: Got it. And I think it's good practice to free core servers from read-only work so that they can be as fast as possible in transaction management...

Ashley: And that is achieved through the important role played by the replica servers.

Tiago: Yeah, but how is the data on these replica servers updated?

Ashley: The data on replica instances are replicated asynchronously. They will periodically ask a core instance for transactions that they haven't yet processed since their most recent request.

Iryna: So you addressed data integrity, with what we've seen with the core servers and the transactions validated by a majority of them. You told us about *scaling*, which we have seen through the replica instances, but you have not yet said anything about *causal consistency*...

Ashley: As you probably know, causality is the link between cause and effect. To have a predictable effect, the cause must be known. If this idea is applied to the data consistency model, the system will ensure that to get a correct read of the data, each of the transactions related to the write operations which persist the data (the cause), must be applied to each of the core instances in the *same order*.

Iryna: That's super complicated. Can you elaborate? And can someone please perform CPR on Brian?

Ashley: Well, let's break it into smaller pieces. The client application sees the causal cluster as a single Neo4j instance–it doesn't care about the cluster. Only the driver associated with the *bolt+routing* protocol needs knowledge of the cluster topology, so it can perform the appropriate routing, which depends on the availability of the instances and the type of transaction to be performed (read or write). The client application will make one write (or even several) by placing a bookmark on the transaction: the bookmark is an identifier that will serve as a reference id for the system. Once this is done, the client application might try to read the data corresponding to this transaction bookmark. There is no guarantee that the Neo4j instance that was called to do the read has received this data yet. The Neo4j instance will therefore consult its transaction logs and, if the bookmark transaction has not yet been passed to it, it will put itself on hold until the other instances have transmitted the data enabling it to find the transaction indicated by the bookmark. This ensures that the application can read at *least* its own records.

Life cycle of the causal cluster

Ashley: Now let's look at the technical aspects of how the causal cluster works. Its functioning is based on a life cycle which uses four protocols:

- *Discovery protocol*
- *Raft protocol*
- *Catchup protocol*
- *Backup protocol*

Though the term *protocol* is often used in networks, here the term doesn't necessarily imply a *network* connotation. In this context, we should define the word *protocol* to mean *a set of rules defining the way it works*.

Discovery protocol

Ashley: When the cluster starts, the first step consists of discovering its core members. Whether the Neo4j instance that discovers the cluster is a core or replica server, the status of the cluster is always reported by core instances.

Brian: What happens when the first server is up and running?

Ashley: The first server will form the cluster and wait for the other members to join. The other members are specified by the `causal_clustering.initial_discovery_members` parameter defined in `[NEO4J_HOME]/conf/neo4j.conf`. If a server comes alive and at least one core server is already present, then this new instance joins the already existing cluster and becomes aware of the cluster topology. If necessary it will do a catch-up of the transactions, then it comes under the management of the transactional protocol (Raft).

Brian: Is it the same for the replica servers?

Ashley: No, replica servers are not involved in the transactional protocol. Replicas are registered with the cluster *whiteboard*. This *whiteboard* is a registry whose job is to maintain the list of available replica servers, and to allow routing of read-only requests from client applications (*bolt+routing*). The whiteboard is kept in core servers memory.

Raft protocol

Ashley: Raft [http://d-booker.jo.my/neo4j-raft] is a consensus protocol that allows the synchronization of logs within a cluster. In the case of Neo4j, it will be used to keep our transactions synchronized.

Brian: What black magic does that?

Ashley: So, every transaction on a core server will be recorded in a transaction log. This record is called a log *entry*. The log entry is replicated on each of the core servers in the cluster, and once enough servers (a consensus group) has recorded this entry in its own log, the transaction is validated. The Raft protocol guarantees the order of the entries in the log, so transactions are always carried out in the same order on each of the core servers.

Brian: What so important about the order?

Ashley: If a core server carries out transactions in the wrong order, the data can be corrupted. For example, suppose one transaction updates a node property of "nam" to be "Brian", and another transaction corrects that same node and property to be "Ashley". If the transactions are done in reverse order, the name will be left as "Brian".

Brian: How does it do that?

Ashley: In the Neo4j Raft cluster, each core server has a role. One of them acts as a leader and the others as followers. The leader maintains a logical clock, that is, a mechanism providing pseudo-temporal reference points necessary for sequencing transactions. The sequencing will be imposed on followers so that they keep the same order of transactions. When a transaction reaches the cluster, the leader records it in its transaction log put a kind of buffer stroke on it using its clock (the word term is used in the official documentation). Then it checks that a consensus is obtained for this transaction with a majority of followers. When this occurs, the transaction is validated in its log (commit) and the Neo4j client is informed of the validity of the transaction.

Brian: I may be missing a pseudo-temporal reference point, but isn't there always a risk that the leader is no longer available?

Ashley: Yes! Good, you're exactly right! If a core server in a follower role detects that the server in the leader role is stumbling, then it assumes the role of candidate for leader, and an election of a new leader takes place. The official documentations says this election takes about 500 ms on average, but in reality the election time is often shorter.

Brian: This sounds like the HA cluster, where the election of the new leader depends on a number of criteria?

Ashley: We'll make a system architect out of you yet, Brian! Indeed, the candidate having the more stable state will be elected leader, which means the one having the highest buffer stroke, the one having the longest transaction log, and the one having the highest transaction ID validated, in that priority.

Brian: What about write operations that happen during the election? Because, I figure in this time span there is no logical clock providing the pseudo-temporal reference points (I'm using "pseudo-temporal" every chance I get) that guarantee the transaction order.

Ashley: Dude, you are seriously on fire! Unlike the HA cluster, which acts as if nothing had happened from the clients's point of view and just sets new entries aside, the causal cluster will switch to read-only mode and return a transaction error to the Bolt clients. The client application is responsible for handling these exceptions by using the retry mechanism built in the Bolt driver, or and setting up a custom *retry* mechanism if the driver proves insufficient.

Catchup protocol

Ashley: Now for the Catchup protocol, and I'm warning you no bad puns about "catchup"...

Brian: You mean like, the optimum Catchup protocol is one squirt of ketchup for every five average size french fries? Puns like that that?

Ashley: Yes, Brian, like that. *Exactly* like that. As I was saying... the catch-up principle consists of updating the transactions of an instance from the information provided by the core cluster. This has to happen whenever a new core server joins the cluster, but the main purpose of this protocol is to synchronize replica servers.

Brian: Let me guess—replica instances periodically ask core cluster for transactions they are missing?

Ashley: I'm awed, Brian. You are really impressing me, Mr Genius.

Tiago: Yeah, well, it's much easier to be a genius when you have the documentation right in front of you!

Ashley: Oh, I thought Brian was... hey, give him a break—he's *reading the docs*, and that's a perfectly valid way to get this stuff down. Anyway, that's the right idea. Replica instances spend all their time responding to read-only requests and updating their local data from past transactions on the core server cluster.

Tiago: That said, there must be a ton of transactions to deal with for a young replica who joins a causal cluster that already has done a lot of work, right?

Brian: Who's reading from the documentation now?

Ashley: Yeah, you bet, Tiago! In this case, if the difference in the number of transactions between the new replica and the core cluster is way too large, so the core cluster base data is simply copied to the replica server.

Tiago: But by the time this copy is completed, other transactions will probably have been committed to the core cluster...

Ashley: True. But that's ok, because the catch-up protocol would resume its original operation, and the replica instance would ask for an update of its transactions through the usual channel.

Backup protocol

Ashley: Well, facing facts in the real world, despite the precautions we take, the system as a whole can, and occasionally will, fail.

Brian: Why? With all these instances and pseudo-temporal replication mechanisms, how could the cluster possibly fail? Surely the pseudo-temporals wouldn't let us down?

Ashley: Because if something can happen, it eventually will happen pseudo-temporals notwithstanding. Let's take a rough example. Imagine that your causal cluster is distributed on virtual machines (VM) and that these virtual machines are running on the same physical machine and depend on the same storage space. If this shared storage space fails, your data will no longer be accessible and in effect it's lost. That's why, whatever fancy database management system you've set up, you need to perform backups on a regular basis. The backup mechanism copies the data from a Neo4j instance of the cluster to a third party storage space, preferably on a different storage site from the one on which the causal cluster is running on. It would really suck to lose the data and the data backups at the same time...

Tiago: Of course, it'd totally blow. But still, I need to ask: are we talking about a *hot* backup? Because otherwise we're still talking about down time.

Brian: Hot backup?

Tiago: Yes, hot backup means we don't need to shut down Neo4j instances in order to backup the data.

Ashley: Absolutely, we really want to keep the database up and running. A backup process consists of running the `neo4j-admin backup` command periodically by passing the address of the Neo4j instance acting as backup server. It's best to designate a replica server for this, so that the core servers focus on cluster and transaction management. The backup tool currently uses the catch-up protocol to collect the data that needs to be backed up. This data will be saved to disk at the location specified in the command.

Tiago: Don't forget to mention that two backup types are possible: *full* database or *incremental*.

Ashley: You're right, it all depends on the parameters passed to the `neo4j-admin backup` command and on the state of your last backup.

Tiago: So, if I'm summarizing correctly, the backup tool will perform a catch-up action on a replica (or possibly even a core instance) for the data it needs to save?

Ashley: Yeah, that's it. We'll see the configuration details of the backup tool a bit later. Let's stay focused on the causal cluster, and now that we've seen the different protocols used, we will set up a cluster and look at its configuration more closely.

Configuration of a causal cluster

Ashley: Configuring a causal cluster is similar to configuring an HA cluster. We'll start by installing three Neo4j enterprise core servers on three separate machines. Then, as for the HA cluster, we will edit the neo4j.conf file for each of these servers to configure the following required elements:

- `dbms.mode`: indicates the Neo4j server installation type. For the causal cluster, this parameter can take one of the following two values CORE or READ_REPLICA. In this example, we'll set: `dbms.mode=CORE`.

- `causal_clustering.minimum_core_cluster_size_at_formation`: this parameter is the number of core instances expected to form the core cluster according to the rule: M=2F+1 where M is the total number of core servers needed to absorb F failures. For example, we can set the cluster to withstand one failure like this: `causal_clustering.minimum_core_cluster_size_at_formation=3`.

- `causal_clustering.minimum_core_cluster_size_at_runtime`: this parameter is the number of core instances expected to adjust the voting set. Only core members are part of this voting set. A majority of core members is required to scale up or down the number of instance failures that may be acceptable. For example, we can set `causal_clustering.minimum_core_cluster_size_at_formation=3` if we don't want the cluster to dynamically adjust below 3 core servers.

- `causal_clustering.initial_discovery_members`: indicates the list of cluster member addresses that will form the cluster. The address of a server consists of its IP (or host name) followed by port 5000. So we choose: `causal_clustering.initial_discovery_members=[ip_core_server_1]:5000,[ip_core_server_2]:5000,[ip_core_server_3]:5000`. The instances listed must be core servers, although this parameter is intended for both core and replica servers.

Caution › *Make sure there are no spaces before or after the = symbol for this parameter.*

The last two parameters complete the configuration and are about connectors, like Bolt for example. These parameters specify the way the server instances are seen outside the cluster:

- `dbms.connectors.default_listen_address`: indicates the default network interface on which this instance of Neo4j will listen for incoming network messages. Setting this parameter to `dbms.connectors.default_listen_address=0.0.0.0` allows the instance to listen to messages arriving from any network interface.

- `dbms.connectors.default_advertised_address`: defines the default address that clients should use to connect to this instance.

Note that these last two parameters can be configured for each of the Neo4j network connectors (HTTP, HTTPS, Bolt, etc.). If everything is configured correctly, all we need to do is to launch the core instances:

```
[NEO4J_HOME_1]/bin/neo4j start
[NEO4J_HOME_2]/bin/neo4j start
[NEO4J_HOME_3]/bin/neo4j start
```

Now I'll add a replica instance:

```
[NEO4J_HOME_REPLICA]/bin/neo4j start
```

Using one of the Neo4j Browser, we can check the cluster status with the `:sysinfo` command.

Figure 4.6 : Causal cluster :sysinfo

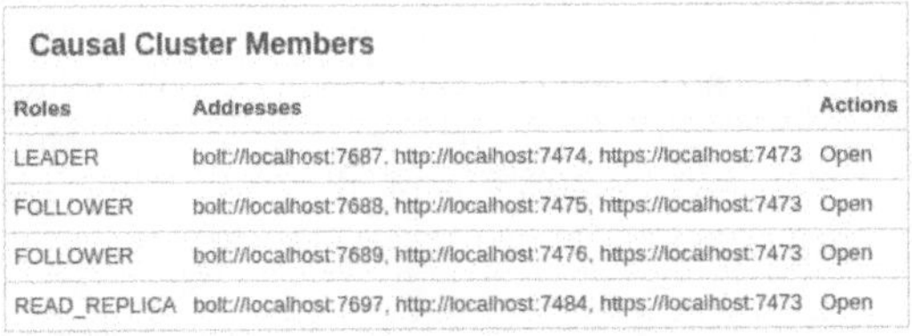

Causal Cluster Members		
Roles	**Addresses**	**Actions**
LEADER	bolt://localhost:7687, http://localhost:7474, https://localhost:7473	Open
FOLLOWER	bolt://localhost:7688, http://localhost:7475, https://localhost:7473	Open
FOLLOWER	bolt://localhost:7689, http://localhost:7476, https://localhost:7473	Open
READ_REPLICA	bolt://localhost:7697, http://localhost:7484, https://localhost:7473	Open

We can also do the same using a procedure: `CALL dbms.cluster.overview()`.

Figure 4.7 : Causal cluster—CALL dbms.cluster.overview()

Tiago: Is it tricky to add another core server to the cluster?

Ashley: No, not at all. We just follow the same configuration process, then launch the server. This new instance will join the cluster automatically. As soon as the new graph instance is updated (via the catch-up protocol), it will become available.

Tiago: How about adding replica instances?

Ashley: That's also easy. Just make sure that the following parameters are set correctly, as I did for my replica instance:

- `dbms.mode=READ_REPLICA`
- `ha.initial_hosts=[ip_server_core_1]:5000,[ip_serv-er_core_2]:5000,[ip_server_core_3]:5000`

Tiago: One final question that I hope is quick: is it possible to remove a core server from the cluster and use it elsewhere in a standalone mode?

Ashley: Pretty odd question, but sure, why not? Yes, it is possible, but you'll need to avoid using an instance listed in the `causal_clustering.initial_discovery_members` parameter and ensure that the initial cluster size remains valid. There are two actions to take:

- stop the instance you wish to remove from cluster;
- run the `neo4j-admin unbind[--database=path_to_database]` command line from the stopped instance.

Now we can use this instance as a *standalone* Neo4j server by setting: `dbms.mode=SIN-GLE`, or we could use this instance to initialize data of another cluster.

Tiago: Powerful! Could I then reintegrate this instance back into the cluster later?

Ashley: No, not if you have used this instance in standalone mode or in another cluster. Remember the transaction identifiers and the Raft protocol clock! There would be no data consistency at all since each system would have applied its own independent transaction references. Let's take a look at the activity logs when the elected core instance leader starts:

```
[...]
INFO [o.n.c.c.c.RaftMachine] Election timeout triggered
INFO [o.n.c.c.c.RaftMachine] Election started with vote
 request: Vote.Request from MemberId{2e415eeb} {term=1,
 candidate=MemberId{2e415eeb}, lastAppended=0, lastLogTerm=0} and
 members: [MemberId{2e415eeb}, MemberId{e0a1ee7c}]
INFO [o.n.c.c.c.RaftMachine] Moving to CANDIDATE state after
 successfully starting election
INFO [o.n.c.m.SenderService] Creating channel to: [66ea1b016791:7000]
INFO [o.n.c.m.SenderService] Connected: [id: 0x02ef9b84,
 L:/172.18.0.2:49106 - R:66ea1b016791/172.18.0.3:7000]
INFO [o.n.c.c.c.RaftMachine] Moving to LEADER state at term 1 (I am
 MemberId{2e415eeb}), voted for by [MemberId{e0a1ee7c}]
INFO [o.n.c.c.c.s.RaftState] First leader elected: MemberId{2e415eeb}
INFO [o.n.c.c.c.s.RaftLogShipper] Starting log shipper:
 MemberId{e0a1ee7c}[matchIndex: -1, lastSentIndex: 0, localAppendIndex:
 1, mode: MISMATCH]
INFO [o.n.c.c.c.m.RaftMembershipChanger] Idle{}
INFO [o.n.c.c.c.s.RaftLogShipper] Starting log shipper:
 MemberId{13748c2a}[matchIndex: -1, lastSentIndex: 0, localAppendIndex:
 1, mode: MISMATCH]
INFO [o.n.c.m.SenderService] Creating channel to: [e094f3d6e071:7000]
[...]
```

Let me translate: Once the usual start-up operations have been carried out, an election is called by the started instance. This instance takes the *candidate* role. We can see that at this point, there are only two candidate instances: `MemberId{2e415eeb}` (the instance we observe doing the logging) and `MemberId{e0a1ee7c}`. Only one is elected leader: (`Moving to LEADER state at term 1 (I am MemberId{2e415eeb})`). So the instance whose logs we are following was elected to the leader role.

Tiago: Might it be instructive at this point to issue a request from a Bolt client using the *bolt+routing* protocol?

Ashley: That's a very good idea for a test. We'll run a test from a Bolt client on a Neo4j causal cluster, then shut down the leading instance and run the test again. But before that I'll follow the Neo4j Operations Manual [http://d-booker.jo.my/neo4j-clustering] to launch a causal cluster inside Docker containers. I'll mount three core servers and one replica server. This script enables me to run this cluster on a single machine, which is convenient for testing purposes.

```
bash neo4j-causal.sh --cores=3 --replicas=1 --erase=true
```

These instances will be accessible through the following Bolt ports:

Table 4.2 : *Ports for causal cluster instances*

Instance name	Port number
core 1	7687
core 2	7688
core 3	7689
replica 1	7697

Ashley: Ok, now that we've started the cluster, let's take a look at the Bolt client which will query and write into this cluster:

```
AuthToken token = AuthTokens.basic(LOGIN, PASSWORD);
Driver driver = GraphDatabase.driver("bolt+routing://
ip_server_core_1:7687",token);

String bookmark ="";
final String name="Nicolas";

try(Session sessionBolt = driver.session()){
  sessionBolt.writeTransaction(new TransactionWork<Integer>() {
    @Override
    public Integer execute( Transaction tx )
    {
      return createPerson(tx, name);
    }
  });
  bookmark = sessionBolt.lastBookmark();
}
driver.close();
```

Parenthetically, note that I get the *bookmark* from our Bolt session. Using this same bookmark for the read operation, I am guaranteed to read the data I just wrote in the previous code, relying on the causal consistency (*read at least your own writes*):

```
try(Session sessionBolt = driver.session(bookmark)){
  Node node = sessionBolt.readTransaction(new TransactionWork<Node>() {
    @Override
    public Node execute( Transaction tx )
    {
```

```
                return findPerson(tx, name);
         }
    });
}
```

Let's take a second to review the Bolt client's activity log:

```
INFOS: Routing information is stale. Ttl 1507028680280, currentTime
 1507028680281, routers RoundRobinAddressSet=[localhost:7687], writers
 RoundRobinAddressSet=[], readers RoundRobinAddressSet=[]
```

First, the Bolt client logging above tells us that it has no routing information (or that this information is obsolete: *Routing information is stale*), so it will connect to the only core instance it knows in order to ask for the cluster topology:

```
INFOS: Got getServers response: [Record<{ttl: 300, servers: [{addresses:
 ["localhost:7687"], role: "WRITE"}, {addresses: ["localhost:7697",
 "localhost:7688", "localhost:7689"], role: "READ"}, {addresses:
 ["localhost:7689", "localhost:7688", "localhost:7687"], role:
 "ROUTE"}]}>]
INFOS: Got cluster composition
ClusterComposition{expirationTimestamp=1507028980343,
readers=[localhost:7697, localhost:7688, localhost:7689],
writers=[localhost:7687], routers=[localhost:7689, localhost:7688,
localhost:7687]}
```

This time the Bolt client is told about the following elements:

- `localhost:7687` has the WRITE role, which corresponds to the leading instance of the cluster. Therefore, write transactions will be directed to this instance.

- `localhost:7697` (replica), `localhost:7688` and `localhost:7689` have the READ role. Consequently, read-only transactions will be directed to one of these three instances.

- Lastly, the following instances: `localhost:7687`, `localhost:7688` and `localhost:7689` (all cores) have the ROUTE role, which means that these instances will be able to redirect requests from the Bolt client.

Then the Bolt client refreshes its routing table by ordering the instances according to their role and their availability:

```
INFOS: Refreshed routing information. Ttl
 1507028980343, currentTime 1507028680345, routers
 RoundRobinAddressSet=[localhost:7687, localhost:7689, localhost:7688],
```

```
writers RoundRobinAddressSet=[localhost:7687], readers
RoundRobinAddressSet=[localhost:7697, localhost:7688, localhost:7689]
```

For example, for the processing of a read-only transaction, the first instance that will be chosen is the replica server (localhost:7697). Let's shut down our leader instance and have a look at the activity logs of our *core_2* instance:

```
INFO [o.n.c.d.HazelcastCoreTopologyService] Core member removed
MembershipEvent {member=Member [core1]:5000 - 55dd625d-
cc5f-4348-9816-4811e40cf995,type=removed}
INFO [o.n.c.d.HazelcastCoreTopologyService] Core topology
changed {added=[], removed=[{memberId=MemberId{2e415eeb},
info=CoreServerInfo{raftServer=2dcfe6f685f3:7000,
catchupServer=2dcfe6f685f3:6000, clientConnectorAddresses=bolt://
localhost:7687
```

This instance receives an event warning that the *core_1* cluster member has just left the cluster. This event is received via port 5000, i.e. the one assigned by default to the discovery protocol. Let us focus on the line:

```
INFO [o.n.c.d.HazelcastCoreTopologyService] Core member removed
MembershipEvent {member=Member [core1]:5000 - 55dd625d-
cc5f-4348-9816-4811e40cf995,type=removed}
```

Continuing with the activity log of the *core_2* instance, we can see a warning:

```
INFO [o.n.c.c.c.m.RaftMembershipManager] Not safe to remove member
[MemberId{2e415eeb}] because it would reduce the number of voting
members below the expected cluster size of 3. Voting members:
[MemberId{e0a1ee7c}, MemberId{2e415eeb}, MemberId{
13748c2a}]
```

This message tells us that this cluster is now fragile as it will not be able to absorb losing any more servers. No leader could be elected if a new core instance crashed. Now let's go back to our Bolt client and run our test again. In the activity logs of the Bolt client, we see the new topology received by Bolt client:

```
INFOS: Got getServers response: [Record<{ttl: 300, servers: [{addresses:
["localhost:7689"], role: "WRITE"}, {addresses: ["localhost:7688",
"localhost:7697"], role: "READ"}, {addresses: ["localhost:7688",
"localhost:7689"], role: "ROUTE"}]}>]
```

Our transaction has succeeded, because a majority of core servers are still available. This majority is composed of the two remaining core instances divided by two plus one, i.e. two instances, which is ok. Let's carry on, and shut down the core_2 instance and call the CALL dbms.cluster.overview() procedure from the last available web browser:

Table 4.3 : Causal cluster–dbms.cluster.overview()

id	addresses	role
13748c2a-aa96-4b70-ae61-a2dc8a12f5e6	["bolt://localhost:7689", "http://localhost:7476", "https://localhost:7473"]	FOLLOWER
ad6b3497-c39a-465a-a19e-337c689f5c3d	["bolt://localhost:7697", "http://localhost:7484", "https://localhost:7473"]	READ_REPLICA

What do we see here, Brian?

Brian: Ain't no leader no mo'.

Ashley: As precisely true as inelegantly stated. The cluster is stuck in read-only mode since no leader can be elected. If I restart the test and follow the Bolt client activity logs, I'll see that this time my write transaction doesn't go through:

```
GRAVE: Transaction failed and will be retried in 8373ms
org.neo4j.driver.v1.exceptions.SessionExpiredException: Failed to obtain
  connection towards WRITE server.
Known routing table is: Ttl 1507117310637, currentTime 1507117010639,
  routers RoundRobinAddressSet=[localhost:7689], writers
  RoundRobinAddressSet=[], readers RoundRobinAddressSet=[localhost:7689,
  localhost:7697]
```

Now the *retry* mechanism starts up, that is: *Transaction failed and will be retried in 8373ms*. It will keep retrying until a timeout is reached (configurable in the driver) or a new leader is elected.

Initialization of a new causal cluster with existing data

Ashley: Imagine that for some reason (such as replacement of physical servers, etc.) we wanted to create a new causal cluster with existing data. In this case, we need to carry out the following actions:

1.   create the core cluster as demonstrated above;

2.   initialize data by one of the methods below;

3.   start the cluster.

We'll look at the three ways we can initialize the data of a causal cluster, which are:

•   from an online system;

- from an offline system;
- with the data import tool.

Initialization of a cluster from an online system

Brian: What, pray tell, is this *online* system of which you speak, oh wisest of the wise?

Ashley: I will tell thee, jejune yet sporadically attentive callow fellow of unenlightened status. By online I mean that the system from which we get the data is a running system. Data can come from a standalone Neo4j server, an HA cluster or another causal cluster. Take, for example, the case of a replica server that would be the only survivor of the cluster we would like to replace.

Brian: The Last of Us... like in the video game...

Ashley: Yeah... moving on and pretending you're inaudible. So I now set up my causal cluster as before but, most critically, I DO NOT start it!

Tiago: If you did so, its graph would be initialized empty... present, but empty.

Ashley: That's right. To initialize the data for this cluster, I'll use the `neo4j-admin restore` command to import the data onto at least one of my core servers. But it's good practice to import to all three. That way the cluster will not only start up faster, but we'll limit the risks of data replication errors:

```
[NEO4J_HOME_1]/bin/neo4j-admin restore
 --from=source_graph_database_folder --
database=target_graph_database_folder_instance_1
[NEO4J_HOME_2]/bin/neo4j-admin restore
 --from=source_graph_database_folder --
database=target_graph_database_folder_instance_2
[NEO4J_HOME_3]/bin/neo4j-admin restore
 --from=source_graph_database_folder --
database=target_graph_database_folder_instance_3
```

Once this is done, we start the cluster and check that our graph database is running on the three instances and that no errors have appeared in the activity logs (`neo4j.log`).

Initialization of a cluster from an offline system

Brian: Let me guess: an offline system is a system that is offline.

Ashley: Brilliant. But being offline doesn't mean that the system doesn't have data. Suppose, for example, that you want to upgrade from a Neo4j community edition to an enterprise edition. In that case, your data source (i.e the instance that manages the source graph database) must be down, so that it won't accept any new transactions, keeping the system stable. Then the data transfer will consist of:

* extracting the source graph data into a folder;
* loading this graph data into an instance of the new cluster.

We can perform these tasks by using the neo4j-admin dump tool followed by the neo4j-admin load tool, with following commands:

```
[NEO4J_HOME_SOURCE]/bin/neo4j-admin dump --
database=source_graph_database_folder --to=dump_folder
[NEO4J_HOME_1]/bin/neo4j-admin load --from=dump_folder/graph.dump --
database=target_graph_database_folder_instance_1
[NEO4J_HOME_2]/bin/neo4j-admin load --from=dump_folder/graph.dump --
database=target_graph_database_folder_instance_2
[NEO4J_HOME_3]/bin/neo4j-admin load --from=dump_folder/graph.dump --
database=target_graph_database_folder_instance_3
```

All that's left is starting the cluster.

Initialization of a cluster using the import tool

Brian: Is this the same import tool that Iryna told us about earlier, about 45 years ago, I think?

Ashley: One and the same: neo4j-admin import. We locate our CSV files and launch the appropriate command, which is:

```
[NEO4J_HOME_SOURCE]/bin/neo4j-admin import --mode=csv --
database=target_graph_database_folder_instance_1 --nodes:Label=nodes.csv
 --relationships:TO=relationships.csv
[NEO4J_HOME_SOURCE]/bin/neo4j-admin import --mode=csv --
database=target_graph_database_folder_instance_2 --nodes:Label=nodes.csv
 --relationships:TO=relations.csv
[NEO4J_HOME_SOURCE]/bin/neo4j-admin import --mode=csv --
database=target_graph_database_folder_instance_3 --nodes:Label=nodes.csv
 --relationships:TO=relations.csv
```

And as in previous cases, we then start the cluster. Remember, we use the neo4j-admin import tool to import data only into core instances and–this is important–only into an empty database.

Conclusion on the causal cluster

Ashley: Ok then, thoughts about the causal cluster?

Tiago: It appears to be much safer than the HA cluster.

Brian: Even so, it's no harder to set up than the HA cluster.

Iryna: It is a bit more complicated to understand, as it's a little more sophisticated. The causal cluster uses a rather recent consensus algorithm which looks much more robust, as Tiago says. The Neo4j team has provided an ambitious and significant option by introducing the causal cluster, in my opinion.

Ashley: That's my opinion, too. We move to a bona fide ACID system from an *eventual* or *timely* consistency system (referring to the CAP theorem [http://d-booker.jo.my/neo4j-en-cap], although we don't have a partition-tolerance dimension because there is no real data distribution). Therefore it's natural that Neo4j wants to encourage using this type of cluster. Even though the HA cluster has been eclipsed by the causal cluster, it seemed important to me to start with the HA cluster study in order to grasp the cluster concept in a simpler context. As you said, Iryna, the causal cluster is a little more sophisticated and more challenging to learn. But bear mind, there's much value in secure transactions. The transactions may be successful or they may be refused (and reported to customers running them), but they are never lost.

Tiago: We can go even further with the causal cluster, right?. For instance we can set up a *multi data center clustering* solution, which spreads the data over different parts of the world, can't we?

Ashley: We can, indeed! With a relatively easy change to the configuration, and by working natively with the *bolt+routing* network protocol. I haven't had a chance to check out how it works, and I don't think our client will be interested in this issue yet. This configuration usually involves cloud solutions providing services around Neo4j. However, if you're curious, then you can take a look at Neo4j Operations Manual [http://d-booker.jo.my/neo4j-multidatacenter].

4.4. Backup and resilience

Ashley: The causal cluster delivers availability and consistency, certainly, but still doesn't guarantee the complete data safety. Strictly speaking, I would consider that to be true because the data cannot be calculated or derived from other data, as it is *user specified*. We should consider the data fundamentally *sacrosanct*.

Brian: I think maybe you're be a bit over dramatic...

Tiago: Actually, no, Ashley isn't overstating the importance of proper data maintenance. Once lost, there is no guarantee that we will be able to regenerate the data again, *ever*.

Ashley: Absolutely. Because there is no perfect system, and there is an ever-present risk of failure with physical storage systems (hard disks, etc.). We need to provide–and this is paramount–a means to save the data regularly to another system which can be used to restore our Neo4j graph back to its last valid state, i.e., to provide *resilience*.

Tiago: You touched on this topic earlier, so I guess we'll now go into finer details of how using these tools?

Ashley: Yeah, that's absolutely the purpose of this part of the study. Note that the basic procedure will be the same whether we are working with a standalone Neo4j instance, an HA cluster or a causal cluster.

Backup server

Ashley: The first thing to do in setting up a backup process is to choose a Neo4j instance that will act as the backup server. For an independent instance, the question isn't applicable, as the single instance itself will act as backup server. In an HA cluster, any of the instances will do. And for the causal cluster, a replica instance, if any, are preferred, using a core instance only if there are no replica instances. Once the instance has been selected, it must be configured in the `[NEO4J_HOME]/conf/neo4j.conf` file in order to activate the network connector used to respond to backup requests. To do this, we:

- set the `dbms.backup.enabled` parameter to the `true` value: `dbms.backup.enabled=true;`
- specify the network interface exposed by the backup instance using the `dbms.backup.address` parameter and providing it with the network interface address (or hostname) on port `6362` (default). The `0.0.0.0` address can be used to listen on all the host machine's network interfaces: `dbms.backup.address=0.0.0.0:6362`.

Once this is done, you need to restart the backup instance, if it was running when the configuration change was made.

Performing a backup

Ashley: To perform a backup, we use the `neo4j-admin backup` command line tool.

TECHNICAL: neo4j-admin backup

The `neo4j-admin` command used in combination with the `backup` parameter allows a number of options to be used:

```
neo4j-admin backup  --backup-dir=<path_to_backup_directory>
           --name=<backup_graph_database_name>
           [--from=<backup_server_address>]
           [--fallback-to-full[=<true|false>]]
           [--timeout=<timeout>]
           [--check-consistency[=<true|false>]]
           [--cc-report-dir=<path_to_report_directory>]
           [--additional-config=<path_to_configuration_file>]
           [--cc-graph[=<true|false>]]
           [--cc-indexes[=<true|false>]]
           [--cc-label-scan-store[=<true|false>]]
           [--cc-property-owners[=<true|false>]]
```

These options are detailed below

Table 4.4 : neo4j-admin backup—options

Option	Default value	Description
`--backup-dir`		Folder where the backup will be saved.
`--name`		Name of the backup. If a backup with the same name already exists then a incremental backup will be attempted.
`--from`	`localhost:6362`	Host machine and port number for Neo4j backup server.
`--fallback-to-full`	`true`	If a incremental backup fails then the old backup will be renamed: `<name>.err.<N>` and a full backup will be performed instead.
`--timeout`	`20m`	Time delay expressed in the `<value>[ms|s|h|m]` format, where the default unit is in seconds. This option is mainly used for debugging purposes and only when recommended by a Neo4j team member.
`--check-consistency`	`true`	Whether or not to launch a database consistency check.

Option	Default value	Description
`--additional-config`		Load additional config parameters from a file. This option is deprecated.
`--cc-report-dir`	.	Folder where the consistency report is to be saved.
`--cc-graph`	true	Performs a consistency check between nodes, relationships, properties, types and tokens.
`--cc-indexes`	true	Performs a consistency check on the indexes.
`--cc-label-scan-store`	true	Performs a consistency check on labels.
`--cc-property-owners`	false	Performs a consistency check on property owners. This validation is very costly in both time and memory.

The backup tool might return any of the error codes described here:

Table 4.5 : neo4j-admin backup—error codes

Code	Description
1	Backup failure
2	Success of the backup but failure of the consistency check
3	Successful backup but inconsistencies were found

Ashley: Here's a small example. I'll first create a folder named backup in my installation folder for the Neo4j instance acting as backup server. Note that this practice is NOT recommended. Use of a physical store system other than the one (or those) supporting cluster members is safer. But to make this easier to explain, we will do it like this:

```
[NEO4J_HOME]$> mkdir backup
```

Then I'll launch the command:

```
[NEO4J_HOME]$> bin/neo4j-admin backup --backup-dir=./backup --
name=graph.db-backup
```

Here is the message that we'll get:

```
Doing full backup...
INFO  [o.n.c.s.StoreCopyClient] Copying neostore.nodestore.db.labels
INFO  [o.n.c.s.StoreCopyClient] Copied neostore.nodestore.db.labels 8.00
 kB
INFO  [o.n.c.s.StoreCopyClient] Copying neostore.nodestore.db
INFO  [o.n.c.s.StoreCopyClient] Copied neostore.nodestore.db 16.00 kB
[...]
```

In this `backup` folder we will find the `graph-db.backup` file.

Tiago: Ok, you've shown us a complete backup, i.e. a backup of the whole graph database. But how do we launch a incremental backup?

Ashley: By default, if a backup with the same name already exists, then the tool will automatically attempt to perform a incremental backup. However, if the backup tool does not find a valid backup then it will perform a full backup (see `--fallback-to-full` option). The incremental backup will include the missing transactions from the previous backup to make it consistent with the current backup server state.

Tiago: But you're forgetting something, aren't you? In fact, the current status of the backup server is maintained through its transaction log, isn't it?

Ashley: Yes, you're right, I need to talk about the notion of a transaction log. In general, the transaction log will not contain all transactions that have occurred since the creation of the graph database. Over time the log would become too large and system performance would suffer. For this reason we'll set up a *retention policy* which enables us to keep only a limited number of operations.

Tiago: So, we have to make sure that our backup is more frequent than the retention frequency set up on the backup server, right?

Ashley: Right! Otherwise, transactions might be missing!

Brian: Uh... time out. I'm not following. How about an example?

Ashley: Sure. Suppose that your transaction log retention policy is two days, that is, you will only keep transaction records that are two days old or younger.

Tiago: And now imagine that you only run a backup every three days, which would be wacko, but it illustrates the point.

Ashley: So you'll miss a day of transactions with each backup. And that's the value of the consistency check that can be applied during backup: the backup is slower, but more secure.

Tiago: To avoid this, you need to plan your backup on a threshold more frequently than your retention policy setting.

Brian: How do we decide on the backup frequency and the retention policy value?

Ashley: There is no universal rule. It depends on how much data you write a day. Usually we run a backup at least once a day. As for the retention policy, it depends on your write volume. The more intense and steady it is, the shorter your retention time.

Tiago: Then you'll need to increase your backup frequency accordingly!

TECHNICAL: Transaction log

The transaction log displays the status of past and present transactions (all operations performed on the graph database or upstream of the database), from their submission to their validation (commit) or their cancellation (rollback). Each transaction is identified with a unique identifier called `txID`. The last known transaction identifier is called `lastestTxID`.

This log is used by incremental backups. It acts as a *source of truth*.

This log is written to one or more `neostore.transaction.db.*` files.

Neo4j writes each new transaction operation into this event log without changing the database. The database will only be modified once the transaction is validated. Because all transaction operations are recorded in this log, it is necessary to set up a retention system to keep only *useful* transactions, i.e. a limited transaction history. Otherwise, the entire transaction history since the graph database was created would be retained, and would eventually cause performance and disk space problems. For this reason, a parameter in the `[NEO4J_HOME]/conf/neo4j.conf` file manages a *retention rule*: `dbms.tx_log.rotation.retention_policy`. Regardless of the settings, the latest non-empty transaction file will be kept.

Table 4.6 : Parameter–dbms.tx_log.rotation.retention_policy

Description	Indicates Neo4j how many transaction operations to keep track of in its transaction log. For example, the 10 days value is used to ask Neo4j to keep only transactions that are 10 or fewer days old in the transaction log. A value indicating 100k txs will keep the last 100,000 transactions in the log.

Values	The allowed values are `true|false` or `number[optional unit]` type. Valid types are • `files`: number of most recent files to be kept; • `size`: maximum disk space that transaction files can consume; • `txs`: maximum number of transactions to be kept; • `hours`: maximum number of hours during which transactions are kept; • `days`: number of days transactions are kept.
Default	7 days

By default, the rotation strategy for the transaction log files is based on size, and the default size is 250 MB. It can be changed using the `dbms.tx_log.rotation.size` parameter.

Table 4.7 : Parameter—dbms.tx_log.rotation.size

Description	Allows Neo4j to rotate a file based on its size. A value of `0` indicates that no automatic rotation will be performed, and that the whole transaction log will be stored in a single file.
Values	The permitted values are expressed in bytes and multiples of bytes: `number[optional unit]`. The minimum value is `1048576` (1MB). The multiples are k (KB), m (MB), g (GB), K (KB), M (MB), G (GB).
Default	262144000

Restore a backup

Ashley: Well, now we know how to back up our data. Always a good thing. But it's even better to know how to restore data, otherwise the backup wouldn't be worth much. In the same way that the neo4j-admin tool offers us a backup option, it offers us the restore option to restore the data into a Neo4j system from a backup.

TECHNICAL: neo4j-admin restore

The neo4j-admin command used in combination with the restore parameter allows the use of a number of options:

```
neo4j-admin restore --from=<path_to_backup_directory>
```

```
[--database=<database_name>]
[--force[=<true|false>]]
```

Restore options are detailed below:

Table 4.8 : neo4j-admin restore—options

Option	Default value	Description
--from		Folder where the backup is available
--database	graph.db	Database name
--force	false	Forces to replace the database if it already exists

Restore a standalone Neo4j server

Ashley: No magic is involved here. There's a modus operandi to follow:

1. Stop the Neo4j server.
2. Launch the restore command.
3. Restart the Neo4j server.

For example:

```
[NEO4J_HOME]$> bin/neo4j stop
[NEO4J_HOME]$> bin/neo4j-admin restore --from=/mnt/backup/graph.db-
backup --database=graph.db --force
[NEO4J_HOME]$> bin/neo4j start
```

Restore a Neo4j causal cluster

Ashley: Still no magic, but this procedure is slightly different from the previous one:

1. Stop all Neo4j core and replica instances.
2. Run the previous restore command on each core and replica instance.
3. If you restore your database on a new cluster (due to a hardware change for example), go back through the causal cluster settings and make sure that the value of the causal_clustering.initial_discovery_members parameter properly reflects the servers on which the restores were made. Also make sure that the values of the causal_clustering.minimum_core_cluster_size_at_formation and

`causal_clustering.minimum_core_cluster_size_at_runtime` parameters match the number of core servers present in this new topology.

4. Restart each instance.

Restore an HA cluster

Ashley: As we are now experts in causal clusters restoration, HA cluster just follows an analogous process:

1. Stop all Neo4j instances of the HA cluster.

2. Run the restore command on each instance.

3. Check the HA cluster configuration usage in the `neo4j.conf` file, in case a new cluster is initialized (same as for the causal cluster).

4. Restart each instance starting with the master instance.

4.5. Logging

Ashley: Now that we know how to set up a highly available system, how to manage the size of our transaction log, and how to backup and restore our data, we should discuss event logs produced by a Neo4j instance. Unlike the transaction log, which is meant to be read by a machine, the various logs we are going to talk about next are human-readable, or maybe I should say nerd-readable: they are textual information about the processing performed by the system. These are of several types of event logs:

* `debug.log`: Neo4j general activity log;
* `gc.log`: activity log for Java Garbage Collector;
* `http.log`: HTTP server activity log of the Neo4j instance;
* `query.log`: CYPHER query logging (enterprise edition only);
* `security.log`: logging of security events (enterprise edition only).

All log files can be configured. Keep in mind that we must manage our disk space according to our needs of our environment (development, production, etc.), we will need to find a balance between the level of detail we want and the disk space we can dedicate to these logs. Only the `debug.log` and `neo4j.log` files are enabled by default. Here are the configuration parameters for the general activity log (`debug.log`):

TECHNIQUE: General logging configuration

This configuration is set in the `[NEO4J_HOME]/conf/neo4j.conf` configuration file and the log files are written to the `[NEO4J_HOME]/logs/` folder.

Table 4.9 : Parameter—dbms.logs.debug.level

Description	Log output level
Values	From the most verbose to the least verbose: DEBUG, INFO, WARN, ERROR, NONE
Default	INFO

Table 4.10 : Parameter—dbms.logs.debug.rotation.delay

Description	Minimum time interval before rotating files (since last rotation)
Values	Duration expressed as `<value>`[`<unit of time<`, time units are: ms (milliseconds), s (seconds), m (minutes); default unit is the second
Default	300s

Table 4.11 : Parameter—dbms.logs.debug.rotation.keep_number

Description	Maximum number of general log files retained
Values	integer value whose minimum is 1
Default	7

Table 4.12 : Parameter—dbms.logs.debug.rotation.size

Description	Maximum size the active log file can have before a rotation is performed
Values	Value expressed in bytes and byte multiples: `<number<`[`<optional unit<`. The minimum value is 0 and the maximum value is 9223372036854775807. The multiples are k (KB), m (MB), g (GB), K (KB), M (MB), G (GB)
Default	20971520

4.6. Memory

Ashley: Here's a question: which part of a machine introduces the longest latency when accessing data?

Brian: The hard drive?

Ashley: Yes, what makes you say that?

Brian: Well, when I run too many programs on my computer, the disk slows down and starts to irritate me.

Ashley: Yeah, and that's probably because it is *swapping*, that is the memory is saturated, so it offloads part of the data it has in RAM to the disk, and then loads the data it needs at the moment. This swapping results in a lot of input/output operations. Accessing data on a hard disk is always slower than accessing data in RAM. Obviously this is all true for Neo4j as well, and we'll see how to configure the memory size used by Neo4j to limit resorting to disk access.

Tiago: Starting with the host machine I would guess...

Ashley: You guess right. Let's assume that we will install our Neo4j server (or our instances) on a dedicated machine. The host operating system (OS) always needs memory space to work. So Neo4j *should* not take up *all* available memory space. One GB is a good base from which we will add the size of the files graph.db/index and graph.db/schema so that the indexes are wholly mounted in memory. This is very important—we could lapse into disk access if insufficient memory is allocated to index storage. And a slow index is a useless index.

$$Memory\ to\ be\ left\ to\ OS\ operations = 1GB + (graph.db/index\ size) + (graph.db/schema\ size)$$

Now let's talk about the *cache (Page Cache)*. The idea of this cache consists of mounting the contents of the files that make up the Neo4j database in memory, namely all files with a name like graph.db/*store.db*. This configuration parameter is specified with dbms.memory.pagecache.size and can be computed as follows:

$$Cache\ size = sum\ of\ each\ graph.db/*store.db*\ file\ size + 20\%\ (for\ new\ incoming\ data)$$

Brian: Uh... I don't see the dbms.memory.pagecache.size parameter in the neo4j.conf file. Am I missing something?

Ashley: Right, that's because it's almost impossible for Neo4j teams to predict the size of this cache for every user who will install Neo4j. It really depends on the use case. However, setting it allows you to better control your environment.

TECHNICAL: Page Cache

This configurational setting is added to the `[NEO4J_HOME]/conf/neo4j.conf` configuration file and is used to cache in memory as much data as possible from the Neo4j database storage files.

Table 4.13 : Parameter–dbms.memory.pagecache.size

Description	Sets the cache size in order to mount storage files in memory.
Values	Value expressed in bytes and byte multiples: `<number<[<optional unit<`. The minimum value is `245760`.
Default	Heuristic calculation based on the available resources of the host machine.

Table 4.14 : Parameter–dbms.memory.pagecache.swapper

Description	Only used in combination with proprietary storage systems (as CAPI flash). Designates the cache system to use.
Values	A character string
Default	

Ashley: Finally, we will configure the JVM on which Neo4j works. We will adjust the *heap* so that our Neo4j instance can run enough operations without diminishing performance.

Brian: Pardon the interruption but what is the *heap* thingy?

Ashley: Without going into too much detail, the memory space of the JVM can be thought of as being split into two parts: the *heap* which is the space reserved for the creation of objects during the execution of the program, and the *non-heap* which is, roughly speaking, the memory space reserved for class loading; this is a static space which doesn't change much.

Brian: Ok, so *roughly speaking*, I get it. We need to decide how much memory space to allocate to the heap so that Neo4j runs as smoothly as possible.

Ashley: That's right, and to do that we must prevent the Java Garbage Collector from being triggered too often.

Brian: Wait, what? The *Garbage Collector?* Do JVMs have some kind of sanitation problem?

Ashley: Yes, kind of. The Garbage Collector is the Java mechanism that automatically cleans up the JVM memory. It reclaims memory that is wasted on objects that are no longer referenced. Too frequent triggering of the Garbage Collector slows down the execution of Neo4j's main tasks, because the collector steals time from the main JVM tasks.

Brian: I'm probably starting to begin to get a glimmer of a slice of the dawn of understanding.

Ashley: Always be digging, Brian! Usually, a size between 8GB and 16GB is sufficient. We will use the `dbms.memory.heap.initial_size` parameter to set the initial stack size (equivalent to the `-Xms` JVM option) and the `dbms.memory.heap.max_size` parameter (equivalent to the `-Xmx` JVM option) to set the maximum size. If we ever want to fine-tune our JVM memory, we can use the `dbms.jvm.additional` parameter.

Tiago: So if I summarize correctly, we determined the size of the memory that must be left to the operating system to work at a minimum level, we set the cache of Neo4j database files and the memory used by the JVM, which amounts to something like:

$$RAM\ dedicated\ to\ OS = RAM\ available - (cache\ memory + JVM\ heap)$$

Ashley: Um, yeah, that's pretty well summarized.

TECHNICAL: initial memory settings

You can use the `neo4j-admin memrec` command to obtain recommendations on memory settings.

This command takes into account the host settings and suggests values for the following `[NEO4J_HOME]/conf/neo4j.conf` parameters:

Table 4.15 : Parameters—pagecache size and JVM heap size

dbms.memory.pagecache.size	Specifies initial heap memory size.
dbms.memory.heap.max_size	Specifies heap memory maximum size.

Default	Specifies how much memory Neo4j is allowed to use for the page cache.

Here is an example output of `neo4j-admin memrec` command:

```
# Based on the above, the following memory settings are recommended:
dbms.memory.heap.initial_size=5100m
dbms.memory.heap.max_size=5100m
dbms.memory.pagecache.size=7100m
```

4.7. Upgrading Neo4j

Iryna: Ashley, you were insisting on updating our Neo4j graph database regularly. Can you explain why and how?

Ashley: Yeah. So, the different software versions of Neo4j are listed with three digits x.y.z, for example 3.2.3. The first digit indicates a level, i.e. a technological breakthrough; the second digit corresponds to a major version; the third digit refers to a minor version. Currently there is a major version of Neo4j every six months.

Tiago: Sure, but that doesn't tell us why upgrading our database regularly is such a big deal...

Ashley: Agreed! Bear with me. First of all, we need to stay up-to-date because new features appear regularly, especially in major versions.

Brian: For example?

Ashley: For example, the causal cluster is a feature beginning in version 3.2!

Iryna: Aren't features sometimes deprecated when we update Neo4j?

Ashley: Yes, this occurred with the `neo4j-shell` for instance, which was replaced by `cypher-shell`.

Iryna: Similarly, `neo4j-backup` is now deprecated in favor of `neo4j-admin backup`.

Brian: So an update can force changes in the way we use Neo4j? More work! It's not worth it!

Ashley: Think of it as job security! In most cases, the Neo4J browser proposes the replacement of features or new features only if there is benefit to the user. Otherwise, there's no point in showcasing them... Technology is going to advance, regardless. If we don't update to new software versions as they come along, we get further and further behind, making catching up that much more difficult.

Iryna: Yes, that's what's known as technical debt...

CONCEPT: Technical debt

The term *technical debt* borrows a financial term (the debt) for use in software development: software represents value, and not updating it in a timely fashion is like contracting a debt... a debt which you will always have to pay, eventually!

You can choose to contract a technical debt on purpose (for example, developing with an older release to ensure meeting a deadline) or involuntarily (for instance, a team practice that results in poorer technology control, non-compliance with coding conventions, etc.). Involuntary debt is the result of faulty planning, and serves no useful purpose. Whatever the case, the important thing is *controlling your debt*, and managing it intelligently, because there will always be a technical debt.

This intelligent management of software quality consists of improving it step by step (thus regularly pushing for quality updates). The same is true at a higher level, where it is sometimes necessary to update the software components that are part of the system architecture.

The first step to paying down debt is always to become aware of your debt, to identify the weak and time-consuming parts of your project that could be improved with an update.

Iryna: Technical debt or not, some components can also help enforce system security.

Ashley: Neo4j successive versions constantly provide patches, some of them relating to security. Applying these patches reduces the software's vulnerability to attack. And as software quality increases, the vendor exposes fewer and fewer security holes.

Iryna: So at the end of the day, if we don't update, we are vulnerable to attack, but if we follow Neo4j suggestions for moving to newer versions regularly, we become progressively less vulnerable.

Ashley: That's partly true! As we will see, security is not just theory, it's also practice. So we've talked about the why. I prepared a Neo4j update guide in order to speed up the how:

Brian: Good idea. My brain is way too full to think or listen any longer!

TECHNICAL: Neo4j Update Guide

Here are the suggested steps to follow when upgrading Neo4j:

- set up a test environment with the new Neo4j version: First update to the nearest major version from the current version, making sure to use only stable version (*release*) and preferentially choosing versions with a minor index higher than 0 (Neo4j teams always get a pulse of feedback when major versions are released, so a patch often comes soon after);
- check the release notes;
- if your Neo4j version is older than 3.0, follow the specific instructions from the update guide regarding to the version you want to update to (generally the guides suggest the application of successive migrations);
- identify the deprecated parameters in the `neo4j.conf` file and adapt these parameters for the test environment (connection to external systems, path to the graph database, network parameters, etc.);
- set the `dbms.allow_format_migration` parameter value to `true` in the `neo4j.conf` file. This parameter is important if the binary structure of the files containing graph data has been modified since the previous version;
- check the impact on the application code (for example, applications using Bolt or Neo4j HTTP APIs);
- perform non-regression tests on all functional aspects (preferably using automated tests);
- if everything went well, make a backup of the production database;
- update the production environment and check that it's working properly;
- once we are sure that the system works properly, set back the `dbms.allow_format_migration` parameter value to `false` in the `neo4j.conf` file. This will lock the data format and prevent accidental updates. And of course, restart the Neo4j instance so that the new version of this parameter is used.

Ashley: I think Jackie is coming back with Varsha... Hope they won't byte us. Get it? B-y-t-e us?

Tiago: Or even nibble a *bit*...

Iryna: Guys, stop, just stop...

Ashley: I hope that people aren't worried about having too little space for HA or causal clusters–there are a lot of *clusterphobic* ops departments.

Tiago: I'm really glad we aren't doing front end navigation pages–those menu bars take a *heap* of *bytes*.

Iryna: I'm going to kill both of you if you don't stop!

Tiago: What, and end up in the *punitentiary*

Iryna (sobbing): ...can't take any more...

Ashley: People should think of their data like the queen in chess, protected at all cost. Neo4j will *serv-er* well.

Tiago: Come on people, focus and try to get a *grep*.

Brian: Awful, just awful! Apparently this section has made a *hash* of your grey matter. I think we should move right on to the *synapses*.

4.8. Debriefing

Varsha returns to the team, as usual, to check on their progress.

Varsha: So, che pasa? Can we give our client iron-clad guarantees regarding the security of their data? Can we impress them with abstruse, intimidating technical terms that will make them feel confident?

Jackie: Uh... sure... why don't we just summarize it all for you...

Varsha (sighing): Okay, but keep it short. As Shakespeare said, "Brevity is the soul of wit and of software client relationships".

Jackie: Well, as far as data security is concerned, you really need to set up a cluster, i.e. a server farm that will ensure data availability.

Varsha: Okay... server farm... good

Jackie: There are two types of Neo4j clusters: First, the historical HA (High Availablity) cluster [146], which is similar to existing high availability systems, and the causal cluster [157], based on the Raft protocol, which is safer from a transactional standpoint and gives us load-balancing performed by the Bolt driver.

Varsha: Wow, I love it... high availability, Raft, Bolt, load-balancing... and causal clus-ter... excellent, both alliterative and sexy, could be the name of a rock band.

Jackie: Uh, sure. As Ashley has always reminded us, there is no foolproof system. We will therefore always need a plan for regular backups of [174] the Neo4j graph database. Thus, in case of generalized failure of the storage system (or for other purposes) we can perform a restore on [180] the data.

Varsha: All right... generalized failure and system backup/restore practices.

Jackie: These backups are based on the transaction log. We discussed this subject, par-ticularly with regard to the retention policy i.e., the ability to keep logs of only a portion of the transactions completed on the graph database.

Varsha: Ooh... retention rules, that's good, and transition logs sounds really sophisticat-ed... go on...

Brian: Don't forget about the pseudo-temporal stuff.

Jackie: We also discussed memory [184] and logging [182] strategies. A good sys-tem is a controlled system, generally speaking.

Varsha: Can we make that *a muscular system is a controlled system?*

Jackie: Sure, whatever. Finally, we discussed the concepts of technical debt and Neo4j migration to a higher version [187].

Varsha: Okay! I think we're highly relevant and legitimate on Neo4j operations; our client shouldn't have any concerns. They're going to love this. Neo4j is equipped with all the tools needed for a live production environment. That being said, there was one point that gave them the willies, especially in these treacherous times...

Jackie: You want to talk about *data security?*

Varsha: Bam.

Jackie: This is the last stop on solution validation trip. We'll brief you after we've discussed security further.

Varsha: I'll leave you to it to do it. Good luck!

5

Securing Data

The data stored in the Neo4j database may include personal data (for instance, customer personal addresses in the graph ordering process), so it is essential to secure this confidential information. To achieve this, we must follow and implement modern security standards, and establish operating procedures to ensure security compliance. Security must be considered a continuous improvement effort (a marathon) rather than a one time effort after a security audit (a sprint).

In this chapter, we will think of security of our Neo4j database as composed of concentric rings:

- first, secure servers and networks;
- second, implement user authentication and authorization, in line with enterprise policy;
- third, secure Neo4j extensions;
- finally, set up permanent monitoring of logs and metrics (audit).

5.1. Briefing

Jackie, Tiago, Iryna, Ashley and Brian meet to discuss Varsha's appointment with the client.

Jackie: Hello everyone. Varsha just had a discussion with the client who raised new questions about the security of the graph database.

Ashley: Let me guess: because it's a new technology, the client doubts the *security maturity* of Neo4?!

Jackie: Pretty much. We need to provide some *security maturity surety*, particularly as regards to data protection. Could you propose a structured approach to security that we could present to the client?

Ashley: We sure can. And let's spell it out very explicitly so there's no ... ahem... *security maturity surety obscurity.* I'd suggest that the minimum effort required is compliance with good security practices on the server hosting the database...

Iryna: ...As well as the network used to access the database!

Ashley: Obviously. Then it's a question of following A.A.A principles.

Brian: A.A.A? American Automobile Association? A bond rating by Standard and Poor's?

Ashley: No, AAA means *Authentication, Authorization, Accounting.* This is also sometimes known as Authentication, Authorization and Traceability, but we'll use AAA as the abbreviation. Authentication is a matter of managing users who will connect to the graph database.

Iryna: And authorization consists of managing different levels of access rights for different users. We're talking permissions or roles: every user will be entitled to perform some specific actions on the database, but not others.

Ashley: Finally, for accounting/traceability, we can use Neo4j logs to audit the actions performed by the users.

Jackie: That's pretty clear. Anything else to add?

Iryna: Yes. If our graph database has extensions...

Jackie: ...which will probably be the case...

Iryna: ...then we need to secure these extensions! That would be a special process.

Ashley: Finally, let's not forget about upgrading our database on a regular basis to benefit from security patches provided by newer versions.

Jackie (taking notes on the fly): Fine, I'll go back to Varsha and the client to explain our approach. On your side, please dig deeper on these topics. Work for you?

All: Yeah!

5.2. Secure servers and network

Ashley: I'll start, because I mentioned the first aspect about server and network security.

Iryna: Please do.

Ashley: In the OSI model, there are seven network layers that must all be covered regarding security... and all of them can be attacked! The AAA principle with authentication, authorization and accounting/traceability is mainly about the application domain (the seventh and top layer). But in addition, we need to secure the six underlying layers!

Figure 5.1 : OSI model (Open Systems Interconnection)

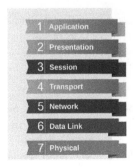

Brian: What does *securing network layers* involve? Sounds waaaaaay too complicated...

Ashley: At the bottom, the physical layer level, the control mechanisms are classic monitoring systems. Regarding the data and network layers, we set up port and protocol controls. *Firewalls* fulfill this role. Usually a DMZ (Demilitarized Zone) is defined. We could place the application server behind a first firewall and the database server behind a second firewall, for example. For the transport, session and presentation layers, the security mechanisms involve controls at the operating system level, including permissions: only specific operating system accounts can run the database software.

Tiago: Maybe you could give us an example using the Linux operating system for the sake of clarity...

Ashley: Sure. We can create a specific Linux user account or group account. Then only that user or a user in that group would be able to run Neo4j and its command line tools. This way, even if evil Dr. Hacker McHackface gets access to the database server, he won't be able to do anything because he'll have limited permissions.

Tiago: Not to mention more advanced mechanisms, such as securing connections to Neo4j...

Ashley: Okay, sure. But right now I'm thinking only about security for Neo4j specifically. Securing connections would fall under security for the application layer:

- disable the HTTP port and leave only the HTTPS port accessible;

- make encryption mandatory on the Bolt protocol connection;

- on a Neo4j cluster, restrict various protocol ports (i.e. 5000, 5001, ...) to machines that are part of the cluster.

The last item can certainly be managed by firewalls. To disable the HTTP port, simply set the `dbms.connector.http.enabled` parameter of the `neo4j.conf` file to `false`.

Tiago: I guess then that to enable the HTTPS port, we would set the `dbms.connector.https.enabled` parameter of the `neo4j.conf` file to `true`.

Ashley: That's right. Then, both the HTTP API and the Neo4j browser will be available on the default `7373` port (and only on 7373). Neo4j provides only a self-signed certificate, so when you connect to the Neo4j browser, your web browser might get a little cranky. Anyway, you have the option of integrating your own certificate if you need strong security from an application client's point of view. Your HTTP traffic between the client and the server will then be encrypted, using the TLS protocol (*Transport Layer Security*).

Tiago: Can you describe for us how this works end to end?

Ashley: Yeah, it goes like this. By default the security of exchanges performed with the Bolt protocol is optional (`OPTIONAL`). This means that the Neo4j server will accept both secure and non-secure exchanges from application clients. To make this security mandatory, we'll set the `dbms.connector.bolt.tls_level` parameter to `REQUIRED`. This way, Bolt clients will now connect with an additional configuration parameter called `TrustStrategy`. Here is a example:

```
final AuthToken token = AuthTokens.basic(USER, PASSWORD);
Config config =
 Config.build().withTrustStrategy(Config.TrustStrategy.trustSignedBy(new
 File(new URI(boltConfig.trustCertFile)))).toConfig();
driver = GraphDatabase.driver(BOLT_URL, token, config);
```

And with that I think we're done with the transport level security.

Brian: Nice. How about the seventh layer?

Iryna: Yeah, let's look at the application layer, and examine the details of authentication, authorization and traceability (AAA).

5.3. Authentication

Brian: Is it possible to forgo authentication when using Neo4j?

Ashley: Yes, it's possible... but we're not going to...

Iryna: If we did have to avoid authentication for some insane reason, we'd just change the value of the parameter `dbms.security.auth_enabled` from `true` to `false`.

TECHNIQUE: Enable or disable authentication

To enable or disable authentication to the Neo4j database, you have to change the value of the `dbms.security.auth_enabled` parameter. The default value of this parameter is `true`.

Caution › When this parameter is disabled (**false** value), both authentication AND authorization are disabled.

Iryna: Fine, but by default this `dbms.security.auth_enabled` setting is enabled, so when connecting to the database you must present a user name and password.

When first connecting to the database, the default identifier is *neo4j* and the default password is *neo4j*.

Figure 5.2 : Connect to Neo4j

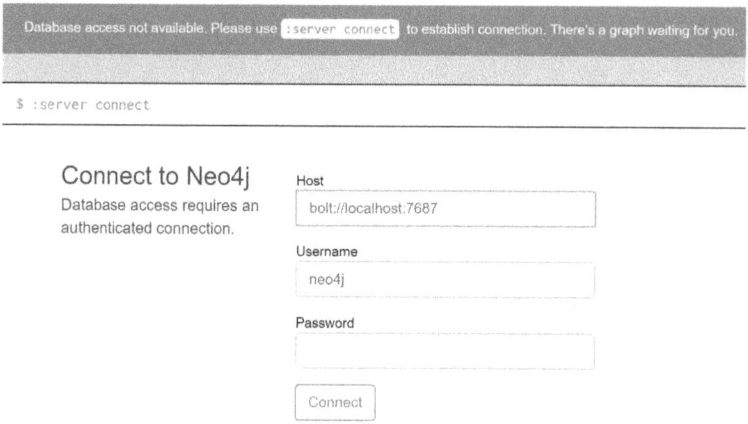

Brian: One question, if you'll forbear my naivete! When you enable authentication, obviously the Neo4j browser will ask you to enter a login and password. But do I also need to provide credentials if I use APIs?

Iryna: When you call the HTTP APIs, you'll have to include an `Authorization` header in your request for so-called *basic* authentication, i.e. with login and password. This is what it's going to look like:

```
curl -H 'Authorization: bmVvNGo6bmVvNGo' http://localhost:7474/user/
neo4j
```

```
{
    "password_change_required" : false,
    "password_change" : "http://localhost:7474/user/neo4j/password",
    "username" : "neo4j"
}
```

Brian: Hold on a second! Where are the credentials? I don't see any in your curl query, just gibberish!

Iryna: This information is passed through the `Authorization` header, and it is base64-encoded, which looks like gibberish to us. For example, the string `neo4j:neo4j` is base64-encoded to `bmVvNGo6bmVvNGo`. That's how your REST request to Neo4j is authenticated!

Brian: Suppose I use the Bolt client and not the HTTP API to connect to Neo4j?

Iryna: Great question! Here is how it works with Bolt... Your application, developed in C#, Java, JavaScript or Python, will connect to the database using a driver. When access to the graph database is authenticated, the driver is instantiated with the parameters required for basic authentication (username and password).

```
public class DriverLifecycleExample implements AutoCloseable
{
    private final Driver driver;

    public DriverLifecycleExample( String uri, String login, String
password )
    {
        driver = GraphDatabase.driver( uri, AuthTokens.basic( login,
password ) );
    }

    @Override
    public void close() throws Exception
    {
        driver.close();
    }
}
```

Brian: I think I get it as far as Bolt is concerned. But where are the `login` and `password` credentials stored? Inside the graph database?

Ashley: Yes, by default. You can get the list of registered users by calling the `dbms.security.listUsers` procedure.

Figure 5.3 : *List Neo4j database users*

```
$ CALL dbms.security.listUsers
```

	username	flags
	"neo4j"	[]

Ashley: But rather than keeping user management in the graph database, you might also delegate it to another system...

Iryna: ...but only if you use the Neo4j enterprise edition.

Brian: Why would you delegate user management?

Ashley: A company's information system probably already has a company directory, where all the users are registered. It makes sense to rely on the company global directory, avoiding user database silos that will need to be kept in sync with the company global directory, a maintenance nightmare. Users cursing our names because they can't get past security...

Iryna: Yes, otherwise we'd quickly end up with the same users stored in a lot of different places...

Ashley: And constant confusion about which is the source of truth! By the way, it is possible to connect Neo4j to an external LDAP (*Lightweight Directory Access Protocol*) directory. But the variety of configurations for these directories makes it difficult to demonstrate a typical configuration. However, we'll talk more about that later after we've discussed how permissions work in Neo4j.

5.4. Authorization

Iryna: The concept of authorization is closely tied to the concept of roles: every user of the graph database is assigned a role, which is in reality a set of permissions granting some particular, well-defined set of actions that can be executed on the database.

Brian: I hear the words, I know what each word means in isolation, but the meaning of the sentence as a whole escapes me. In baby talk, what does that mean?

Iryna: A diagram is worth a thousand words. And a diagram of a graph is even better yet! For Neo4j native roles, we distinguish the `reader`, `editor`, `publisher` (publish), `architect` (design) and `admin` (manage) roles. All these roles allow the user to perform five basic actions: changing your password, managing your user profile, viewing the results of your queries, reading data from the graph, and terminating your own queries.

Figure 5.4 : *Roles and permissions*

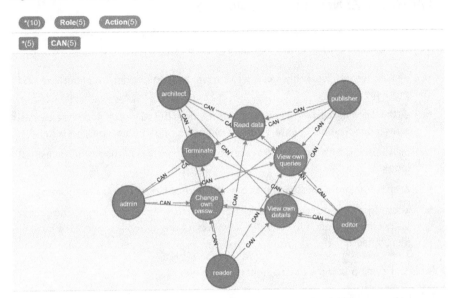

Iryna: In addition, the diagram shows that some actions are allowed for users in some roles but not in others. For example, the editor role allows you to perform writes, updates and deletes on data. These actions are prohibited for the reader role.

Figure 5.5 : *Roles and permissions*

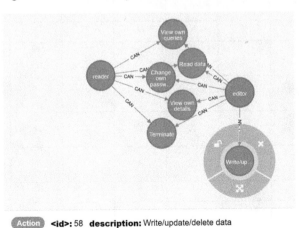

Action **<id>:** 58 **description:** Write/update/delete data

TECHNIQUE: Neo4j native roles

Neo4j enterprise version provides five native roles for fine-grained access control. They are listed below from most restrictive to least restrictive:

- `reader`: grants read-only access to graph data (all nodes, relationships and properties);

- `editor`: grants read/write access to graph data but with restricted write permissions (cannot create or change property names, relationship types, node labels);

- `publisher`: grants read/write access to the graph data with no restriction except indexes;

- `architect`: grants read/write access to the graph data with no restrictions;

- `admin`: grants read/write access to graph data with no restrictions. The admin users can generate a list CYPHER queries that are currently running, as can kill them if needed.

Table 5.1 summarizes the access right of each role.

Table 5.1 : Native permissions and roles

Action	reader	editor	publisher	architect	admin	(none)
Change their own password	X	X	X	X	X	X
Access their own information	X	X	X	X	X	X
Read some data	X	X	X	X	X	
View their own queries	X	X	X	X	X	
Terminate their own queries	X	X	X	X	X	
Read/update/delete some data		X	X	X	X	
Create new properties			X	X	X	
Create new labels			X	X	X	
Create new relationship types			X	X	X	

Action	reader	editor	publisher	architect	admin	(none)
Create/delete constraints/indexes				X	X	
Create/delete a user					X	
Change user password					X	
Assign a role to a user/Remove a role from a user					X	
Activate/deactivate a user					X	
List users and roles					X	
List a user's roles					X	
List all users who have a given role					X	
View all running queries					X	
Terminate all running queries					X	

Iryna: In summary, Brian, we have a set of actions allowed in the graph database: create/delete a user, read some data, update some data, ... In other words, a role is a set of permissions.

Brian: If I understand correctly, users who have the same role have exactly the same access rights on the graph database?

Iryna: Yes, exactly!

Brian: And how are users managed in Neo4j?

Iryna: They are managed with CYPHER, using the integrated procedures starting with `dbms.security`:

Table 5.2 : User management procedures

Procedure	Description
`dbms.security.activateUser`	Activate a suspended user
`dbms.security.addRoleToUser`	Assign a role to a user
`dbms.security.changePassword`	Change current user password
`dbms.security` `.changeUserPassword`	Change a user password
`dbms.security.clearAuthCache`	Clears the authorization and authentication cache
`dbms.security.createRole`	Create a custom role
`dbms.security.createUser`	Create a user
`dbms.security.deleteRole`	Deletes a role (as well as its assignments)
`dbms.security.deleteUser`	Deletes a user
`dbms.security.listRoles`	List available roles
`dbms.security.listRolesForUser`	List the roles for a user
`dbms.security.listUsers`	List users registered in Neo4j
`dbms.security.listUsersForRole`	List users to whom a given role is assigned
`dbms.security` `.removeRoleFromUser`	Unassign a role from the user
`dbms.security.suspendUser`	Deactivate a user

Iryna: Let's look at an example. I'll create a `brian` user who can't write in the graph. I can use the `dbms.security.createUser` procedure. Here's how it looks:

```
CALL dbms.procedures()
YIELD name, signature
WHERE name = "dbms.security.createUser" RETURN name, signature
```

This CYPHER query returns:

Table 5.3 : Procedure—dbms.security.createUser

Procedure	Signature
dbms.security.createUser	dbms.security.createUser (username :: STRING?, password :: STRING?, requirePasswordChange = true :: BOOLEAN?) :: VOID

I can then use the procedure in the following CYPHER query. The "VOID" indicates it doesn't return anything.

```
CALL dbms.security.createUser("brian", "secret", false)
```

I can then check that the user brian exists by calling the dbms.security.listUsers procedure.

```
CALL dbms.security.listUsers
```

The CYPHER query returns:

Table 5.4 : Procedure—dbms.security.listUsers

username	roles	flags
Neo4j	["admin"]	[]
brian	[]	[]

As we can see, the brian user has been correctly created without a default role.

Brian: What's the deal with the *flags* column?

Iryna: flag indicates one or more possible statuses for this user. For example, the is_suspended flag means that the user is disabled, the password_change_required flag means that the user will have to change his password on next login. We can now assign the reader role to this user, using the dbms.security.addRoleToUser procedure like this:

```
CALL dbms.security.addRoleToUser("reader","brian")
```

To verify that the role has actually been assigned:

Table 5.5 : Procedure–dbms.security.listUsers

username	roles	flags
Neo4j	["admin"]	[]
brian	["reader"]	[]

So all is good, the reader role has been assigned to brian user

Brian: How could I verify that I am not allowed to write data to Neo4j?

Iryna: You could just disconnect from Neo4j using the :server disconnect Neo4j browser command. Then you reconnect using the :server connect command, thereby triggering an authentication request from the server. When the authentication page is displayed, you enter the brian login and the *secret* password. Then you'll be re-authenticated. You can use the dbms.showCurrentUser procedure to check the logged in user for the session:

```
CALL dbms.showCurrentUser()
```

Table 5.6 : Procedure–dbms.showCurrentUser

username	roles	flags
brian	["reader"]	[]

Users can always see their own personal data. However, if the user tries to list all users:

```
CALL dbms.security.listUsers()
```

Now an error message results:

```
Error : Neo.ClientError.Security.Forbidden
Permission denied.
```

Which is really quite sad for brian but awesome from a security standpoint. Now let's try a read query:

```
MATCH (o:Order) RETURN o.orderId
```

We get the data correctly:

Table 5.7 : Read-only CYPHER query

o.orderId
20170330-1

If we now try a write query:

```
CREATE (o:Order{orderId:"20170440-1"})
RETURN o.orderId
```

Which flops! No way Neo4j is going to allow reader brian to write to the graph:

```
ERROR Neo.ClientError.Security.Forbidden
Write operations are not allowed for user 'brian' with roles [reader].
```

Basically, Neo4j tells us that write operations are not allowed for the brian user with only the reader role. This is a good thing from a security perspective.

Brian: That's pretty simple, actually.

Iryna: Pretty much, yes.

Tiago: But you can still read *all* the data. That could be bad if there was sensitive data. Is there no way to limit read permissions?

Iryna: Are you talking about data *privacy?*

Tiago: Right.

Iryna: We could accomplish this by by creating *custom* roles, but then we'd need to develop custom permission managers to handle them.

5.5. LDAP directory integration

Ashley: So we've been digging into the authentication and authorization principles na-tively provided by Neo4j. However, as I said before, it is quite possible to delegate these responsibilities to an external directory. Let's see how we can integrate Neo4j with an existing LDAP enterprise directory. Here is an extract from our GraphITs.Tech's LDAP directory:

Figure 5.6 : *GraphITs.Tech LDAP Directory*

```
☐ Root-dc=graphits,dc=tech
   ☐ ou=users
      uid=brian
      uid=christophe
      uid=philippe
      uid=sylvain
   ☐ ou=groups
      cn=reader
      cn=publisher
      cn=architect
      cn=admin
```

We have four users in this directory: *Brian, Tiago, Ashley* and *Iryna*. For this example, we'll create four LDAP groups so that each user is in a different group:

Table 5.8 : *GraphITs.tech LDAP users and groups*

user	group
Brian	reader
Tiago	publisher
Ashley	architect
Iryna	admin

This configuration provides two things: first, Neo4j users will be able to perform *remote authentication* on the external directory; secondly, user group assignment in this LDAP directory will determine the *permissions* each Neo4j user has.

TECHNIQUE: Import GraphITs.tech LDAP configuration

You can import GraphITs.tech LDAP configuration, provided you install the proper software like OpenLDAP, then configure the graphits.tech domain, followed by running the import command:

```
ldapmodify.exe
-x -a
-H ldap://graphitserver.tech:389
-D "cn=manager,dc=graphits,dc=tech"
-f ./ldifdata/ldap_graphits.ldif
-w secret
```

This command means that:

- we configure the graphitserver.tech LDAP server (`-H ldap://graphitserver.tech:389`);

- the LDAP admin account is used to execute the following command: (`-D "cn=manager,dc=graphits,dc=tech"`);

- we import the users and groups described in the `ldap_graphits.ldif` file (`-f./ldifdata/ldap_graphits.ldif`).

Now let's discuss the `ldap_graphits.ldif file`:

First we declare the two directory organizations, *users* and *groups*.

```
dn: ou=users,dc=graphits,dc=tech
objectClass: organizationalUnit
objectClass: top
ou: users

dn: ou=groups,dc=graphits,dc=tech
objectClass: organizationalUnit
objectClass: top
ou: groups
```

Then, we create different groups. Here the groups match the Neo4j roles. Let's take the example of the reader group:

```
dn: cn=reader,ou=groups,dc=graphits,dc=tech
objectClass: groupOfNames
objectClass: top
cn: reader
member:uid=reader,ou=users,dc=graphits,dc=tech
```

. . .

We use the same method for the other groups. Finally, we declare each user to be a group member:

```
dn: uid=brian,ou=users,dc=graphits,dc=tech
objectClass: organizationalPerson
objectClass: person
objectClass: extensibleObject
objectClass: uidObject
objectClass: inetOrgPerson
objectClass: top
cn: Brian Reader User
givenName: Brian
sn: brian
uid: brian
mail: brian@graphits.tech
ou: users
userpassword: test
memberOf: cn=reader,ou=groups,dc=graphits,dc=tech
. . . .
```

And so on for other users belonging to other groups.

Caution › Note the "memberOf" in the above definition for users. This establishes the Neo4j role that the user will have. In the Neo4j configuration file there is a parameter **dbms.security.ldap.authorization.group_membership_attributes** parameter which must be set to "memberOf" for this to work (see the neo4j.conf example below). Whatever value we define this parameter to have, that's the value that must be used in the ldif file above to link the user to a group/role.

Brian: But what about the link between Neo4j and the LDAP directory?

Ashley: This connection is defined in the Neo4j configuration:

TECHNIQUE: LDAP configuration

Delegating user management in a LDAP directory is only available in Neo4j enterprise edition. The parameters used to customize LDAP in the `neo4j.conf` configuration file are:

```
# Type of provider to which we delegate
# authentication and authorization  (here, ldap)
# Default value is "native"
# (when using neo4j internal user management)
dbms.security.auth_provider=ldap

# LDAP server URL
# (one can use a LDAP URL whose default port is 389,
```

```
# or a secured LDAPS URL with default port 686)
dbms.security.ldap.host=ldap://my.ldap.server:389

# Optional : use LDAP admin account to
# access LDAP user attributes
# (if and only if LDAP users don't have the right to access
# their own attributes)
dbms.security.ldap.authorization.use_system_account=true
dbms.security.ldap.system_username=cn=manager,dc=graphits,dc=tech
dbms.security.ldap.system_password=secret

# DN template : Distinguished Name template
# for LDAP users
# the Distinguished Name is the unique identifier
# of any given LDAP user.
# Using a template enables to authenticate
# with LDAP directory without completely specifying the DN:
# Here, cn={0} enables to replace user identifier
# in DN string
dbms.security.ldap.authentication.user_dn_template=\
    cn={0},cn=Users,dc=graphits,dc=tech

# The name of the LDAP base context from which
# user search is performed
# Either we start form the LDAP directory root,
# or from a specific directory
dbms.security.ldap.authorization.user_search_base=\
    cn=Users,dc=graphits,dc=tech

# The LDAP user search filter :
# here we will search the LDAP directory from the CN attribute,
# which stands for Common Name
dbms.security.ldap.authorization.user_search_filter=\
    (&(objectClass=*)(uid={0}))

# This parameter lists LDAP user attribute names
# that contain groups used to match
# neo4j roles
# the value here must match the name in the ldif file which specifies
 the LDAP group


 dbms.security.ldap.authorization.group_membership_attributes=memberOf

# Correspondence between LDAP groups and neo4j predefined roles
# (admin, architect, publisher, reader) :
dbms.security.ldap.authorization.group_to_role_mapping=\
    "cn=Neo4j Read Only,cn=users,dc=graphits,dc=tech"=reader;\
    "cn=Neo4j Read-Write,cn=users,dc=graphits,dc=tech"=publisher;\
    "cn=Neo4j Schema Manager,cn=users,dc=graphits,dc=tech"=architect;\
    "cn=Neo4j Administrator,cn=users,dc=graphits,dc=tech"=admin

# Authentication cache
dbms.security.auth_cache_ttl=1m
```

Ashley: This might be a bit tricky, so let's emphasize the `dbms.security.ldap.authorization.group_membership_attributes` parameter whose `memberOf` value makes it possible to match a given user with the group she belongs to.

Brian: Once we've done our LDAP configuration, how do we re-authenticate with the graph database?

Ashley: Same as before, except that instead of logging in with the default *neo4j* user, you will log in using an LDAP user login and password.

Brian: I think I get it! For example, if my login is `brian` and my password is...

All: Shhh... Don't blab your password!

Iryna (shuddering): Jeez! You don't want to be brought up before the Password Sharing Tribunal of the Department of Security.

Ashley: (loudly, for the hidden Department of Security microphones) Lets pretend your password is `storm`, *(back to normal volume)* then you would enter `brian` and `storm` for the username and password in the Neo4j login prompt.

Figure 5.7 : Connect to Neo4j with LDAP

```
$ :server connect
```

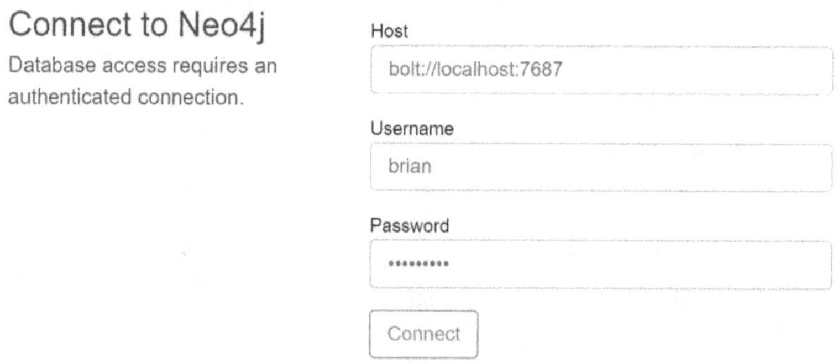

Connect to Neo4j

Database access requires an authenticated connection.

Host

bolt://localhost:7687

Username

brian

Password

•••••••••

Connect

Brian: Now that I am authenticated, what permissions do I have in the graph database? Am I all powerful? Am I the master of my domain?

Ashley: All depends on the roles you have: `admin`, `architect`, `publisher`, `editor` or `reader`.

Iryna: This is in line with the authorization concept we talked about earlier.

Ashley: So, Brian, if you run the CYPHER `CALL dbms command.showCurrentUser` command in the Neo4j browser like you did before, you'll see your assigned role: read-only on the database (reader).

Figure 5.8 : *LDAP user connected to Neo4j in read-only*

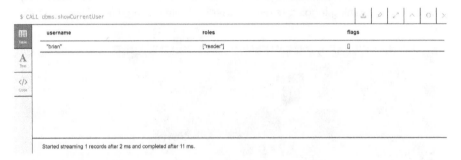

5.6. Traceability

Ashley: Tell me, dudes both male and female, where are we exactly in our AAA security requirements? I think we've dealt with authentication and authorization, so there must be one more thing we need to talk about...

Brian: I know this one!... Auditability, aka traceability!

Ashley: Kudos, Brian, way to keep your head in the game! The traceability requirement is satisfied when we know the answer to the question: *Who does what and when in the graph database?*

Iryna: It's like tracking the actions of the users on the graph.

Ashley: That's it! To satisfy the traceability requirements I can see two viable alternatives: First, only track connections to the graph database (thus answering *who authenticates?* question). Second, track CYPHER queries initiated by users (thus answering *who does what?* question). The security event log addresses the first point. Authentication events are written in the `security.log` file.

Neo4j security logs

The security.log file is located in the Neo4j enterprise edition logs directory: [NEO4J_HOME]/logs.

This file contains timestamped logs of user connections (both failures and successes) as well as containing logging related to user and role management. Here is an example:

```
2017-11-13 12:32:32.569+0000 INFO  [neo4j]: logged in
2017-11-13 15:23:14.234+0000 INFO  [neo4j]: created user `brian`
2017-11-13 15:29:58.739+0000 INFO  [neo4j]: suspended user `brian`
2017-11-13 15:30:43.483+0000 INFO  [neo4j]: activated user `brian`
2017-11-13 15:39:33.959+0000 INFO  [neo4j]: added role `reader` to
  user `brian`
2017-11-13 15:46:00.489+0000 INFO  [brian]: logged in
2017-11-13 15:50:32.563+0000 ERROR [brian]: tried to list users:
  Permission denied.
2017-11-13 16:44:17.873+0000 INFO  [brian]: logged in
2017-11-13 16:44:31.074+0000 ERROR [neo4j]: failed to log in: invalid
  principal or credentials
```

For authentication with the HTTP API, Neo4j recommends deactivating the logs of successful connections to save space. This can be done using the dbms.security.log_successful_authentication parameter in the neo4j.conf file:

```
dbms.security.log_successful_authentication=false
```

Other parameters allow us to manage the volume of logs to be kept:

Table 5.9 : Neo4j security log settings

Parameter name	Default value	Description
dbms.logs.security.rotation.size	20M	Size of security.log file at which the security event log file automatically rotates
dbms.logs.security.rotation.delay	300s	Minimum time interval between each rotation of the security.log file
dbms.logs.security.rotation.keep_number	7	Number of stored security.log files kept

Ashley: So now we know who connected to the Neo4j server, let's capture what the users do, i.e. the CYPHER queries they perform.

Brian: Don't we find CYPHER query logs in a dedicated file?

Ashley: Right again, the `query.log` file.

Brian (checking on his computer): Rats...I don't see that file in the `logs` directory.

Ashley: Chill, dude, that's normal. The `query.log` file is only generated if the `dbms.logs.query.enabled` parameter is set to `true`, and the default value is `false`.

Brian: So if we enable this parameter, then all CYPHER queries are logged?

Ashley: No, setting this parameter to true is necessary but not sufficient. Let us look closer at the parameters you need to set in order to customize your query logging:

Neo4j query logs

The `query.log` file is located in the `logs` directory of the Neo4j enterprise edition:`[NEO4J_HOME]/logs`.

This log contains timestamped events related to CYPHER queries executed on the Neo4j server, as well as information about the client that initiated them. Here is some sample query.log content:

```
2016-10-27 14:31 ... INFO  0 ms: bolt-session bolt   johndoe neo4j-
javascript/0.0.0-dev    client/127.0.0.1:59167 ...
2016-10-27 14:31 ... INFO  9 ms: bolt-session bolt   johndoe neo4j-
javascript/0.0.0-dev    client/127.0.0.1:59167 ...
2016-10-27 14:31 ... INFO  0 ms: bolt-session bolt   johndoe neo4j-
javascript/0.0.0-dev    client/127.0.0.1:59167 ...
2016-10-27 14:32 ... INFO  3 ms: server-session http  127.0.0.1 /db/
data/cypher neo4j - CALL dbms.procedures() - {}
2016-10-27 14:32 ... INFO  1 ms: server-session http  127.0.0.1 /db/
data/cypher neo4j - CALL dbms.showCurrentUs...
2016-10-27 14:32 ... INFO  0 ms: bolt-session bolt   johndoe neo4j-
javascript/0.0.0-dev    client/127.0.0.1:59167 ...
2016-10-27 14:32 ... INFO  0 ms: bolt-session bolt   johndoe neo4j-
javascript/0.0.0-dev    client/127.0.0.1:59167 ...
2016-10-27 14:32 ... INFO  2 ms: bolt-session bolt   johndoe neo4j-
javascript/0.0.0-dev    client/127.0.0.1:59261 ...
```

This logging type can be very resource-intensive and grow fast, so it is disabled by default. To activate it, simply pass the `dbms.logs.query.enabled` parameter of the `neo4j.conf` file to value `true`:

```
dbms.logs.query.enabled=true
```

Other parameters allow to manage the volume of logs to be kept:

Table 5.10 : Neo4j query log settings

Parameter name	Default value	Description
dbms.logs.query.enabled	false	
dbms.logs.query.threshold	0s	Logging queries whose execution time exceeds a certain threshold (valid units: ms (millisecond), s (second), m (minute) and h (hour); default unit is second)
dbms.logs.query.rotation.size	20m	Size of query.log file that triggers log file rotation
dbms.logs.query.rotation.keep_number	7	Number of query.log stored files kept
dbms.logs.query.parameter_logging_enabled	true	Logging parameters for queries that take a longer time to execute than the given threshold dbms.logs.query.threshold

Ashley: So that's it. You've probably noticed that many parameters are common among all logging types.

5.7. Securing extensions

Ashley: We've now seen how to implement the AAA principles of authentication, authorization and traceability, the fundamental principles to be implemented on the graph database itself. However...

Tiago: However, Neo4j is not only a graph database...

Iryna: Right. It can also be enhanced by extensions...

Brian: Extensions? You mean like the APOC procedures?

Ashley: Yes, but not only APOC. There are lots of other Neo4j extensions we'll need to secure.

Brian: Why bother? Don't extensions do things that are well defined and always allowed?

Ashley: Not exactly. Here's an example: imagine you have a Neo4j graph database up and running in production, and imagine we'd like to limit write actions. For instance, we might say only the application server should be allowed to write to the database...

Brian: With you it so far...

Ashley: Well, if at the same time you authorize a given extension to write to the database, you create a security breach: any database user allowed to run this extension can therefore write to the graph, and that breaks our requirement. See?

Brian: Yes, I see... So how do we secure extensions?

Ashley: As I see it, there are three questions to be answered: One, how do we distinguish one extension from the others? Two, how do we restrict the execution scope of the authorized extensions? And three, how are extensions integrated with roles, which comes down to controlling the users able to run such procedures?

Iryna: I like it, nicely structured reasoning. Let me start with the first point, with the `dbms.security.procedures.unrestricted` configuration parameter.

Enable a Neo4j extension

To allow an extension to run on the Neo4j graph database, you should modify the value of the `dbms.security.procedures.unrestricted` parameter in the `neo4j.conf` file. For example, to allow all APOC procedures to run, you fill in the parameter like this:

```
dbms.security.procedures.unrestricted=apoc.*
```

Which means: *all extensions whose name begins with apoc.*.

If we now want to enable brand new procedures developed at graphits.tech, the new value of the parameter would be:

```
dbms.security.procedures.unrestricted=
apoc.*,tech.graphits.procedures.*
```

You might want to restrict the authorized procedures within some extension. This is done using the `dbms.security.procedures.whitelist` parameter in the same way. Note that in this case, only the procedures listed here can be executed.

Tiago: Ok, fine, I'll handle the case where we *don't want* certain procedures to run. Still with us, Brian?

Brian: Yeah, but I'd kill for an example.

Tiago: Sure thing, killer. Suppose that the operator of the graph database wants to authorize only APOC procedures that manage ElasticSearch integration...

Brian: Procedures that start with `apoc.es`?

Tiago: Bingo! In this case we will add a parameter to the `neo4j.conf` configuration file:

```
dbms.security.procedures.whitelist=apoc.es.*
```

Tiago: In this way you can specify within a large library of extensions (`apoc.*`), the list of allowed procedures (`apoc.es.*`, for example).

Brian: Clear as ...uh, clear as...a thing that is really, really clear. And for the third point, how do we control which users are allowed to use which extensions?

Iryna: The first level of controlling user access to extensions is already configured by default in the graph database. And a second level of control is available:

Control the roles authorized to execute extensions

By default, extensions that use write mode (`mode=WRITE`) can only be executed by the `architect`, `admin`, and `publisher` roles. Therefore, the `reader` role is not allowed to execute these extensions.

The `apoc.load.jdbc` procedure, which reads an external relational database, can be executed by any role. But the procedure `apoc.load.jdbcUpdate`, which updates an RDBMS, cannot.

If you want to limit the execution of procedures to specific roles, then you need to use a new configuration parameter: `dbms.security.procedures.roles`.

```
dbms.security.procedures.roles=\
    apoc.jdbc.*:admin;apoc.es.*:publisher,architect
```

In the example above, JDBC procedures (`apoc.jdbc.*`) can only be executed by users whose have the role of `admin`, while Elasticsearch procedures (`apoc.es.*`) can only be executed by users with role `publisher` or `architect`.

5.8. Debriefing

Varsha and Jackie get back to the technical team to get updated on their progress.

Varsha: So, how is the project going?

Jackie: And please, no techno babble this time. Get straight to the point!

Ashley: Ok, well, we've been focusing on the A.A.A (Authentication, Authorization, Accounting) principles: authentication, authorization and accountability/traceability.

Jackie: Let's start with authentication.

Ashley: Neo4j has a native, built-in authentication system but it is possible to use another one, either through an extension, or by connecting to an existing LDAP directory.

Jackie: What about authorizations?

Ashley: Neo4j can manage users and roles, making it possible to limit the scope of permitted actions for a given user based on an Access Control List (ACL).

Varsha: What do you mean by Access Control List?

Ashley: We can have some users read data from the graph, but not change it, while other users will be able to both read and write data.

Jackie: Great, now how about traceability?

Ashley: Traceability is enforced by a two-level logging. The first log level records who connects to the system (as well as other user management actions). Those events are written to the `security.log` file. The second log level identifies who executes which queries. Those events are written to the `query.log` file. It's important to point out that query logging is disabled by default. With these two log levels, if an anomaly is detected in the data, we can track down the query, as well as the user who performed it (and even the client used).

Varsha: I'm guessing that our customer won't have much input on this subject, as it's clear the Neo4j product is mature regarding security, has *security maturity*. Let me thank and congratulate all of you for your work. The information we exchanged through this process is a valuable asset for our client. In fact, even though each of you has specific skills, by now everyone can appreciate what the others are doing. And the team and the project greatly benefit from the shared global knowledge. You should pat yourselves on the back–sharing knowledge, strangely, is not easy and not done well by a lot of groups. But is a key factor for the success of a project!

Brian: Well, it helps that everyone has to explain everything to me.

Varsha: That makes you, Mr. Brian, the most important member of this group!

Brian: It's 'bout time someone realized that!

Appendices

Neo4j OGM and Spring Data Neo4j

1. OGM

OGM (*Object Graph Mapper*) is a library for Java developers, as well as for those using a another JVM based language.

OGM maps between Neo4j data and application domain objects. It will implement querying the database and transforming the query results into objects and vice versa.

To apply business logic to the data, it is convenient to structure it as application objects. Using a driver[1] to manually map the *resultsets* to these objects, we would need to develop low level infrastructure code that has no business value per se. This is often both annoying and cumbersome. OGM allows us to avoid most of this purely boilerplate code, leaving more time to develop apps applying business logic on top of Neo4j.

OGM also offers features such as:

- smart handling of updates;
- simpler transaction management;
- an abstraction encapsulating the protocol used to access the database (such as embedded DB, HTTP, Bolt).

In many ways, OGM is similar to ORM (Object Relational Mapper) often used with relational databases. But there are some noteworthy differences. The main one is that OGM is more tailored to connected data: when loading data, one can specify a loading depth that will be used to traverse the graph down to a given depth, followed by mapping the results back to domain objects. Another difference concerns optimization: because your graph database usually connects heterogeneous data from various data sources. In this use case, you may have different domain models for different applications, each of which represents a partial view of the database. OGM adapts to that scenario and generates CYPHER queries that only fetch nodes and relationships used in the code.

But let's see it in action through some examples.

---

[1]There are different driver types. See the Neo4j java driver manual [http://d-booker.jo.my/neo4j-java-driver-doc].

A first example

We'll work with our catalog graph from the chapter *A Little Bit of Method and Analysis.*

Figure 9 : Our example graph

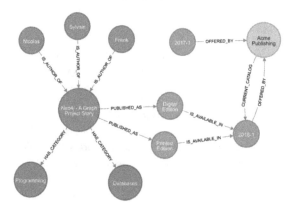

The first step is to annotate our Java objects thereby defining the mapping logic between the database structure and our domain model. This is done like this:

Example 1 : Annotating the Java object

```java
package tech.graphits.catalog.model;
@NodeEntity
public class Person {

    @Id @GeneratedValue
    private Long id; ❶

    @Property(name = "email") ❷
    private String email;

    @Property(name = "name")
    private String name;

    @Relationship(type = "IS_AUTHOR_OF") ❸
    private Set<Book> books = new HashSet<>();

    // getters & setters

}
```

❶ This is a mandatory identifier. The `@GeneratedValue` annotation indicates that the identifier will be a node id assigned automatically by the database.

❷ Object properties are mapped to the database via `@Property` annotations. By default, all attributes are mapped to database fields using the same name, so if they are the same the annotation is optional.

❸ Relationships with other entities are defined and typed with the `@Relationship` annotation.

We can now demonstrate a database search:

Example 2 : *First request*

```
SessionFactory sessionFactory = new SessionFactory(config,
    "tech.graphits.catalog.model"); ❶
Session session = sessionFactory.openSession();

Person nicolas = session.queryForObject(Person.class, ❷
    "match (p:Person{email:{email}}) return p", ❸
    Collections.singletonMap("email",
        "nicolas@graphits.tech")); ❹

assertEquals("Nicolas", nicolas.getName());
assertEquals("Nicolas@graphits.tech", nicolas.getEmail());
```

❶ The configuration and name of the package containing the domain classes.
❷ We want to perform a search returning a type `Person`.
❸ The query to execute, with a parameter named `{email}` as a parameter.
❹ The parameter value to be used in the search is given here.

That's it! It's as simple as that. Let's now dig a bit more into the details.

Installation and setup

Using Maven, we can easily obtain the required dependencies by adding dependencies to the POM file:

Example 3 : *Maven dependencies to use for Neo4j OGM*

```
<dependency>
    <groupId>org.neo4j</groupId>
    <artifactId>neo4j-ogm-core</artifactId>
    <version>3.1.8</version>
</dependency>
```

```
<dependency>
    <groupId>org.neo4j</groupId>
    <artifactId>neo4j-ogm-embedded-driver</artifactId>
    <version>3.1.8</version>
    <scope>runtime</scope>
</dependency>
```

Here we are using the *embedded* version of Neo4j. As the name implies, the database lives (i.e. is embedded) in the same Java process as our Java program. Embedding allows us to easily create a new database on the fly. This is quite handy when writing unit/integration tests, or to process temporary data, hosted in memory. If instead we'd prefer to use a Neo4j database installed on a remote machine we'd just replace the embedded module by the `bolt` or `http` module:

Table 11 : *Available OGM Maven artifacts for the different connection protocols*

ArtefactId	Usage
`neo4j-ogm-embedded-driver`	For an in-memory embedded database. Useful for tests or to work on volatile datasets.
`neo4j-ogm-bolt-driver`	To connect to a remote database using the Bolt protocol.
`neo4j-ogm-http-driver`	To connect to a remote database using the HTTP protocol.

The next step consists of setting up the OGM session factory. We need to declare two things:

- the database connection parameters;
- the name of the package holding the annotated domain entities.

Caution › Make sure to include ALL packages containing entity classes. If you don't you may experience painful unexpected behavior.

There are several ways to create the factory:

Example 4 : *OGM configuration with a properties file, for example a file named ogm.properties for the example below*

```
ConfigurationSource props = new ClasspathConfigurationSource(
    "ogm.properties");
Configuration config = new Configuration.Builder(props)
    .build();
sessionFactory = new SessionFactory(config,
    "tech.graphits.catalog.model");
```

Refer to the OGM user manual [http://d-booker.jo.my/neo4j-ogm-config] for details about the available configuration options.

Example 5 : *OGM programmatic configuration*

```
Configuration config = new Configuration.Builder()
    .uri("bolt://myServer")
    .credentials("user", "my secret password")
    .build();
sessionFactory = new SessionFactory(config,
    "tech.graphits.catalog.model");
```

The latter option is more powerful, because with code we can compute parameters at runtime.

Example 6 : *OGM configuration with a native driver instance*

```
org.neo4j.driver.v1.Driver nativeDriver = GraphDatabase
    .driver("bolt://myServer");
Driver ogmDriver = new BoltDriver(nativeDriver);
sessionFactory = new SessionFactory(ogmDriver,
    "tech.graphits.catalog.model");
```

This approach, using the native driver, is useful when you want to use a new driver version whose configuration options are not yet supported by OGM. You can therefore start using the new driver features without having to upgrade to the latest OGM.

The OGM factory is typically implemented as a singleton, initialized at application start-up time and reused afterwards.

The session

Once the setup done, we can then use the factory to obtain a `Session`. The session provides database access methods to perform searches and data updates, as well as transaction management.

The notion of session is quite close to the notion of session/EntityManager in JPA (Java Persistence Architecture), in the sense that loaded entities are stored within the session and tracked for update management. By this means we can optimize database updates by detecting entities that have been changed, and only perform updates on entities that have been truly modified.

In contrast to the factory which is only setup once at application startup, a session is typically short lived object. We use a session to do a coherent change on a set of data, often under the umbrella of a transaction (though it is possible to have several transactions per session). A best practice is to keep the session and the transaction short lived.

Caution › Unlike the SessionFactory, the session is not thread safe. So it must not be used concurrently by multiple threads.

Data access

The session offers different ways to search for data:

Table 12 : OGM search methods

Method	Use case
load	Loading an entity by id
loadAll	Multicriteria search on an entity type. Offers a rich set of possibilities (such as pagination, graph loading depth)
queryForObject	Search an entity with a CYPHER query.
query	Search for entities or tabular data with a CYPHER query.

The methods `load` and `loadAll` provide a generic approach for searching. We use them to get one or more root entities and their linked entities.

Example 7 : Person search by e-mail

```
Filter emailFilter = new Filter("email"
        , EQUALS, "nicolas@graphits.tech");
Collection<Person> results = session.loadAll(
        Person.class ❶
        , new Filters(emailFilter) ❷
        , 1); ❸

Person result = results.iterator().next();
assertEquals("Nicolas", result.getName());
assertEquals("nicolas@graphits.tech", result.getEmail());

// this loads first level dependant entities
assertEquals(1 , result.getBooks().size());
Book book = result.getBooks().iterator().next();
assertEquals("Neo4j - A Graph Project Story", book.getTitle());

// we've loaded level 1 but not level 2
assertNull(book.getProducts());
```

The parameters of `loadAll`:

❶   The type of root entity to search for.
❷   Search filters on this entity, here only e-mail.
❸   The loading depth.

The usage of `Filters` is especially important for dynamic UIs, and users can do searches with an arbitrary number of criteria. `Filters` allow OGM to build safe CYPHER queries, relieving developers of the cumbersome and error prone work of concatenating strings. The loading depth also enables us to retrieve dependant objects using a single query.

Caution › Keep a close watch on performance when using a larger loading depth! Not only this can result a huge volume of data being loaded, but the loaded objects are also kept in memory until the end of the session. Loading too much data can lead to memory saturation and fatal out-of-memory errors.

The methods `query` and `queryForObject` use CYPHER requests. We'll return to these later.

Search methods provide several possibilities for pagination and sorting.

Example 8 : *Paginated search*

```
Pagination paging = new Pagination(0, 10);
SortOrder order = new SortOrder().add(SortOrder.Direction.ASC, "name");

Iterable<Person> authors = session.loadAll(Person.class, order, paging);
```

Data can be written to the database using the `save` method of the session.

Example 9 : *Creation of an entity*

```
session.purgeDatabase();

Book book = new Book();
book.setTitle("a title");
book.setMainTitle("a main title");
book.setSubTitle("a sub title");

Person author = new Person();
author.setEmail("brian@graphits.tech");
author.setName("Brian");
author.setBooks(Collections.singleton(book));

session.save(author);

assertEquals(1, session.countEntitiesOfType(Person.class));
assertEquals(1, session.countEntitiesOfType(Book.class));
```

```
Filter titleFilter = new Filter("title", EQUALS, "a title");
Book newBook = session.loadAll(Book.class
    , new Filters(titleFilter)).iterator().next();
assertEquals("a title", newBook.getTitle());
```

In this example, we see that the creation is simple and occurs in a *transitive* way: that is, all objects nested under the entity passed as a parameter of the save method will be persisted too. This behavior is configurable. We can specify the saving depth with the second parameter of save, in the same way as with the loadAll example.

Updates are also done with the save method.

Continuing our previous example we can do an update:

Example 10 : *Updating an Entity*

```
book.setSubTitle("a new sub-title");

session.save(author);

newBook = session.loadAll(Book.class, new Filters(titleFilter))
    .iterator().next();
assertEquals("a new sub-title", newBook.getSubTitle());
```

We note here, again, that updates are done on the whole object graph. Though we are passing the author (and not the modified book) to the save method, we also update all entities that are linked to it.

But wait, what about performance? Might saving all objects in cascade be prohibitively costly? In fact, not usually, as OGM optimizes database updates behind the curtain. As discussed before, the modified objects loaded in the session are tracked, and OGM will generate update queries only for those that have actually changed. *In summary*, this frees up an OGM based application from having to manage most of database updates optimizations.

For JPA users

The OGM session operates differently from the corresponding session in JPA. In JPA, any object loaded then modified in memory is automatically synchronized with the database when the session ends. With OGM, updates must be explicitly triggered with the save method.

Data deletions are done through the `delete` and `deleteAll` methods. These work the same as the `load` and `loadAll` methods.

Beyond the basic use cases and CRUD access, real world applications often require more advanced data access via the more powerful CYPHER queries, or for performance optimization, return lightweight payloads.

We can then use native CYPHER statements via the method `query`.

Example 11 : *Aggregation of books and their authors*

```
Result result = session.query("MATCH (p:Person) -[:IS_AUTHOR_OF]->
(b:Book) "+
        "RETURN b.title as title, collect(p.name) as authors "
        , Collections.emptyMap()); ❶

Map<String, Object> record = result.queryResults().iterator().next(); ❷

assertEquals("Neo4j - A Graph Project Story", record.get("title"));
String[] authors = (String[]) record.get("authors");
Arrays.sort(authors);
assertArrayEquals(new String[]{"Frank", "Nicolas", "Sylvain"}
        , authors);
```

❶   There are no parameters in this example, but we could add them if necessary.
❷   Iteration on results.

This approach, though more manual than examples without queries, allows for a lot more flexibility; the developer has full control of the query.

Caution › It is important to always use the query parameters for two reasons:

* *security: this protects database queries from code injection;*
* *performance: if a query is run multiple times, the queries using the exact same strings are cached, and do not require the database to recompute the execution plan.*

The `query` method can also be used for data updates.

Example 12 : *Recompose book titles from main titles and subtitles*

```
Result result = session.query("MATCH (b:Book) SET b.title = b.mainTitle
+ b.subTitle"
        , Collections.emptyMap());

QueryStatistics queryStatistics = result.queryStatistics();

assertEquals(1, queryStatistics.getPropertiesSet());
```

```
assertEquals(0, queryStatistics.getNodesCreated());
```

An additional feature in the above example is that OGM sends back the execution statistics of the query. It can be handy to have a detailed update on what's been modified in the database (number of nodes added/deleted/updated).

Note › The `queryForObject` variant does the same thing as the `query` method, but by mapping query results into a Java object. This eliminates the need to map search results manually.

Properties in detail

In the first example, we've seen entities annotated with `@Property` and `@Relationship`. Here are some important things to know about the annotations:

- they must be set on class attributes. *(using the annotation on accessors was possible in previous OGM versions but is not available from version 3);*

- specifying the name of the database attribute can be done in the annotation but is optional. By default, the database attributes will have the same name as the attributes in the Java objects;

- it is a good practice to set entity and attribute names explicitly with `@NodeEntity(name="…")` and `@Property(name="…")`, as it might prevent bugs. For example, when doing a refactoring, it's all too easy to forget that renaming the attribute name will impact the storage in the database and lead to confusing data inconsistencies;

- Specifying the direction of the relationships is optional. Possible values are:
  - `OUTGOING` (default direction)
  - `INCOMING`
  - `UNDIRECTED`

- we might wish to avoid persisting some attributes of a Java entity. In that case we can add the `transient` Java modifier or mark the attribute with the annotation `@org.neo4j.ogm.annotation.Transient`;

- when working with class hierarchies, the annotations propagate from parent to child classes. There is no need to reproduce the metadata at every level of the hierarchy.

Label management

Neo4j allows you to assign labels to nodes. By default, when creating an entity with OGM, a label with the same name as the entity class name will be assigned to the node (simple class name, without the package name). To use a different label, you can use the annotation like this: `@NodeEntity(label = "Magazine")`.

Sometimes it's useful to have multiple, maybe even dynamic labels on a node. For example, we might want to add tags to a book. In this case, instead of using the annotation `@NodeEntity(label=…)`, we can annotate a class attribute with `@Labels` in this way:

Example 13 : *Multiple labels/dynamics on entities*

```
@Labels
private List<String> labels = new ArrayList<>();
```

When persisting the entity, OGM will automatically update database labels with those contained in the list.

Data-carrying relationships

When a relation has one or more properties, such as

```
(book)-[:HAS_CATEGORY {matching:1}]->(category)
```

using attributes annotated with `@Relationship` is not enough.

In this case we have to define a relationship class to materialize the relationship between nodes and carry the `matching` property between the book and the category. In our example for the HAS_CATEGORY link, we need:

Example 14 : *Relationship class*

```
@RelationshipEntity(type = "HAS_CATEGORY")   ❶
public class HasCategory {

    @Id @GeneratedValue
    private Long id;

    @StartNode   ❷
    private Book book;

    @EndNode   ❸
    private Category category;
```

```
    private Double matching;

    // getters & setters
}
```

❶   We use the `@RelationshipEntity` annotation.

❷❸ The source and target nodes of the association.

And in the book entity, we just add the relationship class as we've seen before.

Example 15 : *Using the Relationship Class*

```
@Relationship(type = "HAS_CATEGORY", direction = Relationship.OUTGOING)
private Set<HasCategory> hasCategories;
```

In the example above, the relationship class is unidirectional, meaning only one side of the association holds the link. But the relationship can also be bidirectional, and both source and target entities declare the relationship entity. Either way is fine, and the choice depends on business needs and modeling choices. The behavior is the same from a technical point of view.

Indexing

`@Index` annotations can be used on entity attributes. They are used at application startup to update the database indexes (the indexes are enforced by Neo4j, not by OGM).

The benefit from defining indexes in the code rather than through queries is that application deployment is made easier in that there is no need to run queries manually. On the other hand, the drawback is that index annotations are less flexible. So be careful when using them in production, or on large data volumes.

Note › *Automatic index creation is available from Neo4j version 3.0 or later. Automatic index creation is enabled by the option* ***indexes.auto=assert*** *in the OGM configuration.*

Going further, the `@Index` annotation can be used with the `unique` attribute, which, as its name suggests, adds an uniqueness constraint on the attribute. If, for example, we wanted to enforce uniqueness of e-mail addresses on nodes of type `Person`, we would code this as follows:

Example 16 : *Index with OGM*

```
@Property(name = "email")
@Index(unique = true)
```

```
private String email;
```

Object identity management

Besides the @Property annotation, the @Id annotation is required to indicate to OGM how to manage updates (whether to create new data or update existing values). Every entity must have an identifier, either explicitly declared in the class with @Id, or inherited from a parent class. There can be only one identifier per class hierarchy.

There are three types of identifiers:

Example 17 : *The different kinds of OGM identifiers, as shown in the example below*

```
@Id @GeneratedValue ❶
private Long id;

@Id @GeneratedValue(strategy = UuidStrategy.class) ❷
private UUID uuid;

@Id ❸
private String email;
```

❶   Technical primary key assigned by the database during the first persist. It is the native identifier of the Neo4j node, and must be of type Long.
❷   Technical UUID generated by OGM or other generation strategy provided by the application.
❸   Business value given by the application code. It cannot be empty.

When the identifier attribute has a non null value in the entity instance, OGM will issue a MERGE statement when persisting it, which results in an update of existing values in the database. Otherwise, a regular CREATE statement will be executed.

Identity management is not an easy topic in object/database mapping field. To determine which attributes to use when comparing 2 entities, should we use technical attributes with auto-generated values such as UUIDs, or business attributes like an e-mail address? There is no definitive answer and it's beyond the scope of this scope of this book to examine identity management strategies. But from an OGM perspective, there are a few guidelines to follow:

* a Neo4j native identifier attribute must never be assigned in the application code;
* the entities can use Java's hashCode and equals methods to compare objects — doing so has no effect on OGM behavior;

- however, if is strongly advised to avoid using a Neo4j native identifier in the hash-Code and equals methods, because when nodes are deleted in Neo4j, the ids of these nodes are reused.

Transactions

One of the main characteristics and strengths of Neo4j, in contrast to other NoSQL databases, is its full ACID support (atomicity, coherence, isolation and durability) for transactions. OGM makes transaction management easier, especially when using HTTP to connect to the database. OGM allows us to avoid having cumbersome HTTP requests to the transaction endpoints. A basic example of transactional call with OGM looks like:

Example 18 : *Usage of transactions with OGM*

```
Filter emailFilter = new Filter("email", EQUALS
    , "nicolas@graphits.tech");
try (Transaction tx = session.beginTransaction()) { ❶
    Person nicolas = session.loadAll(Person.class,
            new Filters(emailFilter)).iterator().next();
    nicolas.setName("Nicolas M");
    tx.rollback(); ❷
    // or tx.commit()
}
```

❶ The Java try-with-resources is used here for an automatic resource management, closing the transaction at the end of the block.
❷ From that point that the session is rollbacked it is no longer usable. No new changes will be accepted within this transactional block.

Note › In an explicit transaction (as in Example 18), if the outcome of the transaction is not made explicit by calling ***tx.commit()*** *or* ***tx.rollback(),*** *a rollback is issued automatically at the end of the transaction. In the case of implicit transactions (as in the other data access examples earlier in this chapter), a* ***commit*** *is done by OGM after every database access.*

The OGM transaction management relies on the current execution thread. This means that when using parallel or asynchronous execution, you have to be careful to avoid nasty surprises.

Clustering

The usage of a cluster requires special attention when developing an OGM based application:

- regarding the transaction types;

- when using bookmarks.

There are two transaction types: write transactions READ_WRITE (default type) and read transactions READ_ONLY.

Using read only transactions is very important when using a cluster. Specifying a transaction as read only makes it possible to dispatch the queries to replica servers, thereby balancing the load amongst the whole cluster, and freeing-up the core servers making them more available for write requests.

Example 19 : *Read access*

```
try (Transaction tx =
  session.beginTransaction(Transaction.Type.READ_ONLY)) {
    // data access here
    tx.commit();
}
```

We've seen in the causal cluster section that bookmarks have to be used when we want to do coherent reads. The OGM session allows us to manage bookmarks in the following way:

Example 20 : *Bookmarks with OGM*

```
try (Transaction tx = session.beginTransaction()) {
    // database access here
    tx.commit();
}
String bookmark = session.getLastBookmark();

// here let's imagine that the session is closed and the bookmark
 returned to the client app
// other things happen...
// and eventually the client app makes a new call,
// passing the bookmark as a parameter

session.withBookmark(bookmark);
// the next database accesses will now be consistent with the updates
 done in the previous transaction
```

Note › The use of bookmarks can introduce latency on database access. Therefore, they should be used only when there is a clear reason, and not indiscrimately.

Intercepting persistence events

OGM makes it possible to subscribe to data update events (inserts, updates and deletions) through *event handlers*. Handlers allow us to intercept updates (events PRE_SAVE/
POST_SAVE) and deletions (events PRE_DELETE and POST_DELETE).

A classic use case is data auditing: tracking who changed an entity and when. To do
that, we might define a parent class holding the auditing information (this is not required
but it makes things cleaner).

Example 21 : *Entity holding audit information*

```
public abstract class AuditableEntity {

    @Property(name="modificationDate")
    private Date modified;

    @Property(name="modificationUser")
    private String modifiedBy;

    // getters & setters
}
```

Then we can inherit from that class for our entities, and code a *listener* class in charge
of handling events, which in our example, updates audit information.

Example 22 : *Update Management Listener*

```
class ModificationTrackingListener extends EventListenerAdapter {
    @Override
    void onPreSave(Event event) {
        if (event.getObject() instanceof AuditableEntity) {
            AuditableEntity entity = (AuditableEntity) event.getObject();
            entity.setModified(new Date());
            entity.setModifiedBy(getConnectedUserName());
        }
    }
}
```

To be triggered, event handlers must be registered, either with the session of the session-
Factory:

- for a temporary usage: in the session through the session.register(eventLis-
  tener) method. The lifetime of the listener will be limited to the lifetime of the session.

- for permanent usage: at the factory level with: `sessionFactory.register(eventListener)`.

The events are triggered:

- when calling the `save` or `delete` methods of the session, with the entity passed as a parameter;
- on all the nested objects for which an update is done (cascade save);
- when updating the relationships, on the `@RelationshipEntity` annotated classes.

2. Spring Data Neo4j

Spring is a popular framework in the Java world. It allows to structure and simplify the software architecture of applications. The Spring ecosystem consists of the framework and a multitude of sub-projects, designed to integrate various technologies in a way that is as simple as possible for developers.

Spring Data Neo4j (SDN for the initiated) is the Spring Data module dedicated to Neo4j.

It does not replace OGM—rather it's complementary. SDN comes on top of OGM, making development and integration with the Spring world easier. Consequently, it shares a lot of characteristics with OGM like annotating the domain model and smart updates of the data.

It's even possible to mix SDN and OGM usage in an application, as the OGM session is setup by SDN and registered as a Spring *bean*, which makes it possible to inject it into application code.

On top of OGM, using SDN brings:

- some automation for generating database accesses;
- declarative transaction management;
- declarative bookmark management;
- exposition of entities as REST resources.

Let's dive in with an example.

SDN Configuration

Let's consider we have a running Spring project. We first have to add some dependencies. Using Maven we add:

Example 23 : *Adding SDN/Spring dependencies*

```xml
<dependencyManagement>
    <dependencies>
        <dependency>
            <groupId>org.springframework.data</groupId> ❶
            <artifactId>spring-data-releasetrain</artifactId>
            <version>Lovelace-SR6</version>
            <type>pom</type>
            <scope>import</scope>
        </dependency>
    </dependencies>
</dependencyManagement>

<dependencies>
    <dependency>
        <groupId>org.springframework.data</groupId>
        <artifactId>spring-data-neo4j</artifactId>
    </dependency>
    <dependency>
        <groupId>org.neo4j</groupId>
        <artifactId>neo4j-ogm-bolt-driver</artifactId> ❷
        <version>${neo4j.ogm.version}</version> ❸
    </dependency>
</dependencies>
```

❶ The best way to manage dependencies with Spring Data is to import the *release train* which defines a set of dependencies consistent with each other.

❷❸ Here we use the Bolt driver.

Then, we need to add some configuration code to setup `spring-data-neo4j` in our project.

Example 24 : *SDN/Spring configuration class*

```java
@Configuration
@EnableTransactionManagement
@EnableNeo4jRepositories("tech.graphits.catalog.repository")
public class Neo4jConfiguration {

  @Bean
  public SessionFactory sessionFactory() {
    return new SessionFactory(configuration(),
      "tech.graphits.catalog.model");
```

```
  }

  @Bean
  public org.neo4j.ogm.config.Configuration configuration() {
    return new org.neo4j.ogm.config.Configuration.Builder() ❶
      .uri("bolt://localhost")
      .credentials("neo4j", "password").build();
  }

  @Bean
  public Neo4jTransactionManager transactionManager() throws Exception {
    return new Neo4jTransactionManager(sessionFactory());
  }
}
```

❶   The configuration is a little different from the one used in the OGM example, just
      to demonstrate a more code oriented method.

In this example we'll use the same entities and the same annotation as in the previous
OGM section. Then we can move ahead and code our data access class.

A first repository

Spring Data uses the *Repository* pattern. A repository is responsible for managing access to the persistence store. In Spring Data, the repository consists of an interface that
describes the methods we need for persistence. The repositories for Neo4j implement
the Neo4jRepository interface.

Example 25 : *A simple repository*

```
public interface SimplePersonRepository
    extends Neo4jRepository<Person, Long> { ❶
    }
```

❶   We use the parameterized types Person (the entity managed by this repository)
      and Long (the type of the @Id attribute).

Without additional coding, we can start using this repository, as SDN provides the basic
data access operations (create, read update, delete).

Example 26 : *Using the simple SDN repository*

```
@Autowired SimplePersonRepository repository; ❶

@Test
```

```java
public void search_for_all_authors() {

  Iterable<Person> all = repository.findAll(); ❷

  List<Person> authors = new ArrayList<>();
  all.forEach(authors::add);
  assertEquals(3, authors.size());
}
```

❶   The repository is injected like any other Spring component.
❷   We use the `findAll` method, which is provided by SDN, to search the list of all authors in the database.

The main operations provided by SDN are:

*   `findAll`;
*   `findById`;
*   `count`;
*   `save`;
*   `delete`;
*   `exists`.

There are also some variants like `findAllById`, `deleteAll`, `saveAll`, etc.

A more advanced repository

On a real project, which typically goes beyond generic data access methods, we need more domain focused operations.

Example 27 : *A repository with additional search methods*

```java
public interface PersonRepository extends Neo4jRepository<Person, Long>
  {

  Person findByEmail(String email); ❶

  Person findByNameLike(String name); ❷

  List<Person> findAllByBooksTitle(String title); ❸

  @Query("MATCH (b:Book)<-[:IS_AUTHOR_OF]-(p:Person) WHERE p.name =
{name} return count(b)")
  int numberOfBooksForAuthor(@Param("name") String name); ❹
```

```
}
```

❶   Search by `email` attribute.
❷   Search with a `LIKE` syntax for authors whose name matches the one passed as a parameter.
❸   Search by an attribute of a related entity. The example here is a search on the master title of the person's books.
❹   By custom CYPHER query.

We can combine multiple search criteria with logical operators like `findByNameOrEmail-Like(String name, String email)`. A wide range of keywords and operators are available. For more details, check the SDN User Guide [http://d-booker.jo.my/neo4j-sdn].

But wow, this looks like magic! We didn't need to write any code, or implement the interface methods. How does it work?

It turns out, at application startup, SDN scans the application to find repositories and analyzes their signatures, looking for methods like `findBy<name of an attribute of the entity>` and generates queries with filters built which accords with the method signature.

Transaction and bookmark management

SDN integrates with Spring transaction management. This makes it possible to use declarative transaction management, simplifying application code. To make a piece of code execute inside a transaction, we just use a `@Transactional` annotation on a method or a bean, and Spring will take care of handling the transaction infrastructure code. The transactions are by default in `READ_WRITE` mode but this can be changed by using the `readOnly` attribute of the annotation.

Bookmarks can also be benefit from the declarative approach. The `@UseBookmark` annotation on methods turns on the memorization of bookmarks every time a transaction completes, and makes sure they are used in the next transaction(s) if necessary. The `@UseBookmark` annotation must be used along `@Transactional`.

To configure, declarative bookmark management has to be enabled via the `@Enable-BookmarkManagement` annotation on the Spring configuration classes.

3. When NOT to use OGM/SDN?

In this appendix we have highlighted the advantages of OGM and SDN. But graph/ object mapping is not always the best choice. In some situations, other approaches are more efficient

For example, suppose you build an application that requires mostly complex CYPHER queries, beyond the OMG/SDN capabilities: because most of the work is done by the database itself through queries, what's the point in making the architecture heavier with a layer of abstraction that provides little value? Another situation is when the domain model is very different from the database model. Trying to "glue" them together with a mapping layer is likely to quickly turn into a headache. In both cases, alternative solutions are probably better. When in doubt, direct use of the Neo4j java driver can be a good solution, leaving time for an adapted architecture to emerge.

Another case which is contraindicated for OGM/SDN is an application with high volume data processing. As already mentioned in this annex, the first-level cache used by OGM/SDN does not allow large volumes of data to be handled efficiently. In this case, it is recommended that you use import/export tools provided with Neo4j, an ETL solution, or even custom developed code. The chapter *Data Import/Export* covers this ground.

OGM/SDN is also probably not well-suited for applications that have long running transactions. In that case, it's better to work as close as possible to the database. An intermediate layer that caches data might cause problems with conflicting updates.

4. Summary

In this appendix we have discussed the use of OGM to simplify mapping between the database and a domain model. In the same way as with an ORM (*Object Relational Mapper*), when using Neo4j in an application with somewhat complex business rules that you do not want to expose on the customer side, a OGM is a real win in time and reliability (less code, fewer bugs).

From a performance point of view, it is also possible to benefit from the smart update management of entities, optimizing exchanges with the database.

Spring users are strongly encouraged to check out the Spring Data Neo4j module, where they will get a good discussion of Spring integration.

CYPHER Reference Card

Here you will find a complete reference of the CYPHER query language. This card is based on the v3.5 Neo4j implementation.

1. Read query structure

General Syntax

```
[MATCH WHERE]
[OPTIONAL MATCH WHERE]
[WITH [ORDER BY] [SKIP] [LIMIT]]
RETURN [ORDER BY] [SKIP] [LIMIT]
```

Identifying data

MATCH
`MATCH (n:Person)-[:KNOWS]->(m:Person)` `WHERE n.name = 'Alice'`
Node patterns can contain labels and properties.
`MATCH (n)-->(m)`
Any pattern can be used in MATCH.
`MATCH (n {name: 'Alice'})-->(m)`
Patterns with node properties.
`MATCH p = (n)-->(m)`
Assign a path to p.
`OPTIONAL MATCH (n)-[r]->(m)`
Optional pattern: nulls will be used for missing parts.

WHERE
`WHERE n.property <> $value`
Use a predicate to filter. Note that WHERE is always part of a MATCH, OPTIONAL MATCH, WITH or START clause. Putting it after a different clause in a query will alter what it does.

Collecting data

RETURN
`RETURN *`
Return the value of all variables.
`RETURN n AS columnName`
Use alias for result column name.
`RETURN DISTINCT n`
Return unique rows.
`ORDER BY n.property`
Sort the result.
`ORDER BY n.property DESC`
Sort the result in descending order.
`SKIP $skipNumber`
Skip a number of results.
`LIMIT $limitNumber`
Limit the number of results.
`SKIP $skipNumber LIMIT $limitNumber`
Skip results at the top and limit the number of results.
`RETURN count(*)`
The number of matching rows. See Aggregating Functions for more.

WITH

```
MATCH (user)-[:FRIEND]-(friend)
WHERE user.name = $name
WITH user, count(friend) AS friends
WHERE friends > 10
RETURN user
```

The WITH syntax is similar to RETURN. It separates query parts explicitly, allowing you to declare which variables to carry over to the next part.

```
MATCH (user)-[:FRIEND]-(friend)
WITH user, count(friend) AS friends
ORDER BY friends DESC
SKIP 1
LIMIT 3
RETURN user
```

ORDER BY, SKIP, and LIMIT can also be used with WITH.

UNION

```
MATCH (a)-[:KNOWS]->(b)
RETURN b.name
UNION
MATCH (a)-[:LOVES]->(b)
RETURN b.name
```

Returns the distinct union of all query results. Result column types and names have to match.

```
MATCH (a)-[:KNOWS]->(b)
RETURN b.name
UNION ALL
MATCH (a)-[:LOVES]->(b)
RETURN b.name
```

Returns the union of all query results, including duplicated rows.

2. Write query structure

General Syntax

Write-Only Query Structure :

```
(CREATE [UNIQUE] | MERGE)*
[SET|DELETE|REMOVE|FOREACH]*
[RETURN [ORDER BY] [SKIP] [LIMIT]]
```

Read-Write Query Structure :

```
[MATCH WHERE]
[OPTIONAL MATCH WHERE]
[WITH [ORDER BY] [SKIP] [LIMIT]]
(CREATE [UNIQUE] | MERGE)*
[SET|DELETE|REMOVE|FOREACH]*
[RETURN [ORDER BY] [SKIP] [LIMIT]]
```

CREATE
`CREATE (n {name: $value})`
Create a node with the given properties.
`CREATE (n $map)`
Create a node with the given properties.
`UNWIND $listOfMaps AS properties` `CREATE (n) SET n = properties`
Create nodes with the given properties.
`CREATE (n)-[r:KNOWS]->(m)`
Create a relationship with the given type and direction; bind a variable to it.
`CREATE (n)-[:LOVES {since: $value}]->(m)`
Create a relationship with the given type, direction, and properties.

SET

```
SET n.property1 = $value1, n.property2 = $value2
```

Update or create a property.

```
SET n = $map
```

Set all properties. This will remove any existing properties.

```
SET n += $map
```

Add and update properties, while keeping existing ones.

```
SET n:Person
```

Adds a label Person to a node.

MERGE

```
MERGE (n:Person {name: $value})
ON CREATE SET n.created = timestamp()
ON MATCH SET
n.counter = coalesce(n.counter, 0) + 1,
n.accessTime = timestamp()
```

Match a pattern or create it if it does not exist. Use ON CREATE and ON MATCH for conditional updates.

```
MATCH (a:Person {name: $value1}), (b:Person {name: $value2})
MERGE (a)-[r:LOVES]->(b)
```

MERGE finds or creates a relationship between the nodes.

```
MATCH (a:Person {name: $value1})
MERGE (a)-[r:KNOWS]->(b:Person {name: $value3})
```

MERGE finds or creates subgraphs attached to the node.

DELETE

```
DELETE n, r
```

Delete a node and a relationship.

```
DETACH DELETE n
```

Delete a node and all relationships connected to it.

DELETE

```
MATCH (n) DETACH DELETE n
```

Delete all nodes and relationships from the database.

REMOVE

```
REMOVE n:Person
```

Remove a label from n.

```
REMOVE n.property
```

Remove a property.

FOREACH

```
FOREACH (r IN relationships(path) | SET r.marked = true)
```

Execute a mutating operation for each relationship in a path.

```
FOREACH (value IN coll | CREATE (:Person {name: value}))
```

Execute a mutating operation for each element in a list.

CALL

```
CALL db.labels() YIELD label
```

This shows a standalone call to the built-in procedure db.labels to list all labels used in the database. Note that required procedure arguments are given explicitly in brackets after the procedure name.

```
CALL java.stored.procedureWithArgs
```

Standalone calls may omit YIELD and also provide arguments implicitly via statement parameters, e.g. a standalone call requiring one argument input may be run by passing the parameter map {input: 'foo'}.

```
CALL db.labels() YIELD label
RETURN count(label) AS count
```

Calls the built-in procedure db.labels inside a larger query to count all labels used in the database. Calls inside a larger query always requires passing arguments and naming results explicitly with YIELD.

Import

```
LOAD CSV FROM 'https://neo4j.com/docs/cypher-refcard/3.5/csv/artists.csv'
AS line
CREATE (:Artist {name: line[1], year: toInteger(line[2])})
```

Load data from a CSV file and create nodes.

```
LOAD CSV WITH HEADERS FROM
'https://neo4j.com/docs/cypher-refcard/3.5/csv/artists-with-headers.csv'
AS line
CREATE (:Artist {name: line.Name, year: toInteger(line.Year)})
```

Load CSV data which has headers.

```
USING PERIODIC COMMIT 500 LOAD CSV WITH HEADERS FROM
'https://neo4j.com/docs/cypher-refcard/3.5/csv/artists-with-headers.csv'
AS line
CREATE (:Artist {name: line.Name, year: toInteger(line.Year)})
```

Commit the current transaction after every 500 rows when importing large amounts of data.

```
LOAD CSV FROM 'https://neo4j.com/docs/cypher-refcard/3.5/csv/artists-
fieldterminator.csv'
AS line FIELDTERMINATOR ';'
CREATE (:Artist {name: line[1], year: toInteger(line[2])})
```

Use a different field terminator, not the default which is a comma (with no whitespace around it).

3. General

Operators

General	DISTINCT, ., []
Mathematical	+, -, *, /, %, ^
Comparison	=, <>, <, >, <=, >=, IS NULL, IS NOT NULL
Boolean	AND, OR, XOR, NOT
String	+
List	+, IN, [x], [x .. y]
Regular Expression	=~
String matching	STARTS WITH, ENDS WITH, CONTAINS

null
•   null is used to represent missing/undefined values.
•   null is not equal to null. Not knowing two values does not imply that they are the same value. So the expression null = null yields null and not true. To check if an expression is null, use IS NULL.
•   Arithmetic expressions, comparisons and function calls (except coalesce) will return null if any argument is null.
•   An attempt to access a missing element in a list or a property that doesn't exist yields null.
•   In OPTIONAL MATCH clauses, nulls will be used for missing parts of the pattern.

Patterns
`(n:Person)`
Node with Person label.
`(n:Person:Swedish)`
Node with both Person and Swedish labels.
`(n:Person {name: $value})`
Node with the declared properties.
`()-[r {name: $value}]-()`
Matches relationships with the declared properties.
`(n)-->(m)`
Relationship from n to m.
`(n)--(m)`
Relationship in any direction between n and m.
`(n:Person)-->(m)`
Node n labeled Person with relationship to m.
`(m)<-[:KNOWS]-(n)`
Relationship of type KNOWS from n to m.

Patterns

`(n)-[:KNOWS|:LOVES]->(m)`

Relationship of type KNOWS or of type LOVES from n to m.

`(n)-[r]->(m)`

Bind the relationship to variable r.

`(n)-[*1..5]->(m)`

Variable length path of between 1 and 5 relationships from n to m.

`(n)-[*]->(m)`

Variable length path of any number of relationships from n to m. (See Performance section.)

`(n)-[:KNOWS]->(m {property: $value})`

A relationship of type KNOWS from a node n to a node m with the declared property.

`shortestPath((n1:Person)-[*..6]-(n2:Person))`

Find a single shortest path.

`allShortestPaths((n1:Person)-[*..6]->(n2:Person))`

Find all shortest paths.

`size((n)-->()-->())`

Count the paths matching the pattern.

Labels

`CREATE (n:Person {name: $value})`

Create a node with label and property.

`MERGE (n:Person {name: $value})`

Matches or creates unique node(s) with the label and property.

`SET n:Spouse:Parent:Employee`

Add label(s) to a node.

`MATCH (n:Person)`

Matches nodes labeled Person.

`MATCH (n:Person) WHERE n.name = $value`

Matches nodes labeled Person with the given name.

Labels

```
WHERE (n:Person)
```

Checks the existence of the label on the node.

```
labels(n)
```

Labels of the node.

```
REMOVE n:Person
```

Remove the label from the node.

Lists

```
['a', 'b', 'c'] AS list
```

Literal lists are declared in square brackets.

```
size($list) AS len, $list[0] AS value
```

Lists can be passed in as parameters.

```
range($firstNum, $lastNum, $step) AS list
```

range() creates a list of numbers (step is optional), other functions returning lists are: labels(), nodes(), relationships(), filter(), extract().

```
MATCH p = (a)-[:KNOWS*]->()
RETURN relationships(p) AS r
```

The list of relationships comprising a variable length path can be returned using named paths and relationships().

```
RETURN matchedNode.list[0] AS value, size(matchedNode.list) AS len
```

Properties can be lists of strings, numbers or booleans.

```
list[$idx] AS value,
list[$startIdx..$endIdx] AS slice
```

List elements can be accessed with idx subscripts in square brackets. Invalid indexes return null. Slices can be retrieved with intervals from start_idx to end_idx, each of which can be omitted or negative. Out of range elements are ignored.

```
UNWIND $names AS name
MATCH (n {name: name})
RETURN avg(n.age)
```

With UNWIND, any list can be transformed back into individual rows. The example matches all names from a list of names.

Lists

```
MATCH (a)
RETURN [(a)-->(b) WHERE b.name = 'Bob' | b.age]
```

Pattern comprehensions may be used to do a custom projection from a match directly into a list.

```
MATCH (person)
RETURN person { .name, .age}
```

Map projections may be easily constructed from nodes, relationships and other map values.

Maps

```
{name: 'Alice', age: 38, address: {city: 'London', residential: true}}
```

Literal maps are declared in curly braces much like property maps. Lists are supported.

```
WITH {person: {name: 'Anne', age: 25}} AS p
RETURN p.person.name
```

Access the property of a nested map.

```
MERGE (p:Person {name: $map.name}) ON CREATE SET p = $map
```

Maps can be passed in as parameters and used either as a map or by accessing keys.

```
MATCH (matchedNode:Person)
RETURN matchedNode
```

Nodes and relationships are returned as maps of their data.

```
map.name, map.age, map.children[0]
```

Map entries can be accessed by their keys. Invalid keys result in an error.

Predicates

```
n.property <> $value
```

Use comparison operators.

```
exists(n.property)
```

Use functions.

```
n.number >= 1 AND n.number <= 10
```

Use boolean operators to combine predicates.

Predicates
`1 <= n.number <= 10` Use chained operators to combine predicates.
`n:Person` Check for node labels.
`variable IS NULL` Check if something is null.
`NOT exists(n.property) OR n.property = $value` Either the property does not exist or the predicate is true.
`n.property = $value` Non-existing property returns null, which is not equal to anything.
`n["property"] = $value` Properties may also be accessed using a dynamically computed property name.

`n.property STARTS WITH 'Tim' OR`
`n.property ENDS WITH 'n' OR`
`n.property CONTAINS 'goodie'`
 	
String matching.

`n.property =~ 'Tim.*'` String regular expression matching.
`(n)-[:KNOWS]->(m)` Ensure the pattern has at least one match.
`NOT (n)-[:KNOWS]->(m)` Exclude matches to (n)-[:KNOWS]->(m) from the result.
`n.property IN [$value1, $value2]` Check if an element exists in a list.

List Predicates
`all(x IN coll WHERE exists(x.property))` Returns true if the predicate is true for all elements in the list.

List Predicates

```
any(x IN coll WHERE exists(x.property))
```

Returns true if the predicate is true for at least one element in the list.

```
none(x IN coll WHERE exists(x.property))
```

Returns true if the predicate is false for all elements in the list.

```
single(x IN coll WHERE exists(x.property))
```

Returns true if the predicate is true for exactly one element in the list.

CASE

```
CASE n.eyes
WHEN 'blue' THEN 1
WHEN 'brown' THEN 2
ELSE 3
END
```

Return THEN value from the matching WHEN value. The ELSE value is optional, and substituted for null if missing.

```
CASE
WHEN n.eyes = 'blue' THEN 1
WHEN n.age < 40 THEN 2
ELSE 3
END
```

Return THEN value from the first WHEN predicate evaluating to true. Predicates are evaluated in order.

List Expressions

```
size($list)
```

Number of elements in the list.

```
reverse($list)
```

Reverse the order of the elements in the list.

```
head($list), last($list), tail($list)
```

head() returns the first, last() the last element of the list. tail() returns all but the first element. All return null for an empty list.

List Expressions

```
[x IN list WHERE x.prop <> $value | x.prop]
```

Combination of filter and extract in a concise notation.

```
extract(x IN list | x.prop)
```

A list of the value of the expression for each element in the original list.

```
filter(x IN list WHERE x.prop <> $value)
```

A filtered list of the elements where the predicate is true.

```
reduce(s = "", x IN list | s + x.prop)
```

Evaluate expression for each element in the list, accumulate the results.

4. Functions

Functions

```
coalesce(n.property, $defaultValue)
```

The first non-null expression.

```
timestamp()
```

Milliseconds since midnight, January 1, 1970 UTC.

```
id(nodeOrRelationship)
```

The internal id of the relationship or node.

```
toInteger($expr)
```

Converts the given input into an integer if possible; otherwise it returns null.

```
toFloat($expr)
```

Converts the given input into a floating point number if possible; otherwise it returns null.

```
toBoolean($expr)
```

Converts the given input into a boolean if possible; otherwise it returns null.

```
keys($expr)
```

Returns a list of string representations for the property names of a node, relationship, or map.

```
properties({expr})
```

Returns a map containing all the properties of a node or relationship.

Path Functions

```
length(path)
```

The number of relationships in the path.

```
nodes(path)
```

The nodes in the path as a list.

```
relationships(path)
```

The relationships in the path as a list.

```
extract(x IN nodes(path) | x.prop)
```

Extract properties from the nodes in a path.

Spatial Functions

```
point({x: $x, y: $y})
```

Returns a point in a 2D cartesian coordinate system.

```
point({latitude: $y, longitude: $x})
```

Returns a point in a 2D geographic coordinate system, with coordinates specified in decimal degrees.

```
point({x: $x, y: $y, z: $z})
```

Returns a point in a 3D cartesian coordinate system.

```
point({latitude: $y, longitude: $x, height: $z})
```

Returns a point in a 3D geographic coordinate system, with latitude and longitude in decimal degrees, and height in meters.

```
distance(point({x: $x1, y: $y1}), point({x: $x2, y: $y2}))
```

Returns a floating point number representing the linear distance between two points. The returned units will be the same as those of the point coordinates, and it will work for both 2D and 3D cartesian points.

```
distance(point({latitude: $y1, longitude: $x1}), point({latitude: $y2, longitude: $x2}))
```

Returns the geodesic distance between two points in meters. It can be used for 3D geographic points as well.

Temporal Functions

```
date("2018-04-05")
```

Returns a date parsed from a string.

```
localtime("12:45:30.25")
```

Returns a time with no time zone.

```
time("12:45:30.25+01:00")
```

Returns a time in a specified time zone.

```
localdatetime("2018-04-05T12:34:00")
```

Returns a datetime with no time zone.

```
datetime("2018-04-05T12:34:00[Europe/Berlin]")
```

Returns a datetime in the specified time zone.

```
datetime({epochMillis: 3360000})
```

Transforms 3360000 as a UNIX Epoch time into a normal datetime.

```
date({year: {year}, month: {month}, day: {day}})
```

All of the temporal functions can also be called with a map of named components. This example returns a date from year, month and day components. Each function supports a different set of possible components.

```
datetime({date: {date}, time: {time}})
```

Temporal types can be created by combining other types. This example creates a datetime from a date and a time.

```
date({date: {datetime}, day: 5})
```

Temporal types can be created by selecting from more complex types, as well as overriding individual components. This example creates a date by selecting from a datetime, as well as overriding the day component.

```
WITH date("2018-04-05") AS d RETURN d.year, d.month, d.day, d.week,
d.dayOfWeek
```

Accessors allow extracting components of temporal types.

Duration Functions

```
duration("P1Y2M10DT12H45M30.25S")
```

Returns a duration of 1 year, 2 months, 10 days, 12 hours, 45 minutes and 30.25 seconds.

Duration Functions

```
duration.between($date1,$date2)
```

Returns a duration between two temporal instances.

```
WITH duration("P1Y2M10DT12H45M") AS d
RETURN d.years, d.months, d.days, d.hours, d.minutes
```

Returns 1 year, 14 months, 10 days, 12 hours and 765 minutes.

```
WITH duration("P1Y2M10DT12H45M") AS d
RETURN d.years, d.monthsOfYear, d.days, d.hours, d.minutesOfHour
```

Returns 1 year, 2 months, 10 days, 12 hours and 45 minutes.

```
date("2015-01-01") + duration("P1Y1M1D")
```

Returns a date of 2016-02-02. It is also possible to subtract durations from temporal instances.

```
duration("PT30S") * 10
```

Returns a duration of 5 minutes. It is also possible to divide a duration by a number.

Mathematical Functions

```
abs($expr)
```

The absolute value.

```
rand()
```

Returns a random number in the range from 0 (inclusive) to 1 (exclusive), [0,1). Returns a new value for each call. Also useful for selecting a subset or random ordering.

```
round($expr)
```

Round to the nearest integer; ceil() and floor() find the next integer up or down.

```
sqrt($expr)
```

The square root.

```
sign($expr)
```

0 if zero, -1 if negative, 1 if positive.

```
sin($expr)
```

Trigonometric functions also include cos(), tan(), cot(), asin(), acos(), atan(), atan2(), and haversin(). All arguments for the trigonometric functions should be in radians, if not otherwise specified.

Mathematical Functions
`degrees($expr), radians($expr), pi()`
Converts radians into degrees; use radians() for the reverse, and pi() for π.
`log10($expr), log($expr), exp($expr), e()`
Logarithm base 10, natural logarithm, e to the power of the parameter, and the value of e.

String Functions
`toString($expression)`
String representation of the expression.
`replace($original, $search, $replacement)`
Replace all occurrences of search with replacement. All arguments must be expressions.
`substring($original, $begin, $subLength)`
Get part of a string. The subLength argument is optional.
`left($original, $subLength), right($original, $subLength)`
The first part of a string. The last part of the string.
`trim($original), lTrim($original), rTrim($original)`
Trim all whitespace, or on the left or right side.
`toUpper($original), toLower($original)`
UPPERCASE and lowercase.
`split($original, $delimiter)`
Split a string into a list of strings.
`reverse($original)`
Reverse a string.
`size($string)`
Calculate the number of characters in the string.

Relationship Functions

`type(a_relationship)`

String representation of the relationship type.

`startNode(a_relationship)`

Start node of the relationship.

`endNode(a_relationship)`

End node of the relationship.

`id(a_relationship)`

The internal id of the relationship.

Aggregating Functions

`count(*)`

The number of matching rows.

`count(variable)`

The number of non-null values.

`count(DISTINCT variable)`

All aggregating functions also take the DISTINCT operator, which removes duplicates from the values.

`collect(n.property)`

List from the values, ignores null.

`sum(n.property)`

Sum numerical values. Similar functions are avg(), min(), max().

`percentileDisc(n.property, $percentile)`

Discrete percentile. Continuous percentile is percentileCont(). The percentile argument is from 0.0 to 1.0.

`stDev(n.property)`

Standard deviation for a sample of a population. For an entire population use stDevP().

5. Schema

INDEX

```
CREATE INDEX ON :Person(name)
```

Create an index on the label Person and property name.

```
CREATE INDEX ON :Person(name, age)
```

Create a composite index on the label Person and the properties name and age.

```
MATCH (n:Person) WHERE n.name = $value
```

An index can be automatically used for the equality comparison. Note that for example toLower(n.name) = $value will not use an index.

```
MATCH (n:Person) WHERE n.name IN [$value]
```

An index can automatically be used for the IN list checks.

```
MATCH (n:Person) WHERE n.name = $value and n.age = $value2
```

A composite index can be automatically used for equality comparison of both properties. Note that there needs to be predicates on all properties of the composite index for it to be used.

```
MATCH (n:Person) USING INDEX n:Person(name) WHERE n.name = $value
```

Index usage can be enforced when Cypher uses a suboptimal index, or more than one index should be used.

```
DROP INDEX ON :Person(name)
```

Drop the index on the label Person and property name.

CONSTRAINT

```
CREATE CONSTRAINT ON (p:Person)
ASSERT p.name IS UNIQUE
```

Create a unique property constraint on the label Person and property name. If any other node with that label is updated or created with a name that already exists, the write operation will fail. This constraint will create an accompanying index.

```
DROP CONSTRAINT ON (p:Person)
ASSERT p.name IS UNIQUE
```

Drop the unique constraint and index on the label Person and property name.

CONSTRAINT

```
CREATE CONSTRAINT ON (p:Person)
ASSERT exists(p.name)
```

(^{a}) Create a node property existence constraint on the label Person and property name. If a node with that label is created without a name, or if the name property is removed from an existing node with the Person label, the write operation will fail.

```
DROP CONSTRAINT ON (p:Person)
ASSERT exists(p.name)
```

(^{a}) Drop the node property existence constraint on the label Person and property name.

```
CREATE CONSTRAINT ON ()-[l:LIKED]-()
ASSERT exists(l.when)
```

(^{a}) Create a relationship property existence constraint on the type LIKED and property when. If a relationship with that type is created without a when, or if the when property is removed from an existing relationship with the LIKED type, the write operation will fail.

```
DROP CONSTRAINT ON ()-[l:LIKED]-()
ASSERT exists(l.when)
```

(^{a}) Drop the relationship property existence constraint on the type LIKED and property when.

```
CREATE CONSTRAINT ON (p:Person)
ASSERT (p.firstname, p.surname) IS NODE KEY
```

(^{a}) Create a Node Key constraint on the label Person and properties firstname and surname. If a node with that label is created without both firstname and surname or if the combination of the two is not unique, or if the firstname and/or surname labels on an existing node with the Person label is modified to violate these constraints, the write operation will fail.

```
DROP CONSTRAINT ON (p:Person)
ASSERT (p.firstname, p.surname) IS NODE KEY
```

(^{a}) Drop the Node Key constraint on the label Person and properties firstname and surname.

^{a}Functionality available in Neo4j Enterprise Edition.

6. Performance

Performance

- Use parameters instead of literals when possible. This allows Cypher to re-use your queries instead of having to parse and build new execution plans.
- Always set an upper limit for your variable length patterns. It's possible to have a query go wild and touch all nodes in a graph by mistake.

Performance

- Return only the data you need. Avoid returning whole nodes and relationships — instead, pick the data you need and return only that.

- Use PROFILE / EXPLAIN to analyze the performance of your queries. See Query Tuning for more information on these and other topics, such as planner hints.

Index

U

UNION, 247
Uniqueness, 15
User management, 200, 203
    LDAP, 210
USING INDEX, 29
USING SCAN, 29

W

Web browser
    :sysinfo, 154
Weighting, 13
WHERE, 246
WITH, 28, 247
Write-Only query, 248

Y

YIELD, 61

About the authors

Nicolas Mervaillie

Nicolas Mervaillie spent over 20 years with Java and Spring in the banking, retail and e-commerce sectors, as a developer, architect and technical coach. He is currently a Senior Consultant at GraphAware where he builds some big Neo4j databases and applications on top of it. He is an Neo4j OGM and Spring Data Neo4j committer, and runs the Graph Database meetup in Lille, France.

Sylvain Roussy

Sylvain Roussy is freelance since a few months. Before he was a R&D project manager at Blueway Software. Developer, trainer, consultant for over twenty years (whether on product, business or technology), he has tested the limits of RDBMS by wanting to design dynamic, flexible and scalable systems. He found answers to his many questions in Neo4j, and has since contributed to his promotion in France, notably by co-organising the Neo4j Meetup in Lyon, France.

Nicolas Rouyer

Nicolas Rouyer has been a Big Data expert at Orange for five years. He spent ten years in Digital Services Companies (ESN) before joining the Orange Group in 2009. He has solid expertise in the Big Data ecosystem and has a keen interest in data governance issues. He gives internal training at Orange on Big Data and runs the Graph Database Meetup in Toulouse, France.

Frank Kutzler

Frank Kutzler earned a PhD in physical chemistry from Stanford University. He taught chemistry for 15 years, until transitioning to software development in 2000. As a software developer, he has worked in Java development, becoming a full stack developer both as a contractor and as an employee. He has worked at a number of companies, most recently Best Buy, Inc.